Journalism 2001

Journalism 2001

Christopher Harper
and
The Indiana Group

CourseWise
publishing

Boulder, Bellevue, Dubuque, Madison

Our mission at CourseWise is to help students make connections—linking theory to practice and the classroom to the outside world. Learners are motivated to synthesize ideas when course materials are placed in a context they recognize. By providing gateways to contemporary and enduring issues, CourseWise publications will expand students' awareness of and context for the course subject.

For more information on CourseWise visit us at our Web site: www.coursewise.com

CourseWise Publishing Editorial Staff

Thomas Doran, ceo/publisher: Journalism/Marketing/Speech
Edgar Laube, publisher: Geography/Political Science/Psychology/Sociology
Linda Meehan Avenarius, publisher: CourseLinks
Sue Pulvermacher-Alt, publisher: Education/Health/Gender Studies
Victoria Putman, publisher: Anthropology/Philosophy/Religion
Tom Romaniak, publisher: Business/Criminal Justice/Economics

Other CourseWise Journalism titles:
Perspectives: Online Journalism, edited by Kathleen Wickham
Walking the HighWire: Effective Public Relations by Merry Clare Shelburne

Cover design by Jeff Storm

Cover photos courtesy of John Daly

The credits for this book appear on page 243 and are considered an extension of the copyright page.

Library of Congress Catalog Card Number: 97-075084

ISBN 0-395-902274

Printed in the United States of America by CourseWise Publishing, Inc.
1379 Lodge Lane, Boulder, CO 80303

10 9 8 7 6 5 4 3 2

A Birthing Story

This book emphasizes storytelling. So I thought it would be appropriate to lead with a story—the story of how this book and its publisher were given birth.

Journalism 2001 and CourseWise Publishing, Inc., are like fraternal twins. We were conceived on a warm July evening in 1996 at a restaurant in Bloomington, Ind. And like many conceptions, this one was an accident.

When Chris Harper and some colleagues went to dinner that night, they had little idea of the ambitious agenda they were about to develop—for themselves and for a new publishing company. As participants in the 1996 **Freedom Forum Teaching Program** at Indiana University, these academics naturally got around to talking about what they like and don't like about teaching. Gradually the conversation drifted toward textbooks. It became quite clear that there was a collective frustration with the current crop of books. Somewhere along the line, the suggestion was made that, together, they write a new kind of textbook for the News Reporting course.

This idea was not taken seriously. At first. Though the group was highly skilled in the basic tenets of journalism, they were young, a bit irreverent and untenured. But the more they discussed the idea, the more they liked the possibilities. They would write a shorter book, drawing directly from their respective professional expertise. They would emphasize good storytelling. They would aggressively incorporate coverage of the "real world" and the new technologies that were changing how journalists work.

When Chris Harper and The Indiana Group agreed to develop a prospectus and shop for a publisher, they thought they were merely agreeing to write the kind of textbook they wanted to use in their courses. They didn't know they were also planting the seeds for a new kind of college publisher.

By the time I met Chris Harper at the August 1996 AEJMC convention, I had seen the prospectus and knew that this would be a special project. What was unclear was how to publish it. Putting Chris and The Indiana Group into the traditional textbook publishing box would certainly sour the flavor of the project. Chris was demanding very specific and unusual things from his publisher: a quick commitment to publish, a fall 97 publication date, light but tight manuscript development with an unusually short production schedule. Furthermore, he wanted his own Web site so he could provide a host of timely web resources to supplement the book.

As we developed plans for *Journalism 2001*, the thought of working exclusively on developing similar kinds of teaching tools for other courses held great appeal. Chris and The

Tom Doran

Indiana Group were not the only ones feeling frustrated with traditional textbooks. It was obvious there were a number of instructors who found textbooks too long, overpriced and uninspired, and who wanted to work with new and better teaching tools. And it was clear that the Internet needed to be included in this tool set.

After securing the rights to *Journalism 2001* with an advance drawn from a personal checking account, I recruited some respected colleagues and together we obtained the financial backing to launch CourseWise, Inc. As we go to press with "2001", CourseWise has seven employees working on more than 20 projects in other course areas that will be published this year with 24 more to come next year! All inspired by the intent behind this exciting new book.

And so, in this space—usually allocated for a "thanks to the authors for a great job"—I need to also add a thank you to Chris and The Indiana Group for providing the spark for this publishing start-up. These are writers who are passionate instructors. As you read *Journalism 2001* you'll feel their enthusiasm for their work. I did. That enthusiasm helped launch a publishing company.

A Word about CourseLinks

We invite you to visit the CourseLinks™ site that was built for the News Reporting course (go to http://www.courselinks.com). CourseLinks™ are carefully developed web resources that are R.E.A.L. learning tools™—meaning they are Relevant, Exciting, Approved and Linked. CourseLinks™ are about studying, not surfing. Chris Harper is the academic editor for this site. Along with an academic editorial board, student interns and the CourseWise team, this site integrates additional content and study tools designed to help you with this course. We think you'll find CourseLinks™ an invaluable resource. It's interesting, sensible and easy to use.

A Final Word

Good luck with your studies! We hope you find *Journalism 2001* and the related CourseLinks™ helpful. Please let us know how we did. Write me at: journalism@coursewise.com

Tom Doran
ceo/publisher

Contents

Preface — xv

Chapter

David Tait

1 Storytelling — 1

Reporting as "Story" — 2
What's It Made Of? — 3
The Reporter's Shopping List — 4
Stories Happen — 5
Sequence, Not Structure! — 5
A Helicopter Crashes — 6
Story as Trap — 8
Sidebar Tips — 10

Anita M. Caldwell

2 Finding the Story — 13

Where to Look — 14
Where You Are — 15
Life in the Past Lane — 16
Best People — 16
School Daze — 17
The Minute Waltz — 19
Building Blocks — 20
Sidebar 1 Adventures and Other Great Stories — 15
Sidebar 2 Tips for Finding Ideas in Neighborhoods, Towns and Cities — 21

Carol Schlagheck, Ph.D.

3 Researching the Story — 23

Strike at the Paper Mill — 24
Fundamental Research Materials — 26
    Telephone Book — 26
    Map — 26
    Newspaper Morgue — 26
    The Local Library — 26
Government Documents — 28

Academic Research, Polls, Surveys 29

Sidebar 1 Tips 28

Sidebar 2 Historic Mansion in Danger? 30

4 Computer-Assisted Reporting 33

Getting Started 34

A Simple Search: Who Is Christopher Harper? 35

The Strategy of a Search 38

Sidebar Web Sites 37

Christopher Harper

5 The Interview 43

Types of Interviews 45

    Adversarial Interviews 45

    Personality Profiles 45

    Background Interviews 45

    Support Quote or Reaction Interviews 46

Doing Your Homework Before the Interview 46

Preparing Your List of Questions 46

During the Interview 47

    Don't Try Too Hard to Be Liked 47

    Make Silence Your Friend 48

Peeling the Onion 48

Should You Tape? 49

The Interview Environment 50

The First Few Minutes: They Can Make or Break You 51

Problem Interviewees and How Not to Be Undone by Them 51

    The Human Brochure 51

    The Controller 51

    The Eloquent Rambler 52

    The One-Syllable Wonder 52

Don't Apologize for Tough Questions: The Hostile Source 52

Identifying Key Quotes 53

Wrapping Up the Interview 53

Pat Berg

Going Off the Record   54

Saying Good-Bye   54

After the Interview   55

Sidebar 1 Tips for Interviews   47

Sidebar 2 A Basic List of Interviewing Rules   50

Sidebar 3 Tips for Taking Notes   54

Christopher Harper

6 Reporting the Story   57

The Changing Newsroom, Christopher Harper   58

Covering Cops and Courts, Michael Mercer   59

Writing Obituaries, Robert E. Wernsman Jr.   62

Telling the Story of Fires, Accidents and Disasters, David Tait   63

Getting the Details of Fires, Accidents and Disasters, Ford Risley   65

Covering Education, Robert E. Wernsman Jr.   66

Covering Speeches and Meetings, Glen L. Bleske   67

Getting Good Quotes, Ginger Rudeseal Carter   69

    Using Attribution   70

The Photographer as Writer, James H. Kenney Jr.   71

Sidebar 1 Cops and Courts   60

Sidebar 2 Obituaries   62

Sidebar 3 Covering Tragedies   63

Sidebar 4 Education   67

Sidebar 5 Reporting Skills for Photographers   71

Robert Unger

7 Covering the Big Story   75

Let People Talk   77

Establish Relationships   77

Keep It Simple   78

Be Polite   79

Build the Story   81

Explain the Unexplainable   81

Do What Is Necessary to Get the Story   83

Be Wary of Rules   83

Sidebar 1 Tips   79

Sidebar 2 Don't Let the Big Story Overwhelm you   82

Glen L. Bleske, Ph.D.

8   Writing the Story   **87**

The Lead   88
Organizing the Story   90
Using Quotes in Your Story   92
Ending a Story   95
Finishing the Story   97
    Improving   98
    Fixing   98
Sidebar 1 Reading to Report   88
Sidebar 2 A Checklist for Fixing Stories   90
Sidebar 3 Words That Cause Trouble   91
Sidebar 4 Do's and Don'ts of Quotes   94
Sidebar 5 The Feature Story   96

Mark Paxton, Ph.D.

9   Editing the Written Word   **103**

Don't Quit with the First Draft   104
Double-Check Your Facts   105
Check Your Spelling   106
Use Only the Number of Words Necessary   107
Make Sure Your Subjects and Verbs Agree   108
Make Sure Your Nouns and Pronouns Agree   109
Watch Out for Sentence Fragments   109
Eliminate Run-On Sentences   110
Use Parallel Construction   111
Be Active, Not Passive   112
Sidebar A Craft or an Art?   113

James H. Kenney Jr.

10   Photographing the Story   **117**

The Craft of Photojournalism   119
News   119
Sports   120
Features   120
Picture Essays and Picture Stories   122
Tools   122
Technique: Light, Composition and Color   124
The Moment   129
The Caption: Getting Words   130
Being an Idea Person   131
Digital Photography   131
Sidebar Tips for Photographers   128

Christopher Harper

11 Broadcast Writing and Reporting   **135**

Script Preparation   138
What Is News   139
Finding What's Important   140
On Location   144
Getting Pictures   145
Editing the Story   146
Sidebar 1 A Radio Host's View   143
Sidebar 2 A View from a Television Anchor   145
Sidebar 3 Videotape Log   146
Sidebar 4 Television Scripts   147
Sidebar 5 Doing Longer Television Stories   148

William Marshall

12 The Law   **155**

"Lawyering" the Media   157
The Media's Role in First Amendment Theory   158
News Gathering   158
Confidential Sources   160
Privacy and Defamation   160
Sidebar Tips for Non-lawyers   162

Ford Risley, Ph.D.

13 Ethics   **167**

Codes of Ethics   168
Ethical Problems   170
    Telling the Truth   170
    Deception   170
    Faking Stories   171
    Plagiarism   171
    Conflicts of Interest   172
    Gifts   172
    Lure of Money   172
    Political Involvement   173
    Invasion of Privacy   173

Solving Ethical Problems   175
Sidebar 1 Ethical Principles   170
Sidebar 2 Food Lion vs. "Prime Time Live"   171
Sidebar 3 Less Obvious Forms of Plagiarism   172

14 Public Relations Practice, Writing and Planning   179

What Is Public Relations?   180
The Journalist and the Practitioner: More Alike Than You'd Think   183
RACE: The Formula for Performance in Public Relations   184
    Research   184
    Action   184
    Communication   185
    Evaluation   185
    The Formula in a Crisis   185
The Basics of Public Relations Writing   185
Media Relations in a Nutshell   187
The Ethical Practice of Public Relations   189
Sidebar A Common Thread   183

Ginger Rudeseal Carter, Ph.D.

15 Advertising   191

The Future   193
Freedom of Speech   193
The Changing Environment   193
Creativity   195
Design   195
Strategy   197
Writing   198
Sidebar Information Is Important   197

Ron Schie

16 Reading to Write   201

Reaching the Reader   202
Identifying the News   203
Writers Read to Accommodate Their Audiences   205
Observation   206
Sidebar 1 Reading to Write   204
Sidebar 2 Tips   206

Robert E. Wernsman Jr.

Michael L. Mercer

17 Resumes, Cover Letters, Work Samples and Tips for Getting a Job   **211**

Preparing to Write a Resume   212
Writing a Resume   214
After the Introduction   215
Work Experience and Other Skills   216
References   217
Writing a Cover Letter   218
Sending Work Samples   220
Hunting for a Job   221
Sidebar 1 An Employer's Rant   214
Sidebar 2 Resume Reels   221
Sidebar 3 First Jobs   222

Christopher Harper

18 The Emerging World of Online Journalism   **227**

Online at the *Chicago Tribune*   230
    Darnell Little   230
    Stephen Henderson   231
Virtual Melanin   231
Writing Online   233

Appendix Style   235
Credits   243
Index   245

Preface

As a journalist, you write the first rough draft of history. You get a front seat at what's going on in your community, your city, the nation and the world. Think about it. You can be there for a city council meeting, and your neighbors depend on you to tell them what happened. You can have a front-row seat to watch the basketball team in the playoffs or the high school football team in the state championship. You can ask questions that anyone would like to ask at a news conference. It's a great job and a great opportunity!

In Idaho, where I was born, the only Moscow I knew was in the northern part of the state. That's where the University of Idaho is located. Because I became a journalist, I had the opportunuty to visit the Moscow in Russia. In fact, I traveled to more than 60 countries and more than 40 states in the United States. And the news organizations paid for my trips!

As a public relations representative, you can help communicate an organization's mission to the public. When Mobil Oil thought the media were making errors in their coverage of the oil industry, the company decided to sponsor its own column in the *New York Times* to make certain the industry's side of the story was told. It worked.

As an advertising executive, you can shape what people think. In 1984, Apple ran an ad during the Super Bowl, touting the computer age. The ad ran only once, but it signaled the beginning of a revolution that's still ongoing today.

I was never the best student. In fact, my first teacher in journalism at the University of Nebraska suggested that I find another major. I was never the best reporter, but I did the best I could to provide information in an unbiased way to the reader and viewer. I can never be objective. To me, that means taking notes and simply presenting information chronologically without exercising judgment about what's important and what's not. As a man from flyover country—the part of the United States between New York and Los Angeles—I have biases, including hating New York and Los Angeles. All I can do is recognize my biases and make certain that my reporting is accurate.

My friends and colleagues who have written chapters for this book are among the best and brightest in the communications industry and higher education. For the past 20 years, Indiana University has invited a group of the finest new communications professors from throughout the country for a series of lectures on research, writing and teaching. The 1996 group included professors from 13 states and Canada with a variety of interests. As a result of The Freedom Forum Teaching Program, the professors decided to provide you with a textbook on communications.

The Indiana group is young—a bit irreverent—but skilled in the basic tenets of communications in newspapers, radio and television, online reporting, photojournalism, public relations and advertising. This book intends to maintain the classic structure of communications education while applying those principles to the year 2000 and beyond.

For those teaching introductory courses, this book offers expertise based on what the authors know and have done in the field. Many journalism textbooks are written by one or two authors with some experience in a few fields and no experience in other aspects of the business. Some authors have spent a long time away from the newsroom, the ad agency or the broadcast booth. I worked for more than two decades in newspapers, wire services, radio, television and online reporting. But I know there are far better experts in other fields among the Indiana Group. One or two authors simply cannot know about all the aspects of communications. Therefore, each chapter is written by someone who has first-hand knowledge about a particular field or issue. A reporter writes about reporting. A broadcaster writes about broadcasting. A photographer writes about photography. A public relations expert writes about public relations. A lawyer writes about the law. An ethicist writes about ethics.

I have taught beginning reporting classes at the undergraduate and graduate levels for newspapers, broadcasting and online disciplines. I have tried the drill-sergeant approach, the nice-guy approach and the variations in between. Although teaching styles may vary among us, the major problem I have faced is how to help students identify how to tell the story. Too often I have my students write before they understand how to tell a story, find a story, research a story and report it. For example, I often put too much emphasis on the placement of attribution rather than on the telling of a good yarn. No, we're not abandoning grammar, punctuation and the other rules of the craft. But if all we teach people is punctuation and the AP style book, we aren't preparing them to tell stories. And that's what journalists, public relations people, advertisers and a whole host of people do every day.

That's where this book begins: how to tell a story. Then you need ideas. Where do you get them? Then we turn to research. Any good story or presentation must concentrate first and foremost on research. Then you have to talk to people. How do you talk to them and interview them? That's the next phase of this book. Then you have to gather some facts: an odd notion called reporting. We focus on a variety of reporting techniques, including how to cover the small story as well as the big story. Included are some tips from a Pulitzer Prize winner. After you've gathered some worthwhile facts, you have to make them comprehensible to your boss, your readers, your viewers, your listeners and yourself. That means writing, rewriting and rewriting. As author Anne Lamott puts it so eloquently in her book *Bird by Bird*, no one ever writes a good first draft. Everyone writes a lousy first draft except for one of her acquaintances who she's convinced made a pact with the devil.

The next section deals with myriad forms of communicating. We analyze photography, broadcasting, television and documentaries. Law and ethics are critical for communicators to know and understand. You are the one who is making the decision, and often that determination is made out in the field. Public relations and advertising provide a key means of communicating with people. Take a look at how to do them correctly.

For students, textbooks can be expensive and dull. We often agree with students like those at the Massachusetts Institute of Technology who offered the following course evaluations:

"Information was presented like a ruptured fire hose—spraying in all directions—no way to stop it."
"What's the quality of the text? 'Text is printed on high quality paper.' "
"The course was very thorough. What wasn't covered in class was covered on the final exam."

We have had students analyze this book in an effort to see if what we are saying is clear and makes sense.

There are tips in each chapter on how to practice journalism, public relations and advertising. A separate section emphasizes how a reporter can read information properly to make more effective use of it. We also explore the growing role of digital journalism and the opportunities in the next millennium. Finally, we can't promise students an internship or a job, but there are some tips from an expert on how to get one.

We have enjoyed putting this book together. We hope you can learn from it and enjoy the means of communicating effectively with other people. The Indiana Group would like to thank the faculty of the Indiana University School of Journalism, particularly Trevor Brown, the dean of the school, and his able assistant, Judy Boruff. We also thank The Freedom Forum for its program. And, of course, we thank our wives, husbands, significant others, children, teachers, parents, students and everyone we forgot to include here.

Christopher Harper
Professor, School of
Communications,
Ithaca College
Idaho Statesman,
Associated Press,
Newsweek,
ABC News and "20/20"

▌ Storytelling

David Tait
Assistant Professor, School of Journalism and Communication,
   Carleton University, Ottawa, Canada
London (Ontario) *Free Press,* Whitehorse (Yukon) *Star,*
Calgary (Alberta) *Albertan* and the Canadian Broadcasting Corp.

Chapter Outline

Reporting as "story"

What's it made of?

The reporter's shopping list

Stories happen

Sequence, not structure!

A helicopter crashes

Story as trap

Sidebar Tips

Native cultures emphasize traditions that include characters, setting, complications and resolution—techniques that should be used in news stories as well.

Reporting as "Story"

Story: Journalists use the word all the time. We're on it, after it, chasing it, shooting it, writing it, cutting it, voicing it . . . or missing it. We're searching for a good one, a great one, a breaking one, a moving one, a chilling one, an offbeat one, a funny or bizarre one, a fair and accurate one and, if we're lucky, someday even a prize-winning one. *Story:* As with art and pornography, the closest we get to a firm definition is insisting we know it when we see it. Good journalists usually do, but how?

As a young reporter, I worked for three years in the newsroom of the Canadian Broadcasting Corp.'s tiny radio station in Inuvik, a town well above the Arctic Circle in Canada's Northwest Territories. We broadcast in English and three native languages, Slavey, Gwich'in and Inuvialuktun. My partner and I did news reports the way we'd been taught in journalism school, and then we passed our scripts to Lois Ross, an American who'd married a local native man and settled in the Arctic many years before.

Lois rewrote our stories, putting together what we'd written with the sound bites we had on tape, so the native announcers had a clear, complete text they could translate on-air into their own languages. I soon realized Lois was doing more than transcribing the taped bits back into the script; she was turning our professional-sounding "news copy" into *real* stories for local native listeners with their own strong oral storytelling tradition. She wasn't adding anything, just telling the story in a clearer way—clearer to any listener anywhere, native or otherwise.

Elsewhere in this book, you'll find chapters on how to spot, research and write "news stories" of all sorts for print or broadcast. Those are crucial lessons for anyone wanting to be a journalist. Here, though, we're going to start by snipping the word news off the front of the term; we'll leave news stories aside for a bit and talk instead of stories, plain and simple, and figure out what Lois knew instinctively: What they're made of and how they work.

The first thing you have to understand about stories is that there's no such thing. Stories don't exist; they *happen.* A story is an event, not an object. It exists in time, not space. It's a performance by the giver and an experience for those receiving it. That's as true for stories told on the page as it is for stories told around a campfire.

As we look toward telling journalistic stories in the 21st century via new media we can't even begin to imagine, we need to free our idea of "story" from the constraints of how we currently experience stories through print, radio and television. As we look forward (to storytelling with telepathy and holograms?), it pays to go back to the basics of storytelling in past ages and our own early lives.

What's It Made Of?

Think of all the stories you heard growing up as a child—whatever continent you or your ancestors are from, whatever language you grew up speaking, whatever culture or class, whether you're male or female. Your stories may have been about people and events completely different from those familiar to the person sitting next to you on the bus or across the classroom, but some aspects are identical.

- Every real story has a **setting,** a place where it happens and a combination of circumstances that provides its context.

- Every real story has one or more **characters,** with some being major players and some playing bit parts.

- Every real story has some sort of **complication** that occurs, triggering the chain of events that makes the story more than just simple description.

- Every real story puts its characters through a **process of responding** to this complication as they try to resolve the problem or conflict, take advantage of the opportunity or achieve their goal.

- Every real story brings this process to a **resolution,** happy or otherwise.

- And every real story includes some sort of **closure** that looks into the future (" . . . happily ever after . . . ") or provides meaning (" . . . and that's why . . . ").

There are far more detailed and scientific ways of breaking down the elements of a story, but they are more useful to linguists or psychologists than to journalists. There are also simpler ways, but they aren't much help: Every story has a beginning, a middle and an end, but so does a piece of string! Simpler isn't always better.

For our purposes, it makes sense to see a story as having these six elements: setting, characters, complication, process of responding/resolving, resolution and closure. Once you get used to them, they're as easy to remember as the classic Five-Ws and One-H (who, what, where, when, why and how). They're also more useful in the field as you dash around gathering information for your story, and at the keyboard on deadline as you sweat blood, trying to tell that story clearly and quickly.

The Reporter's Shopping List

If any *real* story is made of those six elements, so should a *news* story. They may not appear in that classic storytelling order (in fact, starting a news story with "Once upon a time" is a great way to initiate a career change!), but all six should be made clear somewhere in your article, broadcast report or Web site.

Reporters are used to reminding themselves to get the *who, what, where, when, why* and *how* of the news, but those labels don't guarantee they'll get a story and be able to tell it *as* a story. Instead, try using the six elements of a story as your checklist:

Setting: I need to get the *where* and *when,* but, more than that, I need to record the mood, the weather, the colors, the textures of the ground or the floor and walls, the smell in the air, the sounds in the background, the mood of the crowd and the activities going on. It isn't just location. It's total context. I need to be able to set the stage for my story and show how the setting changes as the story unfolds. That means soaking in all these details at the scene and writing them down in my notes, because I won't know for sure which specific bits of description I need until I sit down to write. And I can't trust my memory.

Characters: I need to get the *who*—but who's a "who" in my story? Everyone in the crowd? Just those on the podium or in the fight? Just the ones with mile-long titles and expensive suits? Or the ones with articulate or loud opinions? Well, who are the central characters in the story that's emerging? Who are supporting characters? What do I need to show them *as* characters and not just cardboard cutouts with names, ages and titles? Of course, I need those spelled correctly and written clearly in my notes. But I also need the way they dress and how they're built and how they move, speak and behave. I need to show their characters, to show them as characters in the story unfolding on the stage I'm going to set.

Complication: I need to get all the many *whats* of what happens, but this is a particular kind of *what* that's also partly *why.* What happened or is happening that's making these characters on this stage do what they're doing? News is change, so what's changed for them, when, where and why? If I just note down what they're doing when I arrive or while I'm there, I'll misrepresent what's going on. If I'm there as a reporter, it's probably because there's already been a complication that's triggered what I'm covering. What was it in the eyes of each side? That's more important than recording the confrontation blow-by-blow, showing the angry faces and quoting the nasty words. The start of the story isn't the broken window; it starts with whatever put the rock in the thrower's hand.

Process of Responding/Resolving: The next *what* I need is what that broken window, that complication, set in motion. What happened? What happened next? Who did what and why? What did they think was going on? What were they trying to accomplish? What did they say? How did they feel? What worked? What didn't? Why? Did they know where it was leading? Were they struggling for or against that trend? What did they think would come of the approaching resolution they wanted or feared?

Resolution: Reporters rarely get to cover how something ends, partly because they're usually covering it as it's happening and partly because nothing really does end completely despite appearances. The best a reporter can do is say how the process of events has resolved itself so far for the various characters involved. Where does it stand at deadline?

Closure: This final *what* is the "So what?" If that's where things stand, where does that leave us? What's likely to come next? What's planned or feared? How do the different characters feel about what's gone on and where it seems to be going? What do they say they've learned or think others should learn from what's happened? What would they do differently or wish others had done differently or should do differently next time? Where does this single story fit in the broader context of our world?

As reporters, we work ourselves raw, intrude where we're not wanted, take risks, see things we'd rather not know existed and often break our own hearts—all because we believe the people we serve desperately need to understand their world if they're to have any chance of coping with it. Closure is where we help them to this understanding by making an isolated cluster of events something of use to even those far removed from it.

Return to your newsroom with all those elements in your notebook (and on tape) and you won't just have news to report; you'll have a story to tell—completely, vividly, fairly and meaningfully. Now all you have to do is tell it.

Stories Happen

Remember, however, that stories don't exist; they happen. They're events, not objects. And these events don't happen at the writer's keyboard or the storyteller's lips. They happen in the imagination of the listeners, readers or viewers as they encounter the story elements gathered and skillfully arranged by the storyteller—in this case, by the reporter.

Your journalistic product isn't the eight inches of print that go on page one, those 80 seconds on the nightly news or the text, graphics, audio snippets and hot links on a Web site. Your real end-product is the images these leave in the memory—the minds and hearts of the people who experience the telling of your story as it unfolds. These folks receive it as a stream of words they lift off the page or hear spoken. Their eyes, meanwhile, flit over pictures nearby on the page or flickering by on the screen. These are the fragments from which they compose their own understanding of the story you're trying to tell.

But they don't assemble those fragments the way someone builds a house with bricks or even with a deck of cards. It's more as though they're painting a watercolor picture, one delicate brush stroke at a time . . . on a bubble floating in the air in front of them! One clumsy, careless move and the bubble bursts; the image of the story vanishes.

Sequence, Not Structure!

It's routine to speak of a story's structure, but that's misleading. A structure is architecture, whereas a story is more like dance—it happens as a sequence of intricate steps. As a storyteller, you're the choreographer who designs the order of those steps so the dance flows smoothly, the audience is captivated and the dancers don't trip over each other's feet.

Where do you start the dance? You begin with something that signals that what follows is worth attention. In journalistic storytelling of any kind, that's the story's lead. It should signal there's something coming the audience doesn't already know, something they'll care about because it's nearby, it affects them or it involves someone they care about. And it's something more timely than any previous telling they've heard of this unfolding story.

The lead is usually what's newest, so it's often taken from the story's resolution-to-date or even its closure. That's the big difference between a news story and the classic storytelling sequence: "Three little local pigs are living happily ever after today following a terrifying weekend encounter in Aesop's Acres with a big bad wolf." I'd read on; wouldn't you?

Then if the setting isn't immediately clear, you have to set the stage until it is. Is it enough for your particular audience to say "Aesop's Acres" or "8th and 42nd"? Will they instantly picture the neighborhood and the mix of people? Or do you need to explain where it is, how it looks and what the weather's like at this time of year?

Skip this step or stick this "background" at the bottom of the story, and the mind's eye of your audience will be watching everything that follows through a blurry lens. Don't go overboard, but don't plunge ahead until your audience "sees" the setting. It's amazing what just a few careful words can achieve.

A traditional print story might now give a quick bare-bones version of the story, lasting just a couple of paragraphs, including closure-type comments, and then go into a more detailed retelling.

A broadcast story is more likely to move through the story more chronologically within whatever time is allotted. Either way, the closer the storytelling is to an orderly "unfolding," the more easily the audience will absorb it and the more accurately they'll remember it. That's been scientifically tested, as they say on commercials. People remember stories best when they're told in the classic stages we've talked about. Those who are told a story that's out of sequence will predictably make errors retelling the story at precisely the points where the story's natural sequence was broken.

That doesn't mean all news stories must be told chronologically. That would be awkward, often silly and awfully dull. But it does mean that any variation from the natural, step-by-step unfolding should be done with care. And often the classic unfolding works unexpectedly well.

A Helicopter Crashes

Following is a radio story written by a good reporter on a tight deadline (the names have been changed to protect the embarrassed):

INTRO: More details have been released about a helicopter crash in the Yukon last night. The 27-year-old pilot was killed in the crash. The man was from British Columbia. Police are not releasing his name until the next of kin are notified. However, a Northwestel spokesperson says the crash happened after the pilot had dropped off three company employees in a remote area. Mark Loser reports:

VOICE SCRIPT: The crash took place near the old Tungsten mining site close to the Yukon-Northwest Territories border. It happened in a mountainous area.

The Watson Lake police say they received a mobile phone call from a person at a Northwestel tower site. The call came in at about 6 o'clock last night.

The helicopter that crashed belonged to Frontier Helicopters of Abbotsford, B.C. Another Frontier helicopter was dispatched from Watson Lake. And at about 8 o'clock the wreckage was found.

The pilot, who was the only person on board, was dead.

Mike Carter is a spokesperson with Northwestel. He says the pilot was doing work for the phone company. He had just dropped off three company employees.

Carter says the pilot was on his way back to Watson Lake when the crash happened. He issued a distress signal, which the employees on the ground picked up. One of them phoned the police.

Investigators from the Canadian Transportation Safety Board are trying to find out why the crash took place. The Yukon coroner's office and the police are also investigating.

Mark Loser, Whitehorse

Good reporter, bad report. This storyteller jumps all over the map, literally, and the story unfolds out of sequence. Something happens and then later happens again with a new detail added. The reporter probably worked frantically against the clock, first calling the police and then Carter at the phone company, and then wrote the "story" based on the order the details appeared in the notepad—first what the police said, then what the phone company said.

That pays no attention to the true nature of a story. The result is unclear and inefficient. Now let's see how it would work if we forget it's something called news and instead just tell it as a real story:

Setting: Northwestel has microwave relay towers in the mountainous areas in the eastern Yukon. The only way workers can get to these remote sites is by helicopter.

Characters: A helicopter belonging to Frontier Helicopters of Abbotsford, B.C., was working for Northwestel yesterday. The pilot was a 27-year-old man from British Columbia. He dropped three technicians at a telephone relay tower near the border between the Yukon and the Northwest Territories and flew off alone toward his base in Watson Lake.

Complication: Then the Northwestel employees heard a radio distress call from the pilot.

Process of Responding/Resolving: One of them phoned the police in Watson Lake on a mobile phone. That was at 6 o'clock. Another helicopter went out from the Frontier base at Watson Lake to search for the missing one. It found the wreckage two hours later near the old Tungsten mine site.

Resolution: The pilot of the crashed helicopter was dead.

Closure: Police won't release the pilot's name until they've contacted his family. Investigators from the Canadian Transportation Safety Board are trying to find out why the helicopter crashed. The Yukon coroner's office and the police are also investigating.

Clearer? Now let's slap a timely lead on the top, indicate who said what and recast it as a radio report once again:

INTRO: Police and Northwestel have released more details about a helicopter crash in the Yukon yesterday that killed one man. Rosy Future reports:

VOICE SCRIPT: Northwestel has microwave relay towers in the mountainous areas in the eastern Yukon. The only way workers can get to these remote sites is by helicopter.

The helicopter working for Northwestel yesterday belonged to Frontier Helicopters of Abbotsford, B.C. Its pilot was a 27-year-old man from British Columbia.

Mike Carter of Northwestel says the pilot dropped three technicians at a telephone relay tower near the border between the Yukon and the Northwest Territories and flew off alone toward his base in Watson Lake.

Carter says the Northwestel employees then heard a radio distress call from the pilot. One of them phoned the police in Watson Lake on a mobile phone. Police say this call was at 6 o'clock.

Another helicopter went out from the Frontier base at Watson Lake and it found the wreckage two hours later near the old Tungsten mining site. The pilot of the crashed helicopter was dead.

Police say they won't release the pilot's name until they've contacted his family.

Investigators from the Canadian Transportation Safety Board are trying to find out why the helicopter crashed. The Yukon coroner's office and the police have also started investigating.

Rosy Future, Whitehorse

That's not the only way to write this news story and may not even be the best. It sticks closely to the wording of the original because this is an exercise in sequence, not writing flourishes. Still, it's clearer, shorter and probably easier to write on deadline, since storytelling this way is a reflex. Best of all, it's a proper story, not just a collection of facts. You may not remember every name or number, but the *story* stays with you. And maybe as a real story it means something more to you, too, now that you can picture more clearly what it might have been like to be on that hill, hear that distress call and not know what had happened or to search for hours for a missing friend and finally find his body in the mangled wreckage of his chopper. Sharing that reality is part of reporting.

Story as Trap

Thinking "story" can work for you—but it can also work against you if you aren't careful, getting you into deep trouble or, worse, leading you to do harm to others.

An article in the *New York Times* used a direct qoute from Ted Kaczynski, the Unabomber suspect. The report should have attributed the quotation to the individual who recounted *his recollection* of a conversation with a man *he thought* was Kaczynski.

First, there's a difference between story and myth. Look hard into the events you're covering to find what's really going on. Don't jump to conclusions, or you run the risk of slotting characters unfairly and inaccurately into stereotypical roles: hero and villain, bully and underdog, creative child and domineering parent, Prince Charming and damsel in distress (or vice versa). The list of typecasting clichés is endless and dangerous.

Second, report only as much of the story as you've *really* gathered. Don't connect the dots or fill in the blanks to round out the narrative flow, even just by implication or nuance. The six elements of a story are useful even when you can't get all you need to tell a story completely. The sequencing pattern remains the same for the information that *is* available, but a principled reporter can also draw attention to *what's missing* and the questions left unanswered. Downplaying or glossing over holes in a story can do serious harm. Just ask Richard Jewell in Atlanta, the man who turned out not to be the Olympic Park bomber after all.

Third, as a reporter, the story you're telling is often the story of *being told things* by other people. That's different from retelling their stories as your own, but it's so easy to drift across that line as you get wrapped up in the narrative. In the middle of

Sidebar 1

Tips

1. Remember: Stories don't exist—they happen as experiences for those who read, hear or watch them.

2. Replace the Five-Ws and One-H in your tool kit with the six elements of a story: setting, characters, complication, process of responding/resolving, resolution and closure.

3. Think "sequence" rather than structure. Storytelling is akin to choreography, not architecture.

4. Don't be a slave to chronological unfolding, but depart from it with great care (and clear signposting).

5. Treat any story, be it for print or broadcast, as a story to be told, and read your draft out loud to test how well it works.

6. Before using some fancy literary flourish, ask yourself honestly if you are doing it to serve the audience or to impress your colleagues.

7. In journalism, attribute meticulously. Remember, your story is often about people telling stories of their own. Don't fall into retelling those stories as though they were fact.

8. Read broadly with a critical eye for how the story is being told.

9. Listen with an ear that's hungry to study how ordinary people instinctively tell their stories.

10. Tell stories yourself, and tell them as real stories—no matter to whom, no matter why, no matter about what. Rediscover why the story well told has been the most glorious treasure of humankind since the dawn of language.

an otherwise excellent article in the *New York Times* on May 26, 1996, on the life of Unabomber suspect Ted Kaczynski, these paragraphs are written:

```
    Prof. Donald Saari, of the mathematics department at
Northwestern University in Evanston, just north of
Chicago, said a man he thought was Mr. Kaczynski
appeared at his office, without an appointment, one day
in the spring of 1978.
    Investigators have expressed some doubts about
Professor Saari's account of what happened in what he
said were four or five meetings with the man.
```

Although these paragraphs are cautiously and carefully qualified and attributed, just seven paragraphs later appears the following:

```
    What happened next made a deep impression on the
professor.
    "I'll get even," Mr. Kaczynski said, shaking with
rage.
    Professor Saari next saw Mr. Kaczynski at a lecture
by a British scholar, Joseph Needham, who had written
extensively on the history of science and industry in
China. The subject was gunpowder.
```

Drift sets in, and the writer goes from telling the story of the professor's claims to telling the professor's story as though it were fact. The reporter quotes Kaczynski directly, when the damning words are actually the professor's version of a conversation the professor *says* took place. Ditto with Kaczynski's appearance at the lecture, which is presented as fact instead of attributed to the professor. The distinction is important, especially since Kaczynski was still awaiting trial.

Exercises

1. Simply tell someone—or yourself—a story. It could be a true one about something that happened to you or one you make up entirely. Don't think too hard. That's important. Just let the story come naturally. And listen to how it develops: the order in which it unfolds, the elements you emphasize, the places you pause, the point at which you finally end up.

2. Pick a couple of medium-length spot news stories from the newspaper and rewrite them into a classic narrative style, beginning with setting, then introducing the characters, taking them into the complication, through the process of responding, to the resolution and finally to the closure. Look for elements you need to tell each story this way that may have been left out of the newspaper version. Would including these have made it a better, clearer news story?

3. Take the previous exercise a bit further by numbering the facts in the narrative version of the story in the order in which they appear. Then put these numbers in the order these details appear in the newspaper story. How wildly do they jump about? Is every one of these departures from "natural" story order necessary? Do they help or hinder clarity?

4. Tape some TV and radio news stories and do a similar sort of analysis of them. Do they tend to follow the "natural" story flow more closely? Where do they depart from it? Does the story become harder to follow, even momentarily, at those points? How do the reporters try to make up for this, if at all? How would you?

5. Try approaching an interview you do as a process of extracting an oral story from the person. Deal with each of the elements of "story" in order and draw the details out of the person in chronological order. Watch how he or she responds to that approach and determine whether you found it harder or easier to get all you needed.

Suggested Readings

Cruikshank, Julie, et al. *Life Lived as a Story: Life Stories of Three Yukon Native Elders.* Vancouver: University of British Columbia Press, 1990. This is part anthology of traditional Athapaskan and Tlingit stories from Alaska and the Yukon, part oral autobiography of the three native women, and part scholarly analysis of how the women use stories to preserve their history, understand their world and shape an image of themselves. The scholarly bits are easy reading and fascinating; the women's stories about their lives and their people's past are marvelous.

Markham, Beryl. *West with the Night.* San Francisco: North Point Press, 1983. This is a tremendous story well told. In 1936, Markham became the first person to fly solo from England to North America, but most of this story is about growing up in Kenya long before that, running barefoot at the heels of Murani hunters, then training race horses, then working as a bush pilot over the African wilderness.

White, Theodore. *In Search of History: A Personal Adventure.* New York: Harper & Row, 1978. White's career as a newspaper and magazine journalist took him from Depression-era cities to China and the Pacific in wartime to post-war Europe during the dawn of the Cold War to the Kennedy White House. It's a book full of well-crafted stories about chasing stories. His final one is devastating: White was the first journalist to meet with Jacqueline Kennedy just days after her husband's assassination, and White tells the story of *her* telling the story of that day in Dallas.

2 Finding the Story

Anita M. Caldwell
Assistant Professor, Oklahoma State University
The Hartford Courant, Manchester Evening Herald and the *Tucson Citizen* (freelancer)

Chapter Outline

Where to look

Where you are

Life in the past lane

Best people

School daze

The minute waltz

Building blocks

Sidebar 1 Adventures and other great stories

Sidebar 2 Tips for finding ideas in neighborhoods, towns and cities

An Irish woman finally becomes an American citizen at age 101 after years of failed attempts and misunderstandings.

A 59-year-old woman has been collecting salt and pepper shakers—some dating to the early 20th century. Since the age of 16, she has acquired more than 400 pieces from friends and family who have traveled all over the world.

A street in a Connecticut town was named for a counterfeiter from the 1700s, who escaped the constables by hiding at the bottom of a river and breathing through the end of a long reed until his pursuers passed him. Then he left town.

These unusual, or put-a-smile-on-your-face, stories are what editors at *The Hartford Courant* call "Hey, Martha!" stories. They catch our attention with extraordinary events. They make us stop for a moment and reflect. These wonderful slices of life let our imagination run wild.

One of the most exciting places to find such stories is in communities and neighborhoods. And it is here that many news reporters find their first job or assignment.

Newspapers pursue local stories because of the intimacy they create with the readers. When local events and activities get published, many say it encourages greater participation from people and provides them with an opportunity to become a part of the community.

For the young reporter, what makes covering local news such fun is that in these cities and neighborhoods there exists a link to the past, the present and future. Those who know a place well can vividly recreate the history of the community, carefully weaving interesting and exciting tales.

This chapter will show you where such stories exist and how to find the people who can tell these stories.

Where to Look

One of the first steps to finding great tales is to stop looking at the newspaper as just stories and pictures. Instead consider it a collection of adventures from people all over the world. Every day a group of these people (reporters) brings you (the readers) these wonderful adventures in story form. It's like getting together with a group of close friends as they passionately tell their daily adventures, drawing you in with every word.

A reporter's job is to find stories of adventure, mystery and entertainment. Some of the best places for finding fascinating stories are the diner, the delicatessen, the grocery store and the local bars. Spend time getting to know the people who frequent these places. Reporters don't rely on officials or records alone. In fact, it's usually comments from the people and overheard conversations that tip reporters off to good stories. People are more likely to open up to reporters, especially if something funny or heart-warming is happening.

I was visiting a bar in a neighborhood I covered to find out more information about a girl who may have been run over by her boyfriend one night. Only by visiting the bar again and again and chatting with the regulars did I get the kind of information I needed about the couple. It helped establish who they were, and it put some identifying features to their otherwise anonymous faces.

Visit the police station, the fire house and other emergency care stations. Establish a good rapport with police sergeants, fire and police chiefs, public

Sidebar 1

Adventures and Other Great Stories

What's it like to watch an embalming? How does it feel to get a tattoo? Imagine spending a day watching fertilizer become mushrooms or paper become tea bags. Your readers just might want to know about those things.

The idea list for on-the-job profiles is enormous. Find the wacky, the weird or the not-so-traditional. Construction workers, window washers of tall buildings, stained-glass makers and athletes can make for great stories.

Most stories in this genre can be interesting if you approach them with an appreciation for what the workers are doing and a keen eye for detail. Let your readers smell the pungent embalming fluid that pierces your nostrils as you take in a breath. Let them feel the thousands of rapid needle pricks on their arm, as a brightly colored snake tattoo slowly takes shape.

Spend a day, a night or a few hours with someone at work. See if you can get to ride with a police officer or firefighter for a day, a morning, an afternoon or, better still, a night. In fact, comparing the types of calls and incidents during morning hours and late evening or overnight shifts can show some compelling differences and patterns in crime and medical emergencies. (Think twice, though, before doing this if there's a full moon.)

information officers and, if you can get to them, the police officers and firefighters themselves. Besides the usual crime, fire and medical emergency stories, reporters can find great stories about new equipment, training programs, community programs, the youth police and trends in crime and fire prevention.

The Better Business Bureau or Chamber of Commerce can be a great source for stories. Make a good connection with the presidents of these organizations and others, such as the Rotary Club. You might discover some meaty stories. Let me give you an example, the Better Business Bureaus in Phoenix and Tucson, Ariz., led me to a story that became a three-part series on business scams, which were so pervasive that business owners across the nation fell in their destructive wake. It took state and federal authorities to put a dent in some of these operations.

Where You Are

Think about where you are. Look around with a different eye. How often do reporters pass the same buildings each time they drive through the cities they cover? Take the time to go inside some of these buildings—not just the local government buildings.

When a place grows, many people want to save landmark buildings. Why? Because they are a touchstone to the past, some businesses turn these buildings into new shops that help the local economy. One entrepreneur turned an old Fotomat film drop into a drive-in "Condom Hut."

Wherever you are, make sure you meet the directors of the parks and recreation departments. You can get good stories about new programs. You can also discover any controversies over issues such as land use, complaints about inadequate park supervision and the increase or decrease in the number of accidents at parks or swimming pools.

In many communities, the parks get heavy use from local sports teams for kids and adults. And most places don't have the budget to build more parks as the community grows. How do such limitations affect those wishing to use the parks? What are cities doing about obtaining more space? These questions lead to good stories.

Senior citizens' communities and club houses usually start springing up in growing towns and cities as the population gets older. The seniors may want to sell homes that have become too large for them and younger families move in to take their place.

Life in the Past Lane

Be sure to check where community records are kept. For example, in New England, many records go back to the 1600s. By looking through land transactions, tavern and food bills, pharmacy receipts and school records, you can come across some fascinating stories. The records include buildings that now are considered historic: an old schoolhouse, a museum or a dance hall—another bunch of good stories.

Look for hidden places in town that draw on history. One such story I wrote with the help of other reporters drew terrific town trivia questions: In 1819, what did terrified residents see in the sky over the city? Which resident in the 1870s almost succeeded in a forgery scheme against the Bank of England, was caught and jailed and then wrote a book about his imprisonment? Which resident in 1895 spent more than $8,000 for his gravestone monument, which was made in Italy, insured by Lloyds of London and stands in the local cemetery?

Get together with the clerk, planner, historian and anyone else who can give you information about life in the past. Searching those old records will help, too. Most people are so thrilled that you consider their neighborhood important to write about on a regular basis that they are usually quite helpful.

Best People

When you're about to make those first contacts and visits in the city, neighborhood or town, set up appointments ahead of time with some of the people you want to cultivate as sources. Take them to breakfast or lunch or go for coffee. You're trying to establish a relationship with people to whom you'll look for information. However, the same people also may become adversarial if you have to start digging around in business where they don't think you belong. So make your first impression a good one. Choose a relaxed setting away from the office. These new contacts need to see you as a human being before they see you as "The Press."

Other great people to interview are people who work with senior citizens. You'll get great stories about retired folks who have taken up an unusual hobby or business. Many older adults today are quite active and frequently have the time to get involved in their community. Their personal and civic activities can spark terrific stories, and they can become good sources. It's often the older residents who can make the time to stay through an entire town council or planning and zoning meeting. And council members tend to conduct themselves differently when they see persistent residents in the audience following every agenda item.

Who are other good sources? Rarely does anybody do anything in any community without going through the town or city clerk. From dog and cat licenses, and knowing who's who on every board or commission, or to the documents of yesterday and today that could move politicos up in their career or land them in jail,

Senior citizens often remain quite active and frequently have the time to get involved in their community. Their personal and civic activities can spark terrific stories.

the town or city clerk pretty much "owns" the town or city. A savvy clerk also can alert you to a great story.

Mayors or chief administrative officers are people who can be absolutely invaluable if you can establish a good relationship with them. If you succeed at this, your journalistic life can be quite glorious. If you don't, it can be hell. Repeat this mantra on your way into the city or town or before your next telephone call: "They need me as much as I need them. And I need them as much as they need me."

Basically, city and neighborhood leaders want to tell you all the good stuff that's going on for some good press so everyone's happy. If you're accurate, fair and on top of things, chances are you'll get what you need for your stories and they'll get the feel-good stories they want.

One of the best chief administrative officers I've met had a healthy appreciation for the flow of information. When council or committee members complained to him that I called during dinner or late in the evening for a comment, he asked them if they'd rather have the last word on a story or let their opponent have it. He did a good job balancing the needs of the city with access for the press.

School Daze

Schools are perhaps the most important topic for those who have children and those who pay taxes anywhere in the country. As soon as you've met with the heads of the local government, contact the school principals and superintendent. Meet with the superintendent first. That's the person you most likely will be talking to most often. However, the superintendent may be friendly and charming but awfully closed-mouth. If you're faced with that, get a good connection with the principals, assistant principals or other administrators who are more willing to work with you.

Schools are perhaps the most important topic for those who have children and those who pay taxes anywhere in the country.

Then, ask to attend a faculty meeting early in the year. Once you're there, give out your business card and tell the faculty that you want to know everything they're doing that involves the kids. (See Chapter 6 for more details.) I've been amazed at the creativity public school teachers demonstrate with limited money and resources to make education interesting for students. Toss out some story ideas so they can see what you mean: science fairs, debates, music and art competitions, and cultural fairs, which sometimes involve food along with the music and dress of the culture fairs—a feast for the eyes and tummy. When was the last time you held a boa constrictor or let a tarantula crawl over your hand? Zoo creatures often are brought to schools. Other unusual events happen as well, and people like to read these stories.

Let the teachers know you're excited about what they're doing for the students and the parents should know about the creative minds they've hired. The teachers will feel appreciated.

Tell the faculty to send you a press release or other kind of information sheet well in advance of each event. Encourage them to send lots of material so you have a bevy of choices. Some teachers will have done something newsworthy such as an award-winning program. Alert them, however, that not everything will be covered.

When the time comes to embark on a school story that will center on the students, keep in mind that you might get little comment from elementary kids below the fifth grade. They are adorable and their expressions are priceless, but you'll have to be creative with your questions to get any dialogue going. With junior high and high school students, you'll get an interesting mix. Some students will be quite articulate. Others will speak in incomprehensible half-sentences. I once wrote a "critique" of cafeteria food. I visited and rated all the schools. Judging the food was not difficult. Getting quotable material was virtually impossible. Finally, surrounded by a lively group of high school boys who were all eager to get their name in print, I stated that I would take comments only from the first one who could put a whole sentence together. The group grew silent and exchanged a few glances, but eventually I got some good quotes.

Some of the most heated battles that make great school stories are those in which you hear "high taxes" and "schools" in the same sentence. When people complain about high taxes and unnecessary expenses, all eyes usually turn to the public schools as the culprit. Schools often are the most expensive part of an annual budget. Residents seem to accept the expenses that go with fire and police safety and running the city, but schools are frequently accused of spending money on frills. Don't bother trying to make sense of what people consider a frill. If you were to ask each resident to define "school frill," Webster's would have to put out a new dictionary.

The Minute Waltz

After you've become familiar with who's who in your town or city, start attending meetings such as the planning and zoning commission and the school board. Attend other meetings according to what is on the agenda and what "buzz" you hear.

A day or two before a meeting, plan to spend several hours combing through the board or council's past minutes. Go back at least a year, more if you have time. You'll be able to see patterns of voting, the progress of certain issues and who tends to say what. Be aware, however, that in many communities the minutes include only what the person taking the notes considers most important. You probably won't read much of the banter among the board members, nor will you get the nuances of what they said. But it's enough to make you familiar with pressing issues. Once you've attended a meeting or two, you'll be able to fill in the rest of the picture yourself.

Besides reviewing what the controversial issues have been, it's a good idea to spend a few hours once a week going through past minutes of secondary boards, commissions, committees and advisory groups. Although you should cover most of the primary boards and commissions and speak with the leaders of the various groups on a regular basis, you won't be able to get around to everyone.

Minutes can serve as more than just a summary of a meeting and an outcome of votes. Issues raised in secondary board meetings often make fascinating stories. A conservation commission, for example, deals with the environment. Although I believe a conservation commission should be considered important in many locales, it usually doesn't have the same status as other governmental bodies. But the story ideas generated from a conservation commission can be tremendous as most involve controversial issues such as land use and aquifers. These issues affect public health and safety.

I was once tipped off about a former chemical plant that had gone bankrupt a year before but had not finished cleaning up its chemicals, some of which were said to be hazardous. The company said it had just run out of money to finish the job. The tip led to a four-part series on the issue, including tracking the progress of the cleanup. Besides interviewing officials and company directors, at least those who were willing to talk to me, a good part of my investigation came from looking through past minutes to track whatever history there was on the plant.

Building Blocks

If the words "cover a meeting" imply boredom for a reporter, then add planning and zoning to the phrase and most reporters only hear the Zzzzzzzz. Again, it's all in how you look at the lot that's been handed to you. (See Chapter 6 for more details.)

Some of my most memorable stories came from planning and zoning meetings. A good part of the time, this is the first stop to a real estate developer's residential complex or a new business. So you can track the stages of getting a new business in town or watch how a new apartment or condominium complex is coming along.

Frequent controversy involves resident groups wanting to restrict increased development, which they claim causes increased traffic and threats to children's safety. Other battles involve altering the beauty of the locale—how such development will enhance or detract from the way the neighborhood, town or city looks. Still other issues involve infrastructure. Can the city or town support additional demands on water supplies, fire, police and schools? On the other hand, all growing cities and towns need increased tax bases, so local governments want to encourage businesses to locate there. In any case, these meetings can give you some good stories. Again, if you can't stay for the entire meeting, look through the minutes to see what other issues have come before the group that could be additional stories.

Finally, most of the population in the automobile-oriented decades since World War II has shifted from the aging, landlocked central cities to the suburbs. These are rapidly developing areas that are independent residential, recreational and education centers and regional economic centers. In addition, where someone lives is sometimes different from where someone works. Therefore, those living in the suburbs have as much an interest in news from their own backyard—often more so—than they do from the city center.

When you write stories about a community, people begin to see that you have an interest in where they live. And suburban cities and towns usually are in the midst of growth spurts as people move out from the inner cities. Such growth forces changes in government, infrastructure and amenities such as specialty shops, video stores and retail stores.

In one place I covered, the population grew nearly 30 percent in 10 years. But there still was only one traffic light. Stay abreast of these developments, as they frequently have a tremendous effect on the way the local government functions to provide services and education. Then the people will keep looking to you for your next adventure.

Exercises

1. Pick a town, city or neighborhood, maybe your hometown. In source books or on the Internet, look up the history of the town or city. Find the year it was incorporated, whether it has a charter and when that was established. Identify any previous names or spellings it had and any interesting facts about the town or city. Based on this information, write a story suggestion that focuses on the fascinating history or mysteries of the town or city.

Sidebar 2

Tips for Finding Ideas in Neighborhoods, Towns and Cities

- Go to a bar, a coffee shop or an exercise gym.
- Meet the people in power.
- Meet the rest of the people.
- Get everyone's telephone number and give them your number.
- Ask to be on everyone's mailing list.
- Take people to lunch.
- Visit the kids in school.
- Attend events and fairs.
- Dig through records and documents.

2. Find interesting profiles or a synopsis of prominent people who lived in a particular town or city. Choose three communities of various sizes in population and find the histories or brief biographies of two noteworthy people in each place. Describe what contribution these individuals made to the community or why these people are noteworthy. Write a story proposal on one individual.

3. Split up into groups. Each group should select three towns or cities in the state (within an hour's drive from the campus) that seem interesting for stories. Prepare a list of the places you would go and the people you would interview in those communities to find amusing, anecdotal or unusual facts about historical figures.

4. With the list generated from Exercise #3, each full group or specific individuals within the group should visit one of the communities you selected. Analyze how your preparations and research worked or did not work. Write a story proposal about your visit.

References

DeSilva, Bruce, and John Mura, eds. *The Straight Scoop.* Dubuque, Iowa: Times Mirror Higher Education Group, 1996.

Izard, Ralph S. *Reporting the Citizen's News.* New York: Holt, Rinehart and Winston, Inc., 1982.

Mott, Patrick. *The Quill.* Small-town Leaks, March 1991.

Stamm, Keith. *Newspaper Use and Community Ties: Toward a Dynamic Theory.* Norwood, N.J.: Ablex Publishing Corp., 1985.

Suggested Readings

Hoyt, Mike. "Are You Now, or Will You Ever Be, a Civic Journalist?" *Columbia Journalism Review*. September/October 1995. This article is a good overview of civic journalism and the arguments for and against. For journalists of community reporting, the civic journalism movement brings to the forefront the problems and rewards that exist when writing about a neighborhood.

Murray, Donald. *Writing for Your Readers*. Old Saybrook, Conn.: The Globe Pequot Press, 1983. This book is a delightful collection of practical suggestions for clear writing and good storytelling. Tips from professionals and excerpts of newspaper articles add to the book's real-life advice.

Rosen, Jay. "Community Connectedness." The Poynter Papers: No. 3. The Poynter Institute for Media Studies, 1993. This provides quick, friendly material on the finer points of storytelling. Civic or public journalism is covered in several of the articles. New York University Professor Jay Rosen is the intellectual guru of a movement, which some see as critical to the success of informing citizens.

West, Bernadette, et al. *The Reporter's Environmental Handbook*. New Brunswick, N.J.: Rutgers University Press, 1995. West's book on environmental reporting is a wonderful guide to some of the terms, issues and relationships between journalists and issues dealing with the environment.

3 Researching the Story

Carol Schlagheck, Ph. D.
Assistant Professor of Journalism, Department of English
    Language and Literature, Eastern Michigan University
Bedford (Township, Mich.) *Journal-Herald,* Monroe (Mich.) *Evening
    News* and *News Photographer Magazine*

Chapter Outline

Strike at the paper mill

Fundamental research materials

    Telephone book

    Map

    Newspaper morgue

    The local library

Government documents

Academic research, polls, surveys

Sidebar 1 Tips

Sidebar 2 Historic mansion in danger?

Every day reporters learn something new, whether it's how an athlete feels after a big game or how a water filtration system works. Then they tell their readers.

Reporters go to work each day knowing they could be assigned to cover just about anything. Are you ready? How much do you know about tax abatement? Teacher licensing? Smokestack emissions? Asphalt quality? Farmland preservation? Maybe you need to do some research. You may think we're supposed to ask questions. We're not supposed to know everything going in. Besides, we don't have time for research.

This chapter will explain how—even on deadline—research can save time, can make for more effective interviews and can help you avoid embarrassing mistakes or assumptions. Whether it's glancing at a city directory or spending hours poring over documents in a federal depository, time spent on research is time well spent.

Strike at the Paper Mill

It's a couple of hours before deadline, but your work for the afternoon paper is finished. You're using the extra time to put some finishing touches on a piece for next Sunday's features section: "Ferrets: Fun, Furry Friends." All of a sudden, your metro editor is flashing a scrap of paper under your nose. "Got a call from this guy. Says there's pickets out at the paper mill again. See if you can work up a story for today." "No problem," you answer, grabbing your notebook and heading for the coat rack.

As you drive west on Paper Mill Road toward the river, you realize that you're not exactly sure how to get to the paper mill. You were there once when the plant superintendent won an award for his involvement with Junior Achievement. But that was six months ago, right after you got this job. You're sure if you just stay on Paper Mill Road, you'll run right into the plant.

Thirty minutes later, you've driven over every mile of Paper Mill Road, and there's no paper mill. Reluctantly, you call your metro editor to ask for directions.

"There hasn't been a mill on Paper Mill Road in 10 years!" she shouts. "The only mill left is on River Street. Turn left at the light. I swear. If it had teeth, it'd bite you!" The editor slams the receiver in your ear. You find the plant, you find the pickets and you park your car.

The pickets inform you that they have been negotiating a new contract for eight months and the boss still insists on concessions. Some big jobs are coming up, and the union thinks this is a prime time to show its strength.

"Ask the boss what he's gonna do about this," suggests the shop steward.

"Gee, you know, I met your boss once, but I forget his name."

"Smith. Bill Smith."

"Is he inside?"

"He was, but he left. Guess he couldn't take it."

You head back to the office and start writing your story as you dial directory assistance. "Yes, I need the number of Bill Smith."

"S-M-I-T-H?"

"Yes," you answer impatiently, thinking, "How else would you spell Smith? Geez."

The operator returns, "I have a William Smith on Maple Boulevard, but it's a nonpublished number."

"Thanks, anyway."

Reporters cover subjects that can range from tax abatement and teacher licensing to smokestack emissions and farmland preservation. A good story always starts with good research.

You hang up and add a sentence to the end of your story: "Our Town Paper Mill manager William Smith could not be reached for comment."

You file the story with five minutes to spare. You wait until the assistant copy editor nods at you; then you head out for a well-deserved burger and fries.

When you get back from lunch, the paper is off the presses and the metro editor is glaring at you. "Didn't you talk to the plant manager?" she demands.

"He wasn't at the plant," you whimper.

"You were supposed to call him at home!" the editor yells.

"His number is unlisted."

"I gave it to you!"

Suddenly, you remember the note she had flashed under your nose. It's lying crumpled on your desk. You unfold it: "Bob Smyth home—555-7290."

"Not only did you have his name wrong," your editor says, scowling, "but you also got the name of the mill wrong. It's Our Town Paper Co., not Our Town Paper Mill."

It could happen to anyone, right? In your haste to get to the scene, you forgot about the note. You thought you knew the name of the company. Is it your fault the union steward doesn't know the boss's name? Is it your fault the manager spells "Smith" funny?

The bottom line is the blame for sloppy reporting always rests with the reporter. Even on a tight deadline, a little research could have salvaged this disastrous story.

Fundamental Research Materials

Start with the basics. Your research can begin with guides available to everyone.

Telephone Book

An indispensable tool, the local phone book can help you spell names correctly and find addresses as well as phone numbers. In the case of the paper mill story, the phone book would have told you the proper name of the mill and its address. You also could have looked up the number of the plant manager, if it is listed, and you might have noticed that the phone book has various spellings for the name that sounds like Smith—Smyth, Smythe, Smithe, Schmith.

Map

Keep a local map in your desk drawer and another one in your car. Use it not only to figure out how to get where you're going but to double-check such things as street names and whether two roads intersect.

Newspaper Morgue

Clips or computerized copies of old newspapers stories can give you detail and perspective. In the case of the paper mill strike, you could have looked up the Junior Achievement story you wrote six months ago. That would have told you the correct name of the plant manager, as well as the correct way your newspaper refers to the plant—Our Town Paper Co., a division of National Paper Inc.

Remember that your editor said there were pickets at the plant "again." By checking the morgue, you could have learned that this is the third time in a year that pickets have been set up outside the mill and that the relationship between the union and management has been deteriorating for years. You might also have learned that the former mill on Paper Mill Road was closed 11 years ago after a prolonged strike.

The Local Library

Your public library can be an oasis of free information for adding background and context to your stories. Even on deadline, you can find facts that will be meaningful additions to the information and quotes you have been able to gather. If you hadn't wasted half an hour looking for the paper mill, you might have had time to stop by the library and quickly look up the company in the *Standard and Poor's Register of Corporations, Directors and Executives* or other industry directories. You could have learned such things as the name of the parent company, the number of plants the company has, the locations of those plants, the number of people the company employs, the products it manufactures and the names of top company officers.

Have you hugged a librarian lately? Well, maybe not, but you should know that librarians are up there with secretaries as the folks who can make or break you when you need a piece of information and need it fast. With a source at the local library

A public library can be an oasis of free information for adding background and context to your stories.

who is willing to look up a fact or two, you can get short bits of information over the phone, or by fax, while you work on other aspects of your story.

One great library resource is the *Encyclopedia of Associations,* published by Gale Research. Remember that Sunday feature on pet ferrets? A check of the *Encyclopedia of Associations* can yield a phone number for the president of the National Ferret Owners' Association.

In addition to phone books, maps and clippings, every newspaper office should be equipped with the following:

- City directories. Published for most cities and counties, directories work like reverse phone books. In most, you can look up a phone number and see who it belongs to. More important, you can look up addresses and see who lives there. Say you're working on a story on a house fire and you want to know who lives in the home. Look it up in the city directory. Directories also can be useful when you want to call neighbors in a certain area. For instance, if the school district plans to cut out bus service for residents on Ash and Elm streets, you can look in the directory for the names and phone numbers of residents on those streets and then call them for comments.

- Almanacs. Almanacs are full of great information you might need. How do you spell a sports star's name? What year were the Olympics held in such-and-such a place?

- Dictionaries

- Thesaurus. What word do you really want to use?

Sidebar 1

Government Documents

Government records can range from a simple listing of registered voters to a rundown of who in your community has a permit to carry a handgun. They include such routine material as a village budget to the inventory of toxic substances routinely stored at a local industry. Often called "public records," they can help put the meat on what would otherwise be a bare-bones story. What's often confusing, even to veteran reporters, is where to find the records you seek. After all, each government tends to keep its own records. Although government records increasingly are available online or on CD or tape, most local records must be obtained the old-fashioned way—by walking over to where the records are kept.

If you're following up a rumor that a local employer is going bankrupt, would you start at city hall, the county courthouse, a local library, the state capitol or the closest federal courthouse? If you're trying to find who keeps parking illegally in handicapped parking spots, do you call the mayor, the police chief or the deeds office?

It can be a bewildering task, if you don't know where to look. It can sometimes be formidable even if you do know where to look. As you might guess, local government is the best place to go for "local" information. Most local governments have a clerk, registrar or someone with a similar title who keeps track of all official business—minutes of public meetings, dog licenses, building permits, you name it. Even if the clerk or registrar isn't personally responsible for keeping the records, he or she probably knows where they can be found. Get to know your local clerk, whether at the town, village, city or county level.

Records commonly found at the local level include building permits, property deeds, business registrations, vital statistics, construction and tax liens, handgun permits, registered voters and Uniform Commercial Code statements, which detail borrowing and lending.

State record-keeping systems also vary, but, in general, records are kept whenever people file records with the state government. For example, records of state-licensed professionals—from morticians to beauticians in many states—are recorded at the state level, along with any disciplinary actions that have been meted out to licensees. Hunting and fishing licenses, boat registrations and corporate records also are kept at the state level. Other common state records include driving and automobile records kept by the Department of Motor Vehicles.

Though more and more federal information is accessible via computer and online, federal depository libraries have the "hard copy" version of many federal documents. About 1,400 federal depository libraries exist across the United States. Most look like typical community or university libraries and are known by typical library names. But they hold volumes of federal documents that can be accessed easily. Most carry the federal budget, data from the U.S. censuses of population, housing and economic data, the Congressional Record, the Federal Register, Government Printing Office documents, Supreme Court decisions and The Code of Federal Regulations, which are the rules used to implement laws.

Federal courthouses also are depositories of valuable information. They usually hold a treasure of information, ranging from bankruptcy filings to indictments and the names of parties suing or being sued for breach of federal or civil law. Scads of government offices, not only in the Washington, D.C., area, but scattered throughout the country, also hold a combination of helpful documents. Often, government employees are willing to provide information to reporters over the phone if you know what you need.

Academic Research, Polls, Surveys

Much of the information that comes across a journalist's desk is in the form of research that has been done by public pollsters, university professors, marketing firms and, sometimes, other news organizations. As reporters—and consumers of news and information—we need to know how to separate the reliable research from the bad and how to present it to an audience that might not understand scientific gobbledygook or professional jargon.

Many studies are contradictory. Are vitamin supplements good for you or not? It depends on what study you read. What's the latest on caffeine? Each piece of research seems to say something different. As journalists, we need to help the reader understand and evaluate research, from the latest findings on what causes cancer to a new study on making relationships last.

Frequently, writers are called upon to "humanize" research by finding local people who personify the topic or have informed opinions about it.

How do I use research in my stories?

Remember: You're NOT writing a term paper. Reporters use primary sources. If you're doing an article on the latest "cure" for some disease, you search for experts and information written by researchers, not *Time* magazine. As journalists, we don't quote each other. Go to the original source.

Reporters do not use footnotes. We "cite" experts and works by saying, "according to." Do not make it look as if you talked with someone if you're only quoting his or her printed work. Say, "As Dr. So-and-So wrote in the Journal of . . . ," or better yet, call Dr. So-and-So and get some quotes to perk up the raw data.

We translate jargon and euphemisms for our readers. What exactly is a waste water treatment conduit—a sewer? Say so.

We localize research findings and opinion polls. Has *American Demographics* magazine reported that college students are finding it harder to graduate in four years and are graduating with unprecedented student debt? Report the findings, but find some local college students to support or challenge the alleged trend. Get local quotes.

Sidebar 2

Historic Mansion in Danger?

Gary Jones, a *Daily Bulletin* reporter, had heard a rumor at the barbershop that someone had purchased the old Stoddard mansion from the Stoddards, one of the town's founding families.

The rambling structure was a throwback to the days when lumber and paper barons ruled the town. It had always been held within the family, passed from one generation to the next like a treasured heirloom. However, for the past few years—ever since Martin Stoddard died at 97—it has been vacant, yet well kept. Now the rumor was afoot that it had been purchased dirt cheap and would be converted into apartments. If it were true, it would be news that would shatter the local historical society and disappoint many long-time residents.

Gary's first call was to a Realtor he knew, a Realtor who usually was tapped into the local real estate grapevine. The only thing the Realtor had heard was that the property might have a new owner soon.

His next stop was the county deeds office, where land contracts, deeds and other property records are logged. Fortunately, the deeds office had just been computerized and transactions going back three years had already been entered into the computer. An office worker showed him how to run the computer and how to print out a record of the instrument of sale. All he needed was a name for the seller or buyer or that person's address. Gary sat down and typed in the address: 412 Stone St. Within seconds, the computer returned a transaction report. The house had been purchased from the Stoddard estate by a man named John Wickings. On the screen were the purchase price—$212,000—and the date of sale—Jan. 14 of this year.

Gary had already confirmed that the house had a new owner. But who was Wickings? He punched in the name on the deeds computer again. It hummed for a second, and the screen filled with listing after listing of property transactions, 19 in all. Most appeared to be properties that Wickings had purchased. A couple of them were ones he had sold. From the addresses, they all appeared to be in a run-down area of town. He copied a list of the addresses and the sale dates and prices and headed for City Hall.

His first stop at City Hall was the tax office. Sometimes it's called the appraiser's office or other names. It's where the property tax records are

kept. He knew to go there because the city clerk told him about it when he was researching a previous story. The tax office clerk tapped a few keys on her computer, and up popped the property description for 412 Stone St. The description noted that the house was built in 1901. She pointed at the computer screen again. "He bought a house worth $500,000 for $212,000!"

Now Gary had a better story. He went to work on the addresses he had scribbled down at the deeds office in the county courthouse. He drove by the addresses Wickings owned and approached one house, where he noticed someone at home. An elderly man was sweeping the front porch.

"Hi, I'm looking for John Wickings," he said.

"He owns the house, but he don't live here," the man replied.

"Know where I can find him?"

"Well, I think I got his phone number somewhere." The man disappeared and returned with the number scrawled on a slip of paper.

"He never answers his phone and he doesn't return messages. If you ever talk to him, ask him when he's going to fix my roof," the man said. "It's been leaking for two years!"

After a brief conversation, Gary learned the house long had had a series of structural problems that Wickings hadn't corrected. The man also said Wickings offered to let him move into one of 10 new low-income apartments he was creating at the old Stoddard house on Stone Street. The reporter also found that the landlord had been cited for a variety of violations. Here is what he wrote:

A city landlord who has been cited 15 times in the past year for housing violations has purchased the turn-of-the-century Stoddard mansion on Stone Street and plans to convert it into 10 low-income apartments.

John Wickings is seeking a zoning change for a $180,000 redevelopment project that would include paving a portion of the lush garden area long tended by the late Martin Stoddard.

"My business is none of your business," Wickings said when asked to elaborate on his plans.

Some of Wickings' current tenants said they were interested in how Wickings could redevelop the Stoddard mansion when he can't fix their leaky roofs or repair their plumbing.

That's how research turns into a story.

Exercises

1. Select a building—perhaps the apartment building you live in or the bookstore you frequent—and do some research on it without interviewing anyone. When was it built? Who owns it? What improvements have been made in the past five years? What is the tax assessment?

2. Go to a university library and find two pieces of academic research on a topic. Then find a national expert or an association you could contact for quotes on the subject.

3. Acquire a public opinion poll. Evaluate it based on who funded it, who was studied and what questions were asked. Is it newsworthy?

Suggested Readings

Paulos, John Allen. *A Mathematician Reads the Newspaper.* New York: Basic Books, 1995. This book demonstrates what can go wrong when journalists sprinkle figures and statistics into their stories without understanding them. The book includes examples of articles that miss the mark—and suggests ways to learn from the mistakes.

Weinberg, Steve. *The Reporters Handbook: An Investigator's Guide to Documents and Techniques.* New York: St. Martin's Press. Third Edition, 1996. This is a Bible for reporters. It's filled with tips and resources for obtaining information. More than a textbook, this is a book that many professionals keep on their desks.

Wilhoit, C. Cleveland, and David H. Weaver. *Newsroom Guide to Polls and Surveys.* Bloomington: Indiana University Press, 1980. This cuts through the smoke and helps journalists understand the statistical information they routinely present to their readers. A must for any journalist who wants to report on numbers with confidence.

4 Computer-Assisted Reporting

Christopher Harper
Professor, School of Communications, Ithaca College
The Idaho Statesman, the Associated Press, *Newsweek,* ABC News
    and "ABC 20/20"

Chapter Outline

Getting started

A simple search: Who is Christopher Harper?

The strategy of a search

Sidebar Web sites

The information superhighway: Microsoft guru Bill Gates doesn't like the name, but he called his book, *The Road Ahead*. Technoguru Nicholas Negroponte of the Massachusetts Institute of Technology doesn't like the name either. We're stuck with it, though.

Using a computer and cruising the Internet *are* a bit like driving a car. The object of the exercise is to get from one place to another. That should be pretty simple.

There are a few catches. You do have to know how to start the machine. You have to know the rules of the road. You need to find a good mechanic. What most people need is driver's education on the information superhighway.

General Motors doesn't have a "help line" for people who don't know how to drive, because people buy cars only if they can drive. But a lot of people buy computers and expect miracles. Here's what a GM hot line might sound like if people were to buy cars the same way they buy computers.

HELP LINE: "General Motors Help Line, how can I help you?"

CUSTOMER: "I got in my car and closed the door, and nothing happened!"

HELP LINE: "Did you put the key in the ignition and turn it?"

CUSTOMER: "What's an ignition?"

HELP LINE: "It's a starter motor that draws current from your battery and turns over the engine."

CUSTOMER: "Ignition? Motor? Battery? Engine? How come I have to know all these technical terms just to use my car?"

Here's another one:

HELP LINE: "General Motors Help Line, how can I help you?"

CUSTOMER: "Hi! I just bought my first car, and I chose your car because it has automatic transmission, cruise control, power steering, power brakes and power door locks."

HELP LINE: "Thanks for buying our car. How can I help you?"

CUSTOMER: "How do I work it?"

HELP LINE: "Do you know how to drive?"

CUSTOMER: "Do I know how to WHAT?"

HELP LINE: "Do you know how to DRIVE?"

CUSTOMER: "I'm not a technical person! I just want to go places in my car!"

Getting Started

Okay, let's roll up our sleeves and figure out how to use the Internet. What exactly is the Internet? It was started in 1969 by the Department of Defense to allow scientists to communicate with one another via computer. The system used electronic mail, which sends digital computer language from one computer to another.

Every Internet user has an address like the ones from the U.S. Postal Service. If you want to contact me through electronic mail, my Internet address is charper@ithaca.edu. It's mine; nobody else has that address. The Internet also includes the World Wide Web, one of the hottest networks these days. The Web allows text, graphics, audio and even video to travel from one computer to another.

A browser allows your computer to translate the information from a site on the World Wide Web. In addition, there are discussion groups on the Internet, known as Usenet. These groups use electronic mail to communicate with people with similar interests. That may be cooking, cats, kayaking and, yes, various sexual preferences.

Researching topics is one of the best ways to use the Internet, particularly on the World Wide Web. Again, each address on the Web is unique. Let's start with www.ibm.com Sometimes, you have to type http://www.ibm.com The http:// stands for hypertext transfer protocol, which is simply the type of language the computer uses to talk with another computer. Usually, the address starts with "www", which stands for World Wide Web. The second part of the address—"ibm"—stands for the name of the institution on the Web. In this case, "ibm" stands for International Business Machines. The third part of the address indicates the type of organization. In this case, "com" means commercial, or a business. The other types of organizations on the Web include

Research is one of the best ways to use the Internet, particularly on the World Wide Web. Remember that it is *computer-assisted* reporting, not computer-*completed* reporting.

edu   an educational institution

gov   the federal government

mil   military

org   usually for a nonprofit organization

net   an Internet network

A lot of times you can actually guess an organization's Web address—Ithaca College, for example. The first part of the address is www. The second part is ithaca, and, because it's a university, the third part is edu. Therefore, the Web page of Ithaca College can be found at www.ithaca.edu Try this approach to guess what your school's Web page address is.

A Simple Search: Who Is Christopher Harper?

First and foremost, the computer is a machine. It is no better than what you do with it: Garbage asked for, garbage delivered. Second, the computer is simply a reporting tool. Computer-assisted reporting (CAR) is exactly that—assisted, not completed. The computer is a means for gathering information, like a telephone, a television or an interview.

Let's try a simple cruise through the Internet. For example, you may want to find out if I, Christopher Harper, have any business editing this book or writing this chapter. Let's take a look at how you can find out. There are a variety of useful resources called "search engines," which send out searchers—known as spiders, robots and other weird names—to determine if other Internet sites have something you want to know. Here are some of the search engines:

AltaVista   www.altavista.digital.com

Excite   www.excite.com

Hotbot   www.hotbot.com

Infoseek   www.infoseek.com

Lycos   www.lycos.com

Yahoo   www.yahoo.com

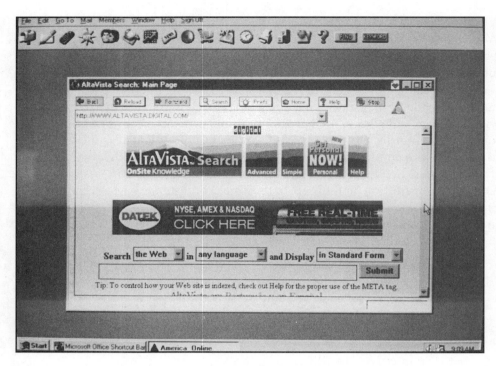

AltaVista is one of the most popular search engines, which allow users to find news and information on the World Wide Web.

There are many more search engines, and you need to find out which one makes life easy for you. Each engine has its own means of searching and its own strengths and weaknesses (please read the instructions, although many people don't). Some engines search only the World Wide Web, whereas some search the entire Internet. If one search engine gets too popular, you can move to another. My preferences tend toward Hotbot, the search engine from *Wired,* which surveys the Internet. But I change from one to another, primarily based on speed of access to the site and speed of the data I receive. I want to receive accurate data quickly. Maybe you have other requirements such as completeness, ease of use or coverage. Try a number of search engines to see what meets your needs.

I select Hotbot for a search. I type Christopher Harper as the search terms and get hundreds of items returned, starting from the best match to the worst match. If you settle for this search, you would see a picture of a Christopher Harper who's not me but someone in Britain. You would have found a Christopher Harper qualifying for the New York Marathon. I can assure you that isn't me. You even find someone from Indiana University looking for a job.

A search is like reporting a story. You start with a general question and then narrow it down. So what do you know about me? You know my name. I taught at New York University. Let's try Christopher Harper and NYU. That narrows the field. The searches can vary from time to time. When I tried it, the first hit was about the Cuban missile crisis. That's me. You can tell from the e-mail address harperc@is.nyu.edu But you will not learn much about me. The second reference includes an article I wrote about customized news services. The third reference provides a reference to my home page, where you can find the classes I teach, the articles I've written and even a picture of me. Now try to write an article about me from what you have found.

Sidebar 1

Web Sites

Keep in mind that Web sites come and go. All of the following sites were operational when this book was published. The main sources of research information include newspapers and news services such as the Associated Press and Reuters. Fortunately, many of these services remain free. All you have to do is sign up for them.

Newslink www.newslink.org provides access to thousands of online newspapers throughout the world.

Editor & Publisher, the organization for journalists, also links a user with online publications at www.mediainfo.com

International news from a variety of countries can be found at www.select-ware.com/news/

The Internet Herald is an online magazine for those born 1963–83 at www.iherald.com

See what you think.

Here are some other subject areas for basic research:

Addresses and telephone numbers

www.switchboard.com

Weather

http://cirrus.sprl.umich.edu/wxnet/

WeatherNet is the Internet's premier source of weather information. This site provides access to thousands of forecasts and images and the Internet's largest collection of weather links. WeatherNet is the most comprehensive and up-to-date source of weather data on the World Wide Web and is sponsored by The Weather Underground at the University of Michigan.

Courts

Federal and state constitutions, statutes and codes

www.law.cornell.edu/statutes.html

This is one of the most complete all-in-one sites with access to state constitutions, statutes, codes and legislation.

U.S. federal and state courts

www.law.emory.edu/FEDCTS/

A service of the Emory School of Law, this point-and-click map to federal courts provides hypertext links to all online federal court sites.

Government

Census

www.census.gov

Freedom of Information Act

www.well.com/user/fap/foia.htm

This guide is intended to be a quick reference on the Freedom of Information Act. It does not substitute for research or consultation with a lawyer on detailed questions. It is intended to address the most common access problems but can't cover everything.

Government Printing Office

www.access.gpo.gov

This is the world's largest publishing house, which issues all the reports of the federal government and more. You can find information about legislation, laws, government reports and much more.

Reference

Bartlett's Familiar Quotations

www.columbia.edu/acis/bartleby/bartlett/

This is a searchable database of quotations made by the famous and the infamous.

Biographies

www.tiac.net/users/parallax/

This site contains biographical information on more than 18,000 people from ancient times to the present day. These are the notable men and women who have shaped the world. Information includes birth and death years, professions, positions held, literary and artistic works, awards and other achievements. It is fully searchable by keyword, name or expression.

Calculators Online

www.sci-lib.uci.edu/HSG/RefCalculators.html

Reporters and editors who can't add and subtract now can calculate foreign exchange rates, local tides, distances between cities, taxes, loan and mortgage rates, the amount of seed needed to plant an acre of different crops and even a quarterback's passer rating on the Calculators Online Web page.

The information really is about Christopher Harper, the author of this chapter. But, in other cases, you should send an e-mail to set up a telephone or personal interview to make certain the information is correct. Remember, it's computer-assisted reporting, not computer-completed reporting. You can't believe anything from the computer. You have to verify it! Make sure it's right! It's your name on that article, and it's no excuse that the source from the telephone, television, personal interview or computer page is wrong. You are responsible for the accuracy of what you report and write.

The Strategy of a Search

The most important part of a search is how you determine what you want to find before you actually begin the search. Let's say that your school has received a major federal research grant from the Centers for Disease Control to conduct experiments to find a cure for AIDS. The $100 million grant will be used to develop and test vaccines on animals to find a cure for the disease. You have been assigned to report a story about the grant and its impact on your school.

First, you have to formulate the questions you want to answer. Write them down. What is AIDS? What cures AIDS? Why are animals used to test vaccines? What are the Centers for Disease Control? Second, identify the important concepts within the questions. AIDS. Animal testing and animal rights. Centers for Disease Control. Your school and its research capabilities. Third, identify search terms to develop the general concepts. AIDS. Animals and animal rights. Vaccines. CDC. Your school and research.

Fourth, are there any variations of these terms that might be useful? HIV is the virus that causes AIDS, so that might be useful. "Animals" may be too broad. Mice and monkeys are often used in experiments. AIDS cures might be a useful combination.

Fifth, prepare the way you want to search and where you want to search.

Most search engines index the words of a document, which increases the number of results. The key problem is that often too many documents are returned.

You may simply want to start with one term such as "AIDS" and then change the search as you go along. That's easy to do with most search engines. It's important to check the specific way the search engine finds relevant information. Click on "help" or "searching" to understand the best way to use the tools. A little reading will save you time.

For the AIDS search, I tried AltaVista, one of the most reliable and complete search engines. You may want to try another search engine or follow along with what I found. Your results may vary because data are added and subtracted every day.

Put "AIDS" into the search form and search the Web in standard form. Hit enter or submit. The search engine identifies thousands of documents matching the query. That's a lot. Fortunately, the sites the engine considers most relevant are listed first. There is one on AIDS treatment, which lists a searchable glossary about treatment at http://avery.charweb.org/health/AIDS/treat.html I choose that location and find lots of information, including *AIDS Treatment News* and the *Bulletin of Experimental Treatment for AIDS*. That sounds interesting, so I choose that site. This site is a text-based series of reports from a "gopher" menu. Gopher is an older searching tool. You might also find FTP—file transfer protocol—sites that provide text-based information, using the basic search techniques. Gopher and FTP sites allow you to transfer the information from another computer to your computer quickly.

Now it's time to see what the Centers for Disease Control and AIDS have in common. The AltaVista search engine again finds more than 100,000 documents. But the first one listed is the National AIDS Information Clearing House at the CDC. The document even provides a toll-free number if you want to ask any questions.

Because AIDS affects so many people in the United States, it may be useful to search the discussion groups on the Internet, known as Usenet. Select search and scroll to "Usenet" on AltaVista and enter the term AIDS. You will find a variety of discussion groups about the disease. Usenet is democracy at its best or anarchy at its worst. Anyone can say virtually anything on many of the discussion lists, so be careful if you choose to ask an e-mail question. Sometimes, it's best to "lurk"—watch the discussion without posting a question or response—and then send specific questions to some of the members of the list. That's a good way to find experts on a particular topic and to set up an interview.

Remember, this process has simply assisted you in gathering information. You now have far more research results in a shorter period of time than any reporter a decade ago ever had. Now you have to use this information to form questions and get answers. Remember, this is computer-assisted reporting, not computer-completed reporting.

Exercises

A journalist's scavenger hunt on the Internet

1. Go to the Internet White Pages site http://www.Four11.com/ and look up the e-mail address for Bill Clinton.

2. It's late at night when you receive an anonymous phone call from someone claiming to be Lamen Khalifa Fhimah (he's kind enough to spell it out). The caller tells you he has information about a plot to blow up a Dow Chemical Co. plant. Who is Lamen Khalifa Fhimah?

3. Some local reservists have been called up to go to Bosnia. Where can you locate more information about U.S. efforts in that region?

4. A new drug known as "roofies" is becoming popular among American teens. What can you find out about "roofies"?

5. Go to the site maintained by Switchboard, a commercial national phone number registry, and look yourself up. Is the information available and current?

6. According to the U.S. Census Bureau, what is the estimated U.S. population as of this moment (within 2,000)?

7. Locate and retrieve a file showing how unemployment rates in the United States compare with those in Japan and Germany.

8. You decide to do a story ranking this state alongside others. You want to compare cost-of-living, employment figures and health statistics. The data you are interested in can be found free of charge on the Internet. Where?

Scavenger Hunt Hints

Hint No. 1

There are two places where you can enter a Web address on Netscape.

1. You can open the "File" pull-down menu and select "Open Location."

2. If Location is shown at the top of your screen, you can highlight the present location and replace it with the new URL, www.Four11.com

Hint No. 2

Look at your question. The name is unique. Use any of the popular Web search engines to look for the words Lamen Khalifa Fhimah.

Hint No. 3

A Lycos search of "Bosnia" returns more than 3,500 hits. You can start to mine these, or you can narrow your search. For example, you can try "Bosnia journalism" or "Bosnia press."

Hint No. 4

Lycos doesn't seem to have much yet on "roofies." You may want to try the same search on a different search engine, i.e., AltaVista at www.altavista.digital.com

Hint No. 5

You could do a search for Switchboard, but remember how easy it can be to simply guess at a web address.

What's the designation for the World Wide Web? www

What's the name of the organization? switchboard

What's the domain for commercial organizations? com

So what is the Web address? www.switchboard.com

Hint No. 6

It should be obvious that census data are on the Census Bureau's site. At least, that's where you'll want to check first. Now you just have to explore a bit to find the population clock. Follow your instincts and common sense.

Hint No. 7

Ask yourself what you are looking for here: unemployment rates. What kind of statistics are unemployment rates? They are labor statistics. Therefore, they are probably kept by the U.S. Bureau of Labor Statistics. It may take some searching to find the statistics you're looking for. The BLS site is loaded. But don't give up too easily. Remember to check gopher and FTP resources as well.

Hint No. 8

This one is a bit tough. One government agency seems to keep the most comprehensive data regarding who lives where, quality of life, health and some labor statistics. It gathers these statistics every 10 years. Visit the Census site and look around. Remember to check gopher and FTP resources as well.

Courtesy of Matthew Reavy, LSU

Suggested Readings

Fulton, Katherine. "A Tour of Our Uncertain Future," *Columbia Journalism Review.* March/April 1996. Ms. Fulton has documented her entry and abilities in the age of computers for *Columbia Journalism Review.*

Harper, Christopher. "Doing It All." *American Journalism Review.* December 1996. This article tracks the work of the digital journalists of the *Chicago Tribune.*

Harper, Christopher. "The Daily Me." *American Journalism Review.* April 1997. This article analyzes custom and personal news services.

Oppenheimer, Todd. "Virtual Reality Check." *Columbia Journalism Review.* March/April 1996. The author has documented the age of computers and reporting for *Columbia Journalism Review.*

5 The Interview

Pat Berg
Lecturer, University of Wisconsin, River Falls
St. Paul Pioneer Press, Minnesota Women's Press and Minnesota
Public Radio

Chapter Outline

Types of interviews

    Adversarial interviews

    Personality profiles

    Background interviews

    Support quote or reaction
    interviews

Doing your homework before the
interview

Preparing your list of questions

During the interview

    Don't try too hard to be liked

    Make silence your friend

Peeling the onion

Should you tape?

The interview environment

The first few minutes: They can
make or break you

Problem interviewees and how not
to be undone by them

    The human brochure

    The controller

    The eloquent rambler

    The one-syllable wonder

Don't apologize for tough
questions: the hostile source

Identifying key quotes

Wrapping up the interview

Going off the record

Saying good-bye

After the interview

Sidebar 1 Tips for interviews

Sidebar 2 A basic list of
interviewing rules

Sidebar 3 Tips for taking notes

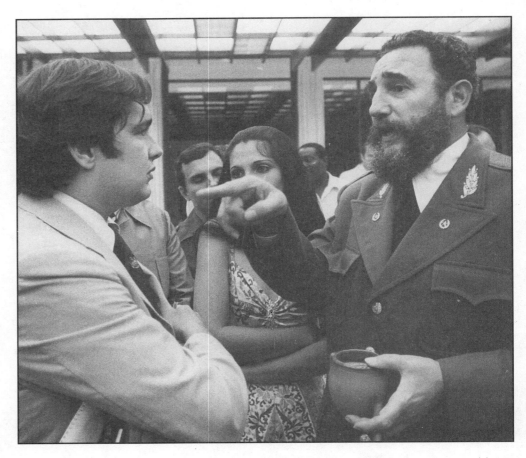

Good reporters always plan their questions ahead of time, especially before going into controversial or adversarial interviews.

News is about people. A garbage collectors' strike, for example, is a story about people—not necessarily about garbage. Your audience wants to know how the strike is affecting them. Behind the piles of uncollected debris, how are the neighbors coping with the mess, the flies, the odor? How are idled garbage haulers spending their time? Has the decaying garbage made anyone sick?

You're covering a scandal at city hall? Again, people are at the center of the story. As a reporter, you must find out what on earth possessed the mayor to appoint his own brother-in-law as fire chief and then say he didn't know about the guy's criminal record. To get these stories, you must talk to people.

Good reporters talk to people who tell stories that interest their audiences. Journalists track down phone numbers. Reporters approach people at the scenes of crimes and disasters. Journalists seek out interesting people at their workplaces and talk to their friends and enemies. Interviewing is exhausting, hectic and nerve-wracking work. It's also exhilarating, somewhat addictive and incredibly fun.

Sometimes interviewing means going to experts and official voices. Other times it means going beyond—or around—the experts. The media are full of predictable quotes from experts and politicians. As a reporter, you need experts and officials, but the best journalists don't stop there. As veteran *Minneapolis Star Tribune* reporters Peg Meier and Dave Wood put it, "We get our kicks talking with regular people."

Find the 80-year-old woman who's threatening to sue the city if those "crooked land developer types" win a permit to put townhouses across the street from her home. Why is she so angry and, perhaps even more interesting, so determined to prevent the project from going forward? If you're sent to the scene of a fatal car accident, look around the crowd for an eyewitness, a "regular person," to interview. The account could turn an otherwise routine brief into a gripping story. Your readers are, after all, regular people. They will notice. So will your editors.

How do you get people to talk? And, once you have them talking, how much of what they say should you try to write down? How do you turn your interview notes into usable quotes? The best reporters never stop refining these skills. In this chapter, you will learn how several veteran journalists use interviewing skills to breathe life into their reporting.

Types of Interviews

Reporters conduct four types of interviews: adversarial interviews, personality profiles, background interviews and support quote or reaction interviews.

Adversarial Interviews

Adversarial interviews are conducted with sources who are involved or thought to be involved in hidden or questionable activities that journalists are trying to uncover. Often such stories involve possible wrongdoing on the part of the source.

Personality Profiles

In a profile, the source's character, life or personality is the story. Profiles are usually written about celebrities such as politicians or entertainers. You may profile ordinary folks during their 15 minutes of fame such as the local high school's valedictorian or the young girl who led her brothers and sisters out of a burning house.

Background Interviews

Reporters conduct background interviews to learn about a story topic before they approach the sources they believe to be at the center of the story. For example, if you are writing about a proposed bill to lower the voting age to 16 in your state, you may want to get background from legislative staffers, child development experts and legislative historians before talking with the sponsor of the bill.

Backgrounding is conducted to get answers to such questions as "Has this been tried elsewhere?" and "Have you found research to support your argument that voting encourages younger teens to stay in school?" The reporter uses the information to formulate in-depth questions for primary sources.

Support Quote or Reaction Interviews

A reporter makes a short telephone call or visit to obtain a perspective on one aspect of a story. Reporters spend much of their time tracking down reaction and support quotes. Writing about the bill to lower the voting age, for example, you'd try to get a reaction quote from a prominent political opponent of the bill's sponsor. You might ask: "You and Senator Smith have disagreed in the past on measures affecting young people. What do you think about this latest proposal to lower the voting age?"

You also need to get reaction quotes from people at the scene of a fire, an accident or a rally.

Doing Your Homework Before the Interview

It is impossible to overstate the importance of knowing information about your source before an interview. Let's say you have an interview with a recording artist. If you were to begin the interview with "What kind of music did you write for your last CD?" the singer would be justified in showing you the door. The most you could hope for would be a superficial conversation with little hope of revealing anything new for your audience.

By contrast, imagine the conversation that could flow from this question: "I know you've said that, as the daughter of a Baptist preacher, you remember singing in church before you knew how to talk. I heard those church roots clearly for the first time in the title track from your latest CD, 'Singing Down the Rafters.' Why are your gospel roots coming out just now?"

Homework involves background document research and background interviews. Prepare for the interview with the singer by talking to her best friend, sisters and brothers, former teachers and parents.

Preparing Your List of Questions

Good reporters always plan their questions ahead of time, especially before going into controversial or adversarial interviews. The advance preparation helps imprint the questions on the reporter's mind. Some reporters bring their question list with them to the interview and freely refer to it. Others prefer to memorize a question strategy in broad outline and leave the list at the office.

If you're not sure how to begin planning questions, ask yourself, "If I could ask this source just one question, what would it be?" Very often, it is a "Why?" question. Why do you oppose this piece of legislation? Why do you want to be mayor? Why do you perform motorcycle stunts for a living? Why did you try to save the dog from the burning building?

Be prepared to juggle several elements of the interview at once: asking the questions, listening to the responses, noting the responses and thinking about what to ask next. It's a delicate balancing act.

Keeping your balance means knowing when to stick to your prepared questions and when to abandon them. "Have a list of questions but don't be too wedded to it," *St. Paul Pioneer Press* reporter Kay Harvey says. "If the conversation opens up other questions, those are usually better ones."

Sidebar 1

Tips for Interviews

Are you ready for an interview? Don't leave the office without the following items!
- Reporter's notebook
- Question list (in your head or in your notebook)
- Your story's key question (it's a good idea to write your most important or most difficult question in your notebook, especially if you think you might otherwise forget to ask it)
- At least two pencils or pens
- Directions to the interview location, including where to park
- Source's phone number
- Change for the phone or carry a cellular phone
- Tape recorder, if you're using one (check the batteries) and a blank tape
- Laptop computer, if you're using one (make sure your interview location is suitable)
- Name of the source's gatekeeper (such as a receptionist or assistant)
- Basic information about your source, including his or her name and job title (check spellings)

Paula Schroeder, host of a public affairs program on Minnesota Public Radio, says she believes that reporters who depend solely on written questions often don't listen to their interview subjects. "Sometimes it sounds like reporters, rather than listening, are just waiting for the person to finish talking so they can ask the next prepared question."

During the Interview

Beginning journalists often make two mistakes in interviews: They try too hard to be liked, and they fear silence.

Don't Try Too Hard to Be Liked

Reporters and sources need each other. They don't necessarily have to like one other. Because you'll be focused on getting answers, you'll find that you can't make every source your friend, especially if you must ask questions your source would rather not answer. The reporter's objective is straightforward—to obtain answers to questions. You and your source might form a pleasant relationship, but only to the extent that it doesn't interfere with your goal—to get the information you need. If you and the source feel good about each other, so much the better.

Sooner or later you're bound to run into a source whose values you despise or who has done something terrible. Don't let that get in your way. A source once tried to fluster me by saying, "Whatever happened to the days when nice girls stayed home?" I ignored the sexist remark and kept on with my line of questioning. His views on women in the work force were not part of my story.

You'll also meet plenty of sources whose company is so enjoyable, whose stories are so engaging that you'll be tempted to buy into their versions of the truth. Beware of this trap.

In short, it's your job to hear whatever your source has to say, even if it means holding your nose while you listen. On the other hand, remember that any one source's version of reality, no matter how compelling, is just that—one version.

Before she conducts an interview, Barbara Walters reads extensive research and carefully prepares her questions.

Make Silence Your Friend

As members of polite society, we are taught to be uncomfortable with long pauses in conversation. We rush to fill in "awkward silences." Unlearn this habit as quickly as you can.

National economics reporter Mike Meyers of the *Minneapolis Star Tribune* sometimes counts silently to 10 after a source has stopped speaking. Often, that's when the source's real story begins to come out. "Silence is your greatest friend," Meyers says. "Simply waiting for someone to finish a thought or to answer your question is the best policy. Ask, 'Why?' and then just sit there. People get uncomfortable with silences, but you know what you're doing, so you're not uncomfortable."

Peg Meier puts it this way: "Shut up. Don't bother to tell about yourself unless asked."

Peeling the Onion

You'll seldom get the real story on the first question. That's why your goal should be to keep the source talking. "You're trying to peel the onion," Mike Meyers says. "What you usually get first is the pat answer, the one he's prepared to give. Often you'll find it's the third, fourth or fifth question that gets the true answer."

Peg Meier had a similar experience while interviewing 104-year-old Jay Zachary, who, according to Meier, was in 1976 "living pretty darn well in St. Paul." Zachary had mentioned two sons and a daughter. Meier asked how many children he had. "Ain't got no children," he replied. Meier was puzzled but kept on with her questioning as if Zachary did have children. Still, Zachary repeated the phrase "Ain't got no children," and paused. Meier and her subject sat for a moment in silence. Then Zachary rewarded Meier's excellent technique. "Ain't got no kids," he said. "Got old people. You get this old and your kids is old people."

Peeling the onion requires two kinds of questions, closed- and open-ended. Closed-end questions seek definite answers, often yes or no but also names, locations and dates. By contrast, open-ended questions ask the source to think out loud about a topic, providing you with angles.

Here is a closed-end question: "Did you know at the time that Mr. Smith had hired a Mafia boss to lobby for his company?" Put this way, the question gets directly to the heart of the matter as defined by the reporter. The source must confirm, deny or refuse to comment on a question the reporter deemed important.

The closed-end question is best when you want to pin down your source; you're ready to get this one answer. If he or she ends the interview immediately afterward, you still have your story. Closed-end questions are the basic thread with which you stitch together your story—the who, what, where and when of the story. If you fail to get these facts, you'll likely not have a story.

Behind these facts, however, you'll find the real meat of the story—the hows and whys. This is what distinguishes a good news story from a police report or the minutes of a school board meeting. To get at the hows and whys, ask open-ended questions.

Here is the Mafia question in open-ended form: "Talk to me about Mr. Smith's connections to the Mafia at the time the money started disappearing. What do you remember?" This opens up the interview to angles you may not yet know about. Open-ended questions are a useful way to keep the source talking until the story comes out.

Open-ended questioning is multi-layered. Each question involves a series of follow-ups known as probers and clarifiers. Here, the basic tools are "Can you say more about that?" (probe) and "What do you mean by that?" (clarifier).

Should You Tape?

Theories vary on the wisdom of taping interviews. Most reporters keep a small recorder (with fresh batteries) nearby to tape sensitive or controversial interviews. In general, reporters rely on good notes rather than tapes. The primary reason is that, in the fast-paced world of news, it's too time-consuming to transcribe tapes. And recorders have a way of giving out just when you need them.

The decision to tape can depend on the type of interview you're conducting. Mike Meyers, whose economics stories often involve adversarial interviews with influential officials and corporate executives, sometimes uses tape to back up his notes. "I occasionally tape interviews with sources who don't trust me or whom I don't trust," he says.

On the other hand, *St. Paul Pioneer Press* pop music columnist and features writer Jim Walsh tapes most interviews. He says he likes to "riff off the source's comments" during his interviews. He finds that in-depth conversation is much easier when he's concentrating on what his source is saying rather than on taking accurate notes.

If you plan to tape the interview, put your recorder where the source can see it. If you're taping a telephone interview, you're not compelled to tell your source that you're taping the conversation in most states. If the source asks, however, tell the truth. Successful reporters are honest with sources.

A Basic List of Interviewing Rules

Always identify yourself.

Always be polite, especially in adversarial interviews.

Always be honest.

Always leave your personal attitudes out of the interview.

Always be yourself.

Never take anything personally.

The Interview Environment

Face-to-face interviewing gives you your best opportunity to observe a source in his or her natural surroundings. For this reason, it's usually a good idea to do an interview at the source's home or workplace rather than in a public setting such as a restaurant. For character profiles, always interview at the location where the source does whatever it is that makes him or her newsworthy. Interview an artist in her studio, for example.

Jim Walsh interviewed Yoko Ono for two hours at her apartment in New York City. An unabashed John Lennon fan, Walsh felt it was important to conduct the interview in The Dakota, the apartment building where Lennon was killed. By conducting the interview face-to-face in Ono's home, Walsh got fascinating insights that would not have surfaced by phone. For example, he knew of Ono's reputation for creating art in every detail of her life, but without visiting her in person he would not have known that she carefully lines up her cigarette butts in the ashtray.

Arrive at your interview a few minutes early. If it's in an office, take a few minutes to notice the general atmosphere and to double-check your source's job title. Once inside the source's office, scan the walls and desk for telling details. If you're interviewing a source at home, pay close attention to details. What does the house say about the way the person lives? Note pictures on the walls, pets, anything that is related to your story. If something strikes you as unusual, make a note of it and ask about it.

Try to sit at a table, facing your source, rather than side-by-side on a couch. Often a source will invite you to sit on the couch because that is where most people entertain guests. Just say you'd rather sit at a table. This arrangement has several advantages. First, it facilitates eye contact. Second, you'll have a hard surface for writing or for placing your tape recorder or laptop. Third, it puts a little "comfort distance" between you and the source. People talk more freely when they have the security of personal space. Get too close, and they tend to clam up.

Expect interruptions, and use them if you can. Phone calls, co-workers barging in, hovering spouses and children running through the house all give you a chance to watch your source interact with people who affect him or her. Observe everything. If your source takes a phone call while you're there, don't leave the room unless asked to do so. Just hearing one side of the conversation might yield an insight.

The First Few Minutes: They Can Make or Break You

You and your source will size each other up within the first few minutes of meeting one another. Your goal is to set the stage for open communication. Be yourself. Shake hands. Introduce yourself, reiterating the name of your news organization and the topic of your story. Keep looking straight into your source's eyes. It's the best way to make a psychological connection and to establish that you are in control of the conversation.

Use the first few minutes of the interview to get a feel for your source. Most reporters accomplish this by spending a few minutes just chatting. This is your chance to listen to the source's speech patterns and estimate his or her attitude toward being interviewed.

Don't let the informal chatting sidetrack your reason for being with the source, however. Keep it short, and be direct and clear about moving into the formal interview.

Mike Meyers says: "If you begin by saying, 'I understand you like golf,' you'll discover you chewed up 10 minutes talking about golf. Instead, I just go right to it. I begin with, 'A lot of people think you should be fired.' I find it rattles them a little and you get better information. I'm there to get information, not to make friends."

Make it a habit to establish how much time the source is willing to spend with you. Then you can make certain to ask the core questions before your time is up.

Problem Interviewees and How Not to Be Undone by Them

Russell Baker once said the reason he left his job as the U.S. Senate correspondent for the *New York Times* was because he spent his life "sitting on marble floors, waiting for somebody to come out and lie to me."

Of course, not all sources lie. But people can be difficult, and it's those who talk frequently with reporters who are often the most difficult to interview. Corporate executives, politicians and government spokespeople are all well-versed in how to get their version of reality published. Other difficulties arise because sources are not used to talking to reporters, or they have something to hide. Be prepared for the following types of difficult interviewees.

The Human Brochure

This source has a rehearsed, rosy version of her company's response to the chemical spill you're writing about. Go to the interview with a set of prepared questions, and keep asking them until you get answers. You'll sound like a broken record. Eventually, you'll get answers.

The Controller

This source tries to make you the subject of the interview with such questions as "How do you like working at *The Times*?" Don't respond to such questions; simply smile and re-ask your question.

The Eloquent Rambler

Many people, especially those who aren't used to talking for publication, can use up your time with useless tangents unless you take control of the situation. A good strategy for handling the rambler is to repeat your central question as often as needed. Use succinct, definite phrasing: "I'm interested to know what you saw that day." Also use probers and clarifiers, and interrupt if you have to: "Why?" "How so?" "That's interesting, but what about . . . ?" "Let's talk more about the accident."

The One-Syllable Wonder

The other extreme—perhaps the most difficult to interview—is the source who forces you to pry answers out of him or her. Chances are this source is frightened at the prospect of talking to you. A sideways approach may work best here. If time permits, interview this source in a series of shorter visits. You'll find that "one-syllable wonders" open up a bit more with each visit.

Sometimes sources clam up because they just don't want to cooperate. In this case, stay your course. "You keep asking the question, and, if you keep getting a one-syllable answer, then give him all the facts and let him not answer them," Mike Meyers says. "Just because he won't give answers doesn't let you off the hook. You still have to ask the questions."

Don't Apologize for Tough Questions: The Hostile Source

Perhaps the most important rule in news reporting is this: Never leave an interview without asking the question you most want answered, no matter how difficult it is to ask. Don't let yourself and your source off the hook just to avoid an uncomfortable moment.

"Trust your instincts," Peg Meier says. "Trust your curiosity. If you want to know, so will your readers. Ask a nun about her sexuality. Ask the mother of a child dying of a genetic defect if she and her husband are considering having another child."

Nowhere is time pressure greater than in television interviewing. In most cases reporters know they'll have only a few minutes with a source, and they don't know before-hand what questions other reporters will ask. In order to get fresh material, they must be ready to select, at the last moment, one or two hard-hitting questions from their prepared list.

As in any art, interviewing has no hard and fast rules. Interviewing for features may call for one set of rules, investigative projects another. Let each circumstance guide you. "Think about how pushy you should be," Peg Meier says. "What is appropriate for this story?" Meier cautions against bravado for its own sake. "Don't spit out tough questions so you can come off as a tough reporter," she says. "Use tact. Imagine how you'd feel on the other end of the interview."

Kay Harvey, who writes about women's health and aging for the *St. Paul Pioneer Press,* agrees. "I've done a successful interview if I can break through the shield of somebody's office or public role," Harvey says. "When I start talking with people rather than interviewing them, people start to give me their best answers."

Many beginning reporters think that people are generally reluctant to talk to the media. Often, the opposite is the case. For a story on compulsive gambling, the *Star*

Tribune's Chris Ison had to call a man whose 19-year-old son had just committed suicide after a disastrous gambling binge. "I didn't think he'd want to talk," Ison recalls, "but once he got started, it was like he really needed to talk. He went on for 45 minutes. And it was such good stuff that we edited it and ran it verbatim as a 50-inch story. His words were much better than anything I could have written."

Keep in mind that your goal is to find out everything your source knows. If you're chasing hostile sources who'd rather have surgery without anesthesia than talk to you about a controversial story, make sure you've fully heard their side before you publish anything.

As Chris Ison puts it: "A lot of reporters don't ask the full question for fear the answer will be a good defense and will hurt their story. This is a big mistake. You want to hear their strongest defense now. The last thing you want is to realize after you've published that they have a stronger defense than you realized."

Here's another, equally important reason to ask everything: Often the source has a plausible explanation for what he or she did. The sooner you find out, the less time you'll spend chasing dead ends.

Identifying Key Quotes

When you think your source is giving you an important quote, immediately tune out everything else. You may still be writing her first sentence when she moves on to another. Keep writing that first sentence. You must get every word right if you plan to quote her directly.

For sentences you plan to quote verbatim, check to make sure that you have the wording exactly right; then mark a big Q in the margin. Take a moment to make sure you can read what you've written. If you have to, ask the source to wait a moment, explaining that you wouldn't want to misquote her. She'll appreciate your effort to be accurate.

It's a good idea to get a usable quote for every perspective covered. That way you'll have plenty of material to put all the pieces together. The bulk of your notes will be used for narrative rather than direct quotation. Abbreviate this material. Concentrate more on the content than the exact wording. Here you can leave out the connective words—a, an, the. Your notes for nonquote material should take the form of fragments and facts such as dates, names, titles and locations rather than complete sentences.

Wrapping Up the Interview

You've closed your notebook—the interview's over, right? Wrong!

As you're packing up to leave, your source may give you your best material. This can happen at the end of an interview with a source who doesn't often talk with the media. Most people don't think in terms of what makes a good news story, so as an after-thought they may toss out bombshell tips without knowing their importance. In addition, people tend to "clear their minds" of surface information before they reveal the heart of the story.

Expect this to happen often—so often, in fact, that many reporters slide a pen into their notebooks to mark the last page of their notes for quick access in case the source starts talking again. It's your job as a reporter to be alert for unexpected information and to follow through when it's offered.

Sidebar 3

Tips for Taking Notes

Every reporter needs an effective system for taking accurate notes during an interview. Some reporters learn shorthand. Most develop, through experience, their own systems of abbreviations. Following is an example of taking notes:

Thelma Fredrickson 55/ 3109 Elm St. "I lv evre am @ 8 for bus go by j's house in 5 yrs i've nvr seen him" accountant

Here is how the entry might appear in a story based on interviews with neighbors of a man named Philip James:

Thelma Fredrickson, who lives three houses from James, has yet to meet her neighbor.

"I leave (lv) every (evre) morning (am) at (@) 8 for the bus, and I go by James's (j's) house," said the 55-year-old accountant. "In five (5) years (yrs) I've (i've) never (nvr) seen him."

Going Off the Record

What if a source asks to be interviewed "off the record"? There are no hard and fast rules here. Chris Ison, who has interviewed hundreds of sources for investigative projects for the *Star Tribune,* says that he seldom, if ever, goes off the record when interviewing a source close to the center of his story. If this means the source won't talk, he takes the question to other sources, where he often gets the same material.

Most reporters don't allow sources to go off the record after the interview. If you've identified yourself as a reporter, and if the source has just given you information you thought was on the record, you have every right to use it. Of course, you may want to carefully weigh the costs of using the information. If the source regularly gives you your best material, you may want to protect the relationship. Ask yourself if this story is important enough to risk losing access to this source in the future.

Many people and reporters don't exactly know what off the record means. It means you cannot publish the information. Most people want to talk on background or not for attribution, which means you can use the material without an individual's name. Make sure you know what "off the record" is and ask the source if you can use the information without identifying him or her by name. Then you need to determine how the source should be described. For example, "a university professor" or "city official" may be acceptable for many people. Try to be as specific as possible in agreeing on the description with the source. To avoid confusion and disagreements with your source about what was on and off the record, you can ask a source to hold "off the record" comments until the end of the interview.

Saying Good-Bye

Finally, thank your source and then ask him or her for permission to call back for clarification if needed. Find out where he or she can be reached between the time the interview ends and your deadline. Write the phone number in your notes and circle it.

Should you let your source check your copy before it's published? No. Many people will ask to do so, either because they think you're naive enough to allow it or because they're unfamiliar with news reporting and believe it's routinely done.

There's no need to apologize; just smile and say no. It is acceptable, however, to read back a part of an interview to a source on technical material to make certain the information is correct. But it's your decision, not the decision of the source.

After the Interview

Go over your notes immediately after the interview. Do this before you get back to the newsroom, if possible, and certainly before your next interview. It takes only a few minutes to make sure you can read your writing and to fill in the questionable details while the interview is still fresh in your mind. Find a quiet place and carefully read every word you've written. This step, so often overlooked by beginning reporters, is one of the best habits a journalist can develop.

Exercises

1. For this exercise, you'll need a reporter's notebook, two pens, a tape recorder (preferably one with a visible counter), a table, a quiet place, 30 minutes without interruptions and one person who will take your interview questions seriously. It's fine if the person is a close friend or a family member. Learn at least one new thing about the person you are interviewing. Do you think you know everything about your mother or brother? If you're a skilled interviewer, you *will* learn something new. After the interview, listen to the tape while following along in your notebook. When you come to a great quote, use the counter on the recorder to mark the spot in your notebook. Listen carefully to those spots several times. Did you get the quotes exactly right? Look for patterns in your notetaking for errors. Work to eliminate them. Did you allow the subject to finish every thought without interrupting? Did you probe for depth without leading the interview subject? Did you ask succinct questions— and then stop talking? Did you focus the interview on one or two good ideas? Did you keep your opinions to yourself? Did you keep control of the interview?

2. Pick someone on radio or television who you think is a good interviewer. Tape a live interview the reporter does and write down the questions. What worked and what did not?

Suggested Readings

Terkel, Studs. *Race: How Blacks and Whites Think and Feel About the American Obsession.* New York: The New Press, 1992. This volume of edited conversations is not a how-to but an example of a master interviewer's work in full bloom. Beginning and accomplished reporters can learn much by listening to the cadence of Terkel's subjects, whom he lovingly quotes at length. Before reading the responses that make up the bulk of the text, students may enjoy reading through Terkel's questions (set off in italics) to observe his technique.

Ward, Jean, and Kathleen Hansen. *Search Strategies in Mass Communication,* Third Edition. New York: Longman, 1997. Ward and Hansen place interviewing in the context of a systematic search for information. Especially useful: This book carefully and explicitly discusses specific aspects of online interviewing. Finally, the section entitled "Sources of Interviewer Error" in the interviewing chapter alerts beginning reporters to real-life newsroom hazards such as unreasonably short deadlines, which can make good interviewing extremely difficult.

References

1. Meier, Peg, and Dave Wood. *The Pie Lady of Winthrop and Other Minnesota Tales.* Minneapolis: Neighbors Publishing, 1985, p. viii.

2. Meier, Peg. *The Last of the Tearoom Ladies and Other Minnesota Tales.* Minneapolis: Neighbors Publishing, 1990, p. xv.

6 Reporting the Story

Christopher Harper,
Ithaca College

Chapter Outline

The changing newsroom by Christopher Harper

Covering cops and courts by Michael Mercer

Writing obituaries by Robert E. Wernsman Jr.

Telling the story of fires, accidents and disasters by David Tait

Getting the details of fires, accidents and disasters by Ford Risley

Covering education by Robert E. Wernsman Jr.

Covering speeches and meetings by Glen L. Bleske

Getting good quotes by Ginger Rudeseal Carter
    Using Attribution

The photographer as writer by James H. Kenney Jr.

Sidebar 1 Cops and courts

Sidebar 2 Obituaries

Sidebar 3 Covering tragedies

Sidebar 4 Education

Sidebar 5 Reporting skills for photographers

For years, budding journalists have been taught traditional areas of coverage known as "beats." These included the police beat, the court beat, the City Hall beat, the education beat, the science beat and a variety of other beats. The term comes from the notion of the cop on the beat, who knows everyone and everything about the neighborhood he or she patrols on foot.

Although beats are still used at many news organizations, the beats are taking on an interdisciplinary approach such as the immigration beat. An immigration beat cuts across more traditional beats and would include the police, courts, City Hall, education and a variety of other beats. At times, the subject-driven rather than building-driven beats may involve teams of reporters with specific knowledge and expertise. This chapter starts with an examination of new trends in the newsroom and then examines reporting in more traditional beats.

The Changing Newsroom

Is the *Orange County Register* the newspaper of the next century? Executive Editor Ken Brusic isn't sure, but he hopes so. "This is one of the few competitive markets left in the nation," he says. The *Register* has nearly 400,000 subscribers in Orange County, while the *Los Angeles Times* has nearly 200,000 there. No longer can the *Register* depend on its bedrock, conservative reader who supported Republican candidates. Today, the county has more than 2.5 million people with an increasing amount of diversity. Nearly two-thirds of the county remains white. But more than 25 percent is Hispanic. Ten percent is Asian, and 2 percent is black.

"Orange County is a place of contrasts. You can find million dollar homes with million dollar yachts, or you can find 15 people living in a garage," Brusic says. As a result of the changing diversity of the community, in 1989 the *Register,* which is privately owned, started to rethink what the newspaper should be. Today the *Register* is known as the "newspaper without walls." Beats do not exist. Teams cover a variety of subjects, including health, environment, government and technology. Each team has a leader, but all reporters, photographers and researchers operate in a democratic, give-and-take reporting enterprise. For example, the team that won the 1995 Pulitzer Prize for investigating the fertility clinic at the University of California–Irvine reported to a team leader, not the business editor, health editor or city editor.

Here are some of the other changes the newspaper has made:

- The newspaper cooperates with an in-house television station that broadcasts 24 hours a day. The newspaper reporters are often expected to file broadcast stories on specific subjects and host programs on special issues. A reporting team that went to the South Pole, for example, hosted a one-hour program.

- Each reporter files online stories for the *Register's* electronic newspaper.

- All the reporters have their own Internet home page so that the copy desk knows where they live and what they do. That can be important when an earthquake or power outage occurs.

- The newspaper has an Intranet system so that all reporters maintain telephone numbers and sources that anyone in the newspaper can access.

"The important skills needed for this newsroom are critical thinking and flexibility," Brusic says. "It's pretty clear to me that people cannot come into this newsroom unless they realize that one day they might be on radio, the next day on television, another day online and another day writing for the newspaper."

Joe Ames headed the team that covered the county's bankruptcy and the team for the 1996 election campaign. "What you really start doing is listening to your readers. This has changed the way we go about covering the conventions and politics," he says. The newspaper polled the community to determine important issues. The top choices included education, job security, taxes and the deficit. Therefore, the newspaper provided the usual fare of the horse race of the election, but the *Register* also focused on these particular issues. "We don't cover abortion because the research shows it's way down the list," Ames says.

Despite a plan to take the newspaper into the next century, most reporters at the *Register* admit they're not entirely certain that they're heading in the right direction. "We're on a journey, and we're simply trying to figure out how to survive," Brusic says.

Joe Ames, a former *Miami Herald* reporter, is pleased to see the experimentation, although he, too, is searching for what works and what doesn't. "You can't have a newspaper that's all investigations. You can't have a newspaper that's all listening posts. You need all the pieces to the puzzle," he argues. So far, the experiment has provided the *Register* with a Pulitzer Prize and a slight increase in circulation. As Brusic notes, however, any increase in circulation is a lot better than what's happening at most newspapers, which are losing readers.

Covering Cops and Courts

By Michael Mercer, Auburn University

Crime affects everyone. That's why covering cops and courts is so vital to a newspaper. Reporters can be assured they'll be covering a well-read beat that can lead to many breaking, exciting, heart-wrenching and bizarre stories.

One of the biggest tasks in covering this beat is knowing the vocabulary. If you're going to cover this beat effectively, you'll need to become expert in knowing the language of the street as well as the beat. And what you don't know, you must ask. Make sure the answer you get and the one you write is translated for the reader.

Unfortunately, this is one of the beats where it's easy for a reporter to fall into the jargon jungle. Never forget: You're not writing for the cops or the courts; you're writing for the reader.

Too many stories come in from this beat laden with legalese and jargon that, if used at all, must be translated. The more you use the language that comes with the profession and is not as well known on the street, the more time you'll spend interpreting the story. It's better to go into the story simplifying the language rather than trying to impress a reader with how much you know, which you have to explain.

For example, before using the words *aggravated assault* in a lead, tell why the charge was made. *Aggravated assault* could cover a mountain of possibilities. If a victim was hit on the head by someone, say so. Don't just say so-and-so was charged with aggravated assault and then in the second paragraph say someone was hit on the head.

Sidebar 1

Cops and Courts

Cop Terms

Almost every newsroom has a police scanner. Following are some of the codes you'll hear:

10.4 Acknowledgment

10.5 Repeat message

10.10 Investigate

10.13 Assist police officer who may be in danger

10.30 Robbery in progress (a robbery is a crime against a person)

10.31 Burglary in progress (a burglary is a crime of obtaining property)

10.33 Report of explosives

10.34 Assault in progress

10.81 Ambulance needed

10.83 Dead on arrival

10.84 Fire

10.85 Need additional unit

Codes in the 10.40s are the most important police calls. These mean serious trouble.

10.41 A call for three sergeants and 15 officers

10.46 A call for one lieutenant, eight sergeants and 40 officers

10.70 Big trouble: Dispatch everyone available.

Court Terms

Felony: Serious crime such as murder or stock fraud

Indictment: A formal, written charge framed by prosecutors and approved by a grand jury

Misdemeanor: Literally, poor demeanor or resisting arrest, littering, jaywalking or smoking in a public building

Subpoena: A court statement ordering the recipient to appear in court. If the individual does not appear, he or she faces a fine or other court penalties.

Summons: A court statement to appear on a specific day to answer a charge in the court. That's what you get when you have a traffic violation you decide to challenge.

Although covering cops and courts can simply be a matter of record, try to secure the records backing up your story. Remember, police reports you see at the station or complaints at the sheriff's department sometimes are at least third-hand information. Often, an officer has made out the report, but it's transcribed or read to you by someone who was not even the investigator or is a desk-bound superior. And, if you have time, double-check the spellings of the names of the people involved, locations, addresses, time and any other pertinent information. Also be sure to attribute the source appropriately.

The court scene calls for a special commitment to allot your time for covering the trial, starting with previews of trial-related stories and coverage of the jury selection. Use plenty of quotes to make the trial come alive for readers, making sure you report the outcome and do any appropriate follow-ups.

Covering the cops-and-court beat also requires cultivating and developing a rich variety of sources from the police department janitor to the judge's special clerk. Sources can tip you off to a lot of stories. The more interesting the story is, the more likely you'll be tipped off. The sooner you become expert at knowing your sources, the sooner you'll be able to find stories on this beat. It's likely the stories will be more in-depth as well.

The police and the court system provide vital stories to a news organization because crime affects everyone. Reporters cover a well-read beat that can lead to many breaking, exciting, heart-wrenching and bizarre stories.

Keeping tabs on cops and courts is a good beat for a reporter regardless of experience. It's often the first beat a new reporter will have or be trained in to back up a veteran reporter. Making the rounds regularly on this beat will lead to many good stories because of readers' high interest in crime and the criminal justice system. You either know victims or you have been a victim in some respect because crime affects everyone.

Don't just be reactionary in cops-and-court coverage. Editors value highly an enterprising reporter, one who not only covers the events as they happen but who can spot trends and anticipate events. Those who try to get the story behind the story are encouraged to do so.

Telling the reader how much the criminal justice system costs is a good place to start. Dealing with crime is a matter of public record. Readers pay to have officers patrol the streets and catch the criminals. They also pay judges to administer the laws passed and to see that justice is served.

Write about the people who run or are affected by the criminal justice system. Readers want to know more about those who investigate crimes as well as those who do the time. Don't be afraid to go in-depth to point out pluses and minuses in the criminal justice system.

Sidebar 2

Obituaries

Following is what you need to find out for an obituary:

Is the time, the date and the place of services complete?

Do birth and death dates coincide with the age?

Are names correct and complete?

Is the stated number of survivors consistent with your list?

Do chronological career events coincide with age and locations?

For what will people most remember this person? Why? Who recalls?

Writing Obituaries

By Robert E. Wernsman Jr., Texas Tech University

Imagine your writing preserved for future generations—handed from one to another as part of the family history. Writing offers few guarantees of immortality, but filed, stored, tucked in family Bibles, the efforts of an obituary writer live on, unlike the vast majority of one day's headlines and lead stories. These stories strike home like no other.

How do we treat obituaries? Too often, we consider them a burden to avoid, an assignment for the novice or the intern. Too often obituaries occupy the lowest rung on the journalistic ladder. Don't take this job until you're ready to do the subjects justice. Your writing rings with life only when you see an obituary as the mark of someone's life and no mere report of death. Treat this mini-profile as news of any impending service and final testimony of a life lived.

Many newspapers treat these reports as part of the daily churn of news events—the obituaries are often printed in reduced type, tucked away with little color and no flair. Some profit-conscious managers convert this information into a money source, charging families for the right to see obituaries in print. Other publications regularly report deaths of community members for their doubtless news value. Broadcast venues often report only the most significant community members' deaths.

Regardless of the situation, your responsibility as obituary writer is to present an accurate, reflective report of someone's life. Information may come directly from family members or can be channeled through a funeral home representative. Written documentation from such sources is ideal and all the more accurate if provided through a form your news operation develops. Don't forget: The news, beyond word of death, is time, date and place of any service. Death affects more than the immediate family, and the public needs to know when services will occur.

Double-checking the facts always serves your journalistic interests. Inaccuracy remains the biggest complaint, by far, about obituary reporting. The finality of both the occasion and the report makes the audience all the more alert to accuracy.

Let's start with the basics: Confirm that the person is actually dead by calling the funeral home. It's imperative to do so if you want to avoid pranksters with a warped sense of humor and considerable media embarrassment, while better serving your audience.

Sidebar 3

Covering Tragedies Any complete story about a tragedy should include the following information: Time of the incident Location of the incident Number of victims Names, ages and addresses of victims	Possible causes Reaction from survivors and witnesses Monetary amount of damages Physical details and description Historical context and significance

Too often, writers assigned this responsibility have little or no experience with death and the circumstances surrounding it. The process of death has touched few of them, and obituary reading seldom generates much interest among high school or college students. To a family, however, the obituary is a lasting memory of a loved one.

Beyond accuracy and completeness, the most crucial aspect of obituary writing is including a quotation or comments from a family member. Only in this way can you hope to more completely illuminate a life for your audience.

Telling the Story of Fires, Accidents and Disasters

By David Tait, Carleton University

Smoke had already stopped pouring out of the old gray three-story house. One woman was dead. I was on the front sidewalk with two other reporters, waiting for the body to be brought out. The front door opened and firefighters led out the ambulance crew, carrying the covered body on their stretcher. The firefighter in front half asked, half ordered us to move back. "Whaddya think we're gonna do?" asked a TV reporter. "Rip off crispy bits as it goes by?" That hard-boiled-reporter act may sound tough in the movies, but on the street it just sounds stupid. And it's as stupid as it sounds because it gets in the way of doing the job.

At fires, accidents, shootings, knifings, floods, mud slides and bombings, reporters more often than not arrive late, stay safe, watch others risk their lives, are spared the most horrifying sights and leave early to file their stories. There's nothing very tough about that.

Writing about deaths and injuries can become routine to reporters, so they may forget that, to those directly involved, the victims, friends and families, neighbors and witnesses, what's happened is more likely a unique, immeasurable horror. A parent's shock and grief at a child's death is just as absolute when a little girl dies in a "routine" highway crash as it is when the child dies in a terrorist bombing or a flood that decimates five counties. There should be no difference in how a reporter approaches people caught in disasters of either magnitude. But approach we must, as reporters, if we are to be able to tell their stories and draw a broader meaning from their catastrophe. It's a role that often earns reporters contempt as vultures or ghouls, but it doesn't have to be that way.

Expressions of grief in the words of ordinary people can be devastatingly powerful. Reporters should show sensitivity in approaching victims and eyewitnesses.

Following is a kinder metaphor. In all our communities, we as neighbors stand witness to each other's baptisms, bar mitzvahs, marriages, retirements and funerals. We do so to signal that we place importance on both the transitions and the people they involve. Our willingness to stand witness lends dignity and weight to whatever the proceedings. In that same way, a reporter standing in the rain at night on the shoulder of a highway, watching as emergency crews pry the body of a young man from the wreckage of his car, is standing witness on the community's behalf to a tragic transition, one that happened too suddenly for invitations or notices. Rather than a heartless intrusion, the reporter's presence can be an act of respect that can dignify rather than disrupt . . . if done right.

First, in all you do at and around the scene of an emergency, clearly convey in words and body language that, to you, whatever has happened is of singular seriousness. You may have covered two events just like it the day before and doubt this one will even make tonight's newscast or tomorrow's paper, but that in no way diminishes its impact on and meaning to those involved, whose stories you hope to tell. Not all reporters realize this. You see them standing in clumps, gossiping and laughing about other things as they wait; keep away from the pack to avoid guilt by association.

Second, ask people about how they experienced the event personally. What happened? Where were they? What did they hear first? What did they see? What did they see happen next? What did they do? What did they think then? How did they feel? A colleague of mine loathes that last question. "How do you *think* she feels?" she roars, appalled, when imagining reporters questioning the mother of a dead child. I don't know exactly and wouldn't presume to guess. I'd demonstrate my respect for that mother and her loss by asking her gently to speak for herself. Expressions of grief in the words of ordinary people can be devastatingly powerful. Besides, people want to talk. It helps.

Third, remember that even witnesses of sudden calamities are victims of a sort. Treat them accordingly. Seeing death happen, seeing a bloody body or seeing someone writhe in agony can deal a wicked wound to the soul. That's not poetry; that's fact. I know. Through a ghastly coincidence, the first three bodies I saw as a young reporter were all headless—two highway crashes and a suicide on a train track. I also watched a man I knew well die right in front of me in an awful accident. Those memories are like scars. No one at the scene of any disaster is just a bystander.

Fourth, don't overlook how other professionals at the scene are affected by adrenaline, exhaustion, disappointment, guilt, grief and other very human feelings. You as a reporter do have to get the details of how five children died of smoke inhalation in their home. However, the coroner you're trying to question actually had to see and touch those five tiny bodies, huddled together just inside the front door. And those sullen volunteer firefighters standing off to the side are thinking, If only I'd dressed faster, driven a little faster, run a bit harder, maybe. . . .

If these sorts of stresses make cops, firefighters or others in the immediate aftermath of emergencies get impatient with reporters, so what? Good reporters don't let brusque or even insulting treatment rattle them. They look beyond it, recognize there are real people in those uniforms and find ways to portray their humanity and emotions as part of the story. Good reporters don't shoot back wisecracks about "crispy bits" to play tough. Instead they gather and tell complete and moving stories about the sometimes horrible human experience, day after day, against the clock, despite abuse, tears, accusations, slurs and stomach-turning sights and smells. And, yes, there is something truly tough about that.

Getting the Details of Fires, Accidents and Disasters

By Ford Risley, Pennsylvania State University

When arriving at the scene of a tragedy, you must concentrate on getting enough information for a bare-bones story as quickly as you can. In other words, seek to answer as many of the "who, what, when, where, why and how" questions as possible.

To get that information, find a police officer or another emergency worker— ideally, someone in charge. Remember, with a breaking story, some of the information will not be available until later. For example, emergency officials will not release the names of victims until a relative has been contacted, and officials often are reluctant to discuss the cause of a disaster until an investigation has been conducted.

Once you have the basic facts, find eyewitnesses, victims and others who can fill out the story with quotes, color and other details. You should also use your powers of observation and note the sights, sounds and smells in order to provide a vivid picture of the scene to your audience.

Keep in mind that establishing communications with your newsroom is essential. You may have all the facts and may have written an outstanding story, but it will never be seen or heard if you can't get it back to your news organization. Fortunately, many news organizations today supply reporters with two-way radios or cellular telephones. But remember that these can fail, so have back-up communications in mind.

When covering a tragedy, continually keep in mind the deadlines you're working under. Editors expect as complete a story as you can provide them when covering a calamity, but they also expect you to meet deadlines so that the story can get into print or be put on the air. Always make sure that you give yourself enough time to write the story and then get it back to your newsroom.

As a reporter, you often will be given greater access to accident scenes than is the average citizen. Even so, it is important that you stay out of the way of emergency workers, so they can do their job. You should also respect the privacy of distraught victims or the family and friends of the injured and dead. Be sensitive and do not try to interview people who are visibly grieving. There is almost always a better time to get their comments and reactions.

Covering Education

By Robert E. Wernsman Jr., Texas Tech University

Providing news coverage of school boards is no simpler than working any other beat and, in many respects, is more complex. It carries implications as serious as any. Education is the foundation of the future—of your community, your state, this nation and all the nations these students will one day influence.

Ask yourself, who are the three most influential people in your life besides your parents? Invariably, a teacher graces such a list. This is the impact of education in your community. Budgets, buildings and contract bargaining may be the most obvious and easily found news stories you'll write, but focusing on the people making decisions is the heart of quality coverage. Stories about people attract readers.

Reflecting the human impact of district board members' decisions is a sure way of serving your audience's needs and interests. Human elements populate all decisions: budgets, choices on closing school facilities in times of shifting dollars and population, even breakfast and lunch nutrition. What roles do taxpayers play in the availability of facilities after school hours or in the emphasis on the arts and sports? Only the attentive reporter will learn and tell. Every one of these areas is rife with human drama and impact.

Visit the schools. Talk to the teachers; gain and respect their confidence. Nothing impresses a teacher more than a good student. Approach your coverage of this beat as an eager student, interested in gathering the facts, understanding the personalities involved and clearly conveying them to your audience. You'll find sources willing to share their experiences and insights, which can bring life to your education reporting.

Visit the students. They are the recipients of all these efforts to educate, propelling them through childhood to early adulthood. What happens to them through this process is of great importance to society and your community. Reflect school board decisions in light of these students, and your stories will illuminate, attracting and enlightening your audience.

Know the numbers. The financial aspect of education may seem overemphasized, but numbers reveal a community's tangible support of its future through learning. An organization can adopt a mission statement, but expenditures reveal its true mission. If you want to understand the system, follow the money flow. Budget coverage requires a review of the numbers, comparisons of previous budgets and an analysis of expenditure choices. Research, review and reasoning—all are

Sidebar 4

Education

Following is a list of what you need to do to cover education:

Know your district.

Visit the schools.

Visit the classroom.

Talk to the students.

Take the students' tests.

Attend nonathletic school events.

Understand the budget.

Know the budget makers and money spenders.

Know the past to comprehend and convey trends.

Never forget: This beat's focus is the world's future.

crucial. Obtain the documents, sit with a willing school district accounting supervisor, talk with a retired principal, see the dollars in action in the classroom.

Here's a tale from the front. An education reporter faced a crucial decision. Immediately before a school bond issue election, the superintendent refused to release documents regarding expenditures during the previous year. The reporter obtained the documents, including reference to nearly $100,000 in expenses from a questionable account. What should the reporter do?

The publisher chose to produce a special edition: a report on the $100,000 expenditure withheld from the public seemingly until after the vote. Coverage of every tax vote requires that the reporter give examples of the dollar impact on individual audience members. The reporter should always reveal the impact of any increase or decrease according to the taxable property, relating this information in terms most accessible to the audience. In this case, the reporter wrote that a $50,000 home's value multiplied against the bond issue's impact resulted in an annual tax bill increase of $137.

Delivered by the postal service to all households in the district, the special edition's coverage reached beyond the usual subscribers. The process of double-checking its content included reading and rereading, both by the five-member staff and by outside, trusted observers. What could have been award-winning stands instead as a humiliation for want of a decimal point. The calculation for the taxable impact of the bond issue for that $50,000 home actually was not $137; it was $13.70. The impact of this mistake haunted the publisher out of town within months and out of the news business for years.

Do your homework, focus on people in the educational process, pursue the truth and always know the advantages of successful mathematical calculations. Recognize that your audience's perception of education as an expense or an investment is directly related to your news coverage.

Covering Speeches and Meetings

By Glen L. Bleske, California State University, Chico

I'll always remember the first speech story I wrote as a student. It was my first *A*. It seemed easy to take all that I had learned in my beginning reporting class and to create a story. I began with a paraphrase of the most interesting thing the speaker said. I followed it with a good direct quote that expanded the lead. From there I alternated between paraphrase and direct quote, re-creating the speaker's main points. At key places, I added background about the speaker and details about where and when he spoke. I ended with a strong direct quote that summarized the speech.

Meeting stories are similar to speech stories, except that you have more than one speaker. Reporting about what happens at a meeting is something that almost every reporter has to do in his or her career. Often, the challenge is how to make a dull but important story interesting. Following are a few tips for reporting speeches and meetings:

You have to pay attention and listen well. A good reporter develops an ear that recognizes main ideas as they are being said. It is almost as if the reporter is writing the story while listening.

You have to know the subject. You can often get an agenda and interview people before a meeting. Find out what is expected to happen. Know what the effects of proposed actions will be. For some speeches, you can get a copy of the remarks ahead of time.

While tape recorders can be handy devices for meetings and speeches, you'll often have short deadlines for writing your story. You won't have time to transcribe the tape, so be sure to take good notes. As a journalism student, you can practice speech and meeting stories by using a VCR to videotape a speech from C-SPAN, which broadcasts dozens of meetings and speeches every week. Take notes and then replay the speech to see how well you did.

Begin your stories with something interesting. If you think it's interesting, so will your readers. For meetings such as the city council, tell readers how some action might affect them. Don't make a rookie mistake and begin with "The city council met," or "President Clinton gave a speech." Focus on what was said or what was accomplished.

Sometimes meetings and speeches can be complicated to report. Some speakers ramble. Sometimes meetings are filled with boring procedures and details. The key is to focus on the most important idea of a speech or the key result of a meeting. Develop one idea at a time. Provide adequate background so a reader understands what happened. And try to be interesting.

All too often, government meetings lead to "Dull but Important" stories. Such stories are reported under the ideal notion that the public needs to know what elected officials are doing. At most of these meetings, the best stories uncover what public officials are doing with taxes: How is the money being spent, who is getting it, where does the money come from, why is the money spent. It's hard to believe that such stories are dull. They don't have to be. Covering government can be one of the most exciting beats in journalism.

The best way to make your government reporting interesting is to focus on people and the effects of government actions on people. The reporter's job is to translate government actions into easy-to-understand stories. To accomplish this, as a reporter you need to

1. Be informed. You have to become an expert on how government works. Cities, counties and states all have layers of responsibility that are outlined by law and administrative codes. Learn the background.

2. Get out of the office. Government affects people, and people comprise the government. Every law, government action, proposal and policy have a face behind them. The only way to understand government is to know the people. You must develop sources who'll share with you the inside news, who'll explain complex

actions, who'll help you do your job. If you're working the city beat, you should be spending time at City Hall. Know the secretaries, guards and janitors because they know what's going on.

3. Work the meeting. A good reporter isn't satisfied with what happens on the podium. Interview people who speak at the meeting. Pay attention to even the most boring segments of the meeting. Listen. Ask questions. For example, a reporter once stumbled on a great story when a county council, without discussion, denied a request for an occupational license for a fortune teller. It all seemed routine during the meeting, but, when the reporter dug into the files, a compelling story of fraud and greed emerged.

4. Educate yourself. Attend workshops that provide background on issues. Attend meetings that are intended as briefings. Collect and clip news stories, pamphlets, books and magazines. Keep files on topics that keep popping up on your beat. Every city hall reporter should have files on sewage treatment, federal revenue sharing and dozens of other recurring subjects. Be sure to collect meeting agendas and the background documents that are critical to covering stories.

5. Remember that insider angles are boring. You need to know the inner workings of government, but most of your readers don't care. Always remember your audience. Avoid government jargon by translating for your readers.

6. Be sure your story has the basics. Tell your readers who voted how and why. Clearly state the effects of the vote and what happens next.

7. Put people in your stories. A rezoning debate isn't about land; it's about people who live next to the land that is being rezoned.

Getting Good Quotes

By Ginger Rudeseal Carter, Georgia College & State University

There's no doubt that good quotes lend a lot to print reporting. As herbs and spices add to great food, quotes add their own special flavor to a story. Quotes can add boldness, authority or a subtle blend of humor. Used properly, a quote can add dimension to any writing. Used too little, too much or incorrectly, quotes can ruin a story, as too much salt can ruin a pot of soup.

Leland "Buck" Ryan, director of the School of Journalism and Telecommunication at the University of Kentucky and author of *The Editor's Toolbox,* has a concise approach to using a quote in a story. A good quote should fit one of the following circumstances:

- Someone said something unique. This is an emphasis on what's said.

- Someone said something uniquely. This emphasizes how it's said—for instance, "The police are not here to create disorder; they are here to preserve disorder." (The late mayor of Chicago, Richard J. Daley, 1968)

- Someone unique said it. "I knew Jack Kennedy. I worked with Jack Kennedy. Senator, you're no Jack Kennedy." (Lloyd Bentsen to Dan Quayle, 1988)

Using these three examples, it's easier to evaluate a quote for a story. But, along with the dos, there are don'ts for using quotes. First, don't use a quotation that merely repeats a transition. For example, the following transition reads:

The meeting will be one of the highlights of the conference weekend, director Bill Lewis said.

But then the quote that follows is a disaster.

"This meeting will be one of the highlights of the conference weekend," Lewis said.

If you don't think professionals do this, look at the news section of your paper. Pick another quote or revise the transition, but don't waste time repeating yourself.

Second, don't make up something to fit the space. For instance, one might manufacture a quote for the football coach who always says the same thing after every win. Don't do it. Make time to find the quotes.

Third, keep quotes in context. Once I interviewed a school superintendent about an outbreak of head lice at an elementary school. As parents know, this is a widespread problem that carries a stigma of uncleanliness. I thought I'd found a sensational scoop. However, the quote I used made the superintendent sound disinterested because he'd minimized the problem. He called me on it, and he was right. I'd used his words incorrectly.

Fourth, make only the slightest grammatical corrections to a quote, and only when necessary. This is one of the most controversial issues journalists face today. There's a fine line between changing verb tense and removing an "um" or "ah." Most reporters do some light housekeeping on quotes.

If you're worried, however, that you're changing too much, you probably are. Consider the alternatives. First, you can paraphrase any quote, as long as you keep the meaning intact. To do this, take off the quote marks and clean it up. Second, you can use a "partial quote," or "snippet," the key phrases of a quote.

Using Attribution

Journalists use attribution to supply credit for and credibility to news stories. One might think attribution is a difficult subject, but it's as simple as a single, monosyllabic word: *said* (*say* for present tense).

The word *said* is the journalist's utility pole. Utility poles bring us power. They serve a purpose, and we depend on them. We don't always notice them, but we know the poles are there. They don't take much away from the surrounding landscape. The same is true of the word *said* as an attribution; it's utilitarian. It gets the job done, allowing the surrounding quotes and copy to shine, and it offers neutral credibility.

"But wait!" you say, "I want the source of my quotes to show emotion!" Consider the previous sentence. Exclamation points make the reader see that the words are emphasized. To use *exclaim* rather than *say* would be redundant with the exclamation points.

Think about this sentence: "She sighed." How does someone sigh? Why not use "She said with a sigh"? You can use such words as *stressed, asserted, maintained* and *replied,* but what do these words really mean? Said.

How should the words be ordered in attribution? I was taught that the name and title come first, then the *said:* "Jill Smith, president of the student council, said." This order is best because it's the order in which we speak and think. However, many newspapers today, permit the use of "said Jill Smith, president of the student council." Either way, the verb of attribution is *said.* Check your publication's style sheet for its preferred order.

As a sage once said, why use a big word when a small, understandable one will do? *Said* is, hands down, the best word for attribution in news, features and press releases.

Sidebar 5

Reporting Skills for Photographers
Good writing for photographers starts with good reporting skills. When you are on assignment, start with the basics. Answer these questions:

Who is the story about?

What is the story about?

Where is the story taking place?

When is the story happening?

Why did the story happen?

How did the story happen?

Be thorough when gathering information. Gather enough information for a story, even if you end up writing only a caption.

The Photographer as Writer

By James H. Kenney Jr., Western Kentucky University

Television characters rarely treat photojournalists kindly. There was Jimmy Olson, the wet-behind-the-ears photographer from "Superman" whom everyone ordered around. He didn't seem to possess a competent mind of his own. Then there was Animal, the photographer from the series "Lou Grant," who rarely showered. He was given the nickname because of his uncontrolled facial hair and disheveled appearance.

Combine these fictional characters with some questionable character traits of real photographers and you have the makings of a stereotype. Photographers have been working hard over the years to shed this image. Some have successfully transformed themselves from mindless followers to inspirational leaders in the newsroom. One way they have overcome the stereotype is by combining their pictures with quality writing.

This writing goes beyond generating photo captions, which should be required writing for any photographer handing in pictures to a news desk (see Chapter 10 for a discussion about writing captions). Many photographers have not only photographed big projects but have written the story for them as well.

Photojournalist John Kaplan has written the stories for many of his projects such as his essay on children in the countries of the former Soviet Union and his Pulitzer Prize-winning essay on being 21 years old in America.

The idea of writing your own stories is not to usurp writers but to complement them. Sensitive conditions in some stories such as a complicated medical operation require that only one person be present at the scene. I have covered news events where a writer was not there or could not get there. My first priority was to record the event visually. But I made sure I came back with background information, quotes and the telephone numbers of those involved in the story. Once I was back in the office, I could either write the story if deadlines permitted or pass along the information to a reporter. I did not consider this to be doing a favor for the reporter; I considered it my responsibility as a journalist.

Photojournalists are reporters with cameras. Part of that reporting requires us to ask questions and write down information. This contributes significantly to the quality of both the pictures and the written story.

Many photographers fear writing. Perhaps they have told themselves that they take pictures because they can't write. However, many of those who try writing discover a hidden talent. Great writers pull from the same well of creativity as do great photographers; they just use different instruments to express themselves.

The key ingredient in writing for impact is to listen for interesting quotes from your subject in much the same way as you look for storytelling visual moments. This attaches a human element to the information. Once back at the office, don't ruin all that good reporting with bad grammar and spelling; you have a dictionary and a newsroom full of editors who can look at your story before you submit it. Ask questions, but try to find an editor who is not on deadline. There's no shame in having your work corrected, only in missing mistakes that run in the newspaper. Ask the person looking at your story to edit it out loud. Listen to the editing process. The best way to gain confidence in your own editing abilities is to observe how it's done.

Taking responsibility for writing will not shed all of the photojournalist's stereotypes. But it changes attitudes toward photographers in the newsroom. Progressive editors recognize the value of a journalist who can report with both photographs and words. Good writers value another "ear" on assignment, a photographer who can provide interesting quotes and other information to supplement the writer's story. Continued commitment to being a complete journalist is the best way to make the Jimmy Olson and Animal stereotypes become a distant memory.

Exercises

1. Visit a local police station and talk to the community relations or press office about what documents are available to a reporter in your area. Ask to see some of those records. Analyze them and determine the most important elements in the reports.

2. Pick any court and go see a trial, either civil or criminal. Talk to the attorneys about what's going on. Visit the clerk of the court and see what documents are available. Isolate the most important elements of that day's testimony and write a 400-word analysis. Don't try a news story just yet.

3. Go to the local fire department and talk with the public relations officials or the local chief. Walk around the fire station and talk with the firefighters. Ask them what they do and why they do it.

4. Collect obituaries appearing between six and 12 months ago, sufficient for three per student. With the names of survivors, a directory and a telephone, pursue the investigative task of surveying at least one family member. Avoid duplication, calling no family more than once. This assignment combines sensitivity toward a subject's life and the family's grief with real-world journalistic responsibility for basic, factual information. Explain you're a member of a journalism class assigned to analyze obituaries for accuracy and completeness. Cordially request the family member's participation but honor any refusals. Among the questions to be asked are the following: Was the obituary accurate? Resolve any factual discrepancies. Did the obituary accurately reflect the life of the person? Did the writer express any

assumptions? Were family members or close acquaintances contacted and quoted? If contacted at the time of the original obituary, what would this family member have said for publication? Record the quotation and repeat it for the interviewee. Is it accurate, word for word? Is there anything else the family member wants to include?

5. Practice writing speech and meeting stories by using a VCR to videotape a speech from C-SPAN, which broadcasts dozens of meetings and speeches every week. Take notes and then replay the speech to see how well you did.

6. Consider this quote from a small-town sheriff in a news conference, "There's no question in my mind that this murder was premedicated." You know he means "premeditated," but that's not what you have in your notes or on your tape. You need to use it. Should you change it?

7. Research the lawsuit of Jeffrey Masson versus Janet Malcolm of the *New Yorker*. Who was right?

Suggested Reading

Buchanan, Edna. *The Corpse Had a Familiar Face.* New York: Diamond Books, 1991. This book about crime in Miami remains a classic. Buchanan won a Pulitzer Prize when she covered the cops for the *Miami Herald*.

7 Covering the Big Story

Robert Unger

Associate Professor, Professional Writing Program, University of Missouri–Kansas City

Chicago Tribune and *Kansas City Star*

Chapter Outline

Let people talk

Establish relationships

Keep it simple

Be polite

Build the story

Explain the unexplainable

Do what is necessary to get the story

Be wary of rules

Sidebar 1 Tips

Sidebar 2 Don't let the big story overwhelm you

The only difference between the big story and the routine assignment is how it is perceived (first) by the editors and (second) by the readers. For the reporter in the trenches, the same fundamentals apply. Bill Jones, the late and much-beloved managing editor of the *Chicago Tribune,* laid that out very clearly 26 years ago to rookie reporters. "If you can make it on the streets of Chicago," he said, without a hint of a smile, "you can cover any story in the world."

He was right. Those "rookies," though now scattered all over the world, have so far won over a dozen Pulitzer Prizes. And each did it on fundamentals every bit as applicable in Biloxi as in Beirut.

That means every story's preparation and execution are essentially the same, at least in spirit. Your research for the big story may be waiting on a hotel fax machine or in your e-mail, thrown together by someone in your newspaper's morgue while you were asleep on an airplane. Your interviews may be arranged over a cellular phone while you're standing in line for a rental car and holding a screaming baby for the harried young mother in front of you. But you still better have done your homework, no matter how hard you had to cram.

The good reporters learn all this long before they need to use it. They aren't just sitting around waiting for the big story to drop in their laps. That's why someone covering the metropolitan sanitary district reads all he can about unrest in the Middle East, and the reporter in the suburbs keeps up on her Spanish. It's why reporters who want to be correspondents routinely devour three or four newspapers a day; they aren't stuck on their own stories in their own section of their own newspaper.

Most of the time what's really different about the big story is what you bring to it—precious little. By definition, most stories are big stories because whatever it is that's happening doesn't happen all the time. So, if you want to do it well (and if you want your editor to send you out on the big story a second time), you'd better get creative fast. That's because there's only one ironclad rule: The bigger the story, the better the competition.

I once spoke to a few hundred managing editors at a convention in Louisville, Ky., and jokingly posed a situation for them: You're on your way to a big story just outside Bleeding Gums, Mont., and you know your competition is following on the next plane. You get to the little airport, and only two rental cars are available. One is a cheap little model that will cramp your legs but please your penny-pinching publisher. The other is a luxurious sedan that costs a small fortune. Which one do you rent? The editors puzzled over that one a bit and finally split almost evenly in their choices. They were all wrong. You rent both cars so your competition finds herself afoot—and you have the story to yourself.

There's more than a grain of truth there. On the big story, you have to live by your wits because there simply are no grooves to follow and, if you're doing it right, the herd is somewhere *behind* you. There's no time, and no reward, for subtlety.

In short, you do what works. There's almost never time for the network-building process of beat reporting, and your paper's "clout" that got you close to sources back home petered out somewhere over Wyoming. It's all up to you. Every choice, whether it involves ethics, professionalism, accuracy, fairness or just plain dignity, is yours to make. And, despite that cellular phone in your pocket, you'll make those choices alone. Like no other, the big story, because of so little time and so much distance, is the reporter's story.

And there's another hard reality. Given today's move-em-into-management theories for young newsroom hotshots, your editor may have no useful concept of what working so far off the leash is all about. So depend on yourself first, last and always.

In the end, big stories are simply too diverse to accommodate a convenient list of dos and don'ts, but experience does suggest a few guidelines that may be helpful. None are rules; there would be far too many exceptions. And they are not all equally important; you'll have to rank them for yourself.

Let People Talk

The first guideline is to let people talk, about anything. Soak up who they are, not just what they have to say. Above all, be sincerely interested in them and let them know it. You won't be able to fake it, because good people can spot a phony. Examine yourself from the first day you head out with a notebook. If you can't feel their joy, if you can't share their pain, do something else. Turn in your pencil and move on.

That route can get a little rocky, of course, as it did for me one cold night in early 1983. I was in North Dakota covering the aftermath of tax resister Gordon Kahl's deadly shootout with U.S. marshals. Kahl, the harmless loudmouth, was suddenly Kahl the killer, and if anybody knew where he was hiding no one was telling. I'd spent a week with his friends and family in Texas and then North Dakota, repeatedly asking the question, Where would Gordon run? In my gut I knew no one would tell me.

Then somebody did. It was at a little gathering, almost a party but more of a wake. By then I knew the little clan and understood their foibles and philosophical fragilities but liked them anyway. I was standing against a wall, enjoying a full stomach and warm thoughts, when a new friend whispered one word in my ear: *Mena.*

There it was. I had it. To my astonishment, I'd been entrusted with something that outsiders just couldn't know. Yet, in a very few moments, I realized that knowing Gordon Kahl was headed for the hills around Mena, Ark., was not necessarily a healthy state in the middle of his Posse Comitatus true believers. What if my confidant had second thoughts? What if there arose a need to repair the indiscretion? I soon made my excuses and raced to my computer and then on to my newspaper to apply a proven journalistic principle: When you know something that someone might want to erase, tell the world.

After that, I thought a lot more about the whole concept of listening, and I hope I moved further up the scale from sympathy toward empathy. Maybe I saw a little more clearly that, contrary to the pop song of a few years ago, in journalism it's the song, not the singer. It's always about them; it's never about us.

That can be hard to keep in mind sometimes—during the Gulf War, for instance, when the generals and admirals showcased their triple penchants for preening, posturing and propaganda. Journalists' reaction, however, soon turned the rooster parade into a strutting cockfight. In Saudi Arabia, reporters finally had to ask for nontelevised briefings because even their own preening for the cameras was blocking the story. Good professional questioning and follow-up got mixed up with competition for air time—even among the print reporters. For a while, the singers lost the song.

Establish Relationships

Another guideline for getting the big story is, if there's a kid involved, play to the kid. People like people their kids like. More than that, strangers need some reason to trust you and your intentions. Kids have great radar for sincerity, and their parents know it. They can take you miles in minutes—or they can shut you out.

The key to getting a story often is to make a connection with people who are reluctant to talk to reporters. Author Robert Unger practices what he preaches: "If there's a kid involved, play to the kid. People like people their kids like."

When militant Lakota Sioux occupied a tiny state park in South Dakota's Black Hills a few years ago, I went up to see what it was all about. For one thing, the park was not far from Wounded Knee, a place twice stained with the blood of red-white hatreds. This time, a Sioux already had been picked off by a sniper from the ridge that separated the park from a white and hostile housing area. So I wasn't surprised when the nervous young guards at the Sioux's makeshift checkpoint wanted a peek at my bag. There were no guns in sight, but the guns you can't see are always the worst kind.

When I got inside, no one in the little compound—a few teepees and a new sweat lodge—would talk to me. But why should they? Police all over the world have been playing reporter for years. I needed a wedge, and an old hoop nailed to a couple of boards and a tree seemed as promising as any. The half-flat basketball wouldn't bounce. But, with four inches of snow on the ground, that didn't matter much. Within five minutes, a little boy about six years old was retrieving the ball for me. Within eight, he was standing on my shoulders, alternately shooting toward the hoop and dropping the ball on my head. Within 15 minutes, his father had invited me inside a hot, stuffy teepee for some bad coffee and good conversation.

Likewise, if you're trying to reach a man or boy, pay respectful attention to his horse, dog or camel. Or flirt a little with Grandma or tease Uncle Fred. The key is to make a connection quickly, to start a mini-friendship or to offer a hint of trust. Your editor may think she's paying you to report, analyze and write. She's not. She's really paying you to connect somehow with at least a thousand distinct personalities every year. Without a connection, there's no story or, worse, there's a bad story.

So it's not really about animals, kids and Uncle Fred at all. It's about reading where people are and meeting them there. You may pound on a door in Manhattan, but in the countryside you let them see you *before* you see them. Make noise when you drive up. Linger around the car. Walk slowly. Give them time to come to the door, walk out on the porch, call their neighbor or load the shotgun if that's what makes them feel more comfortable. Former Senator Bill Bradley, once a professional basketball player, called this vital tool "a sense of where you are." You have to bring that sense to your court, too.

Keep It Simple

Choose the simple route to a story. Any big story is complicated enough without your making the reporting complicated, too.

Mike Kelly, columnist and editor at the *Omaha World Herald,* tells how he and his editors fretted for days over how and when to fly an interpreter to Ft. Chaffee, Ark., to help their reporting team interview thousands of Cuban boat people herded there in 1980. Finally, they found just the right person and sent him south at considerable cost. "We'd just arrived inside the camp," Kelly said, "when I saw this big guy standing in the middle of hundreds of refugees, waving a $50 bill, and yelling, 'Anybody want to be an interpreter?' He had 10 takers in five seconds, all of them fluent—and cheap. We'd spent a lot of time and money for what he got in a heartbeat."

Actually, I hired two interpreters that day so that one could always listen while the other translated—with a substantial bonus promised if either caught the other rearranging fact or nuance in the journey between Spanish and English.

Artificial complexity always works against the story. During the Gulf War, for instance, the American military told journalists it was just too difficult, too costly and logistically impossible to hook up reporters with hometown military personnel

Sidebar 1

Tips

Take care of yourself—physically. Factor in your rest time and guard it tenaciously. If you need a day off or an hour nap, take it. Of one thing you can be certain: If you wait for someone in the office to tell you to take care of yourself, you'll be wearing dirty underwear and keeping your eyes open with toothpicks. And, if you run out of gas, your story does, too.

However, that advice does not excuse the Middle East correspondent who told his office for three weeks that he was waiting in Paris for a visa to Algeria, when, in fact, he could have picked one up at that time by simply arriving at the Algiers Airport. For that matter, neither does it excuse the Washington correspondent who swears that certain club memberships are a must for committing good journalism, D.C.-style.

It *can* mean, however, that a motel's location is more important than its price tag, no matter how many memos you receive about cost cutting. And it *can* mean that dinner with a friend is a legitimate expense account item even if it doesn't yield a scoop.

Contrary to the folks in accounting, a telephone call to your son after his track meet does *not* necessarily require a personal calling card account. And a movie in your room (disallowed by the beancounters) is far less expensive than drinking half the night with your buddies (an allowed expense).

Sometimes your own mental health just has to come first. In 1982, after a long season of off-year election coverage, I found myself in eastern Tennessee reporting on Jim Cooper, a bright young man who was fighting Cissy Baker for a seat in Congress. He asked me one day how I liked politics. "I hate it," I answered, and at that moment I really did. He asked what kind of stories I liked, and, when I said I liked good people features, he started telling me about the Melungeons. "They're olive-complected, light-haired, often blue-eyed folks who have always lived way back up Snake Hollow, and nobody knows where they came from or when they got here," he said. "See ya later," I said, heading for my car. The result was a wonderful story with the best lead I've ever written. I had dozens of calls the day it ran (as opposed to exactly none on my political coverage). When I last checked, Cooper still had a copy of the Melungeon story on his office wall. And I survived Campaign '82.

in the war zone. Many deeply disappointed reporters, specifically sent there to write about local units, spent weeks fighting for that special access, and they usually lost. A far simpler solution, it seemed to me at the time, was to bend the military's rules, drive as far north toward Kuwait as roadblocks would allow and pull into one of the several truck parking areas. Then, donning a brand new blue Kansas City Royals baseball cap that fairly gleamed in the desert sun, I waited for homesick kids and friendly neighbors to jump at the connection with home. Word moved up and down the rows of trucks faster than I could have, and all I had to do was fill my notebook. That cap never failed. Of course, I also had another hat, a brown one that looked remarkably like an officer's hat, which I wore at roadblocks. But that's another story.

Be Polite

Be a gentleman or a lady, in the old-fashioned sense of those words, anytime you can. Manners, civility and respectfulness cost nothing, and life's too short to squander it on being the stereotypical journalistic jerk portrayed in the movies. Leave the macho posturing at the high school or college newspaper. And save your genuine toughness for those times, which indeed *will* come, when you really need it.

Plain bad manners almost got me killed during the Intifada on the West Bank in 1988. My interpreter and I had stopped on a narrow street in front of a mechanic's garage to ask directions to a specific address. As always happens in the hospitable and curious Middle East, everyone in the shop came out to see what we wanted. My friend introduced us while I fought with a wrinkled map and irritably chewed on the pipe I smoked at the time. Hearing my name, I half-heartedly tried to say hello, but the word somehow wrapped around the pipe stem and came out as something the wary Palestinians mistook for Hebrew. Within 30 seconds the car was surrounded by every man and boy in the neighborhood, and a couple of hundred Arab fingers pulled at bumpers and fenders, intent on dumping me on my allegedly Jewish head. Some fast talking and a lot of forced smiles barely saved the day. We eventually lingered more than an hour over coffee and juice in the back of the shop while the Palestinians apologized repeatedly for what was, in fact, a direct consequence of my own rudeness.

Manners, respectfulness and a touch of grace once were and still should be a reporter's ideal. The Journalist's Creed, composed by Walter Williams decades ago, includes the pledge "I will not write as a journalist what I would not say as a gentleman." The word *gentleman* should imply a far higher standard than, unfortunately, it does today. No professional code of ethics, no matter how encompassing or precise, can make up for the loss.

In fact, no institutional code of ethics will ever relieve you of the responsibility of creating your own. No code of ethics will cover the human situations that really matter or give you all the answers when you need them most. On the big story, especially, when you're out there by yourself and headed for Page One, you'd better be armed with something more.

In 27 years of reporting, of covering stories in virtually every state and several foreign countries; after five presidential election campaigns, a couple of wars and countless riots; in witnessing the birth of nations and the slow death of civility—I have never heard a conversation among working correspondents about codes of ethics. Yet in bars, bistros, cafes and courtyards all over this planet I've heard and asked scores of questions about right and wrong, good and bad, fair and unfair, about the very essence of good journalism.

In the end, a good reporter must maintain balance according to her or his own internal gyroscope, that very delicate instrument set in motion years before by good teachers and finely tuned over a lifetime by editors, colleagues, sources and readers. And, finally, those toughest choices are tempered in a place that poets call the heart, or maybe the soul.

Many journalists today want to deny and hide most of that. They seem to prefer an illusion of separateness, as if the practice of journalism, the researching and telling of stories, is as mechanical as the building of cars, each story as inevitable in its outcome as is the composition of a Chevrolet.

In fact, journalism's role as the first rough draft of history is the result of choice built on choice built on choice. And a crucial first choice, no matter how we label it, is bound up with the old-fashioned concepts of "lady" and "gentleman." In short, what sort of person do I choose to be? What personal rules and standards do I bring to the game? Who am I?

Journalistic "Jerks," though proliferating, hardly dominate the profession. In fact, journalism is replete with genuine ladies and gentlemen. One, however, stands above the rest, at least in my book. David Broder, a veteran political reporter for the *Washington Post,* is the consummate journalist, fiercely competitive, tenacious and highly respected by everyone even remotely connected with the cut and slash of politics. He's also a fine, kind, generous and gentle man. And he's proof positive that you don't have to be mean to be good.

Build the Story

Find someone who knows a little more about the story than you do; then build from there. Reporting even the biggest story is just about that simple. It's the same way you cover the school board or city hall. However, on the big story, you have to build faster.

David Halberstam, author and former correspondent for the *New York Times,* once said that the worst feeling in the world was getting into a strange town, working the motel phone and then waiting in the gut-eating fear that no one would return your calls. He's right, but someone always does. Piece by piece, the story builds.

Just remember to reach for the right pieces. I've made a special point, over the years, of being nice to janitors, cleaning staff people, secretaries and guards in parking garages. They give access a whole new meaning, and they know about office dynamics.

Likewise, I got more insight into hatred, prejudice and resentment in one afternoon with a dozen Palestinian children in a Bethlehem living room than the political leadership of both sides could provide in a month. In Bosnia, the aid and charity workers knew as much about the shifting front lines as the United Nations Protection Force ever did. And I'm convinced a certain tired mother in Chiapas knew more about real economics, the kitchen table variety, than did Mexican President Carlos Salinas, despite his Harvard degree.

However, there's good reason to tap the acknowledged experts, too. Almost every subject under the sun, no matter how obscure or arcane, is somebody's consuming passion. And seasoned journalists know there's a very good chance somebody's already done their research for them, whatever the subject. The key is finding that person.

In Canada, when Quebec was making loud noises about secession, I found myself curious about the evolution of attitudes that had brought our neighbors to that dangerous point. A string of phone calls led me to a professor at Montreal's McGill University. "What impact has the church and public school affiliation in Quebec had on nationalistic aspirations among Quebec's Francophones?" I asked. "By age, gender, location or income level?" he responded. "I'll be right over," I said. I later walked away with six ways of looking at the question and seven different answers. But it was a start.

Explain the Unexplainable

Even on the biggest or most complex story, look for the comprehensible that explains the incomprehensible. That usually involves getting out of the way and letting people tell the story in basic, elemental terms, in ways that they understand and your readers will understand. When you experience an "Aha!" moment, don't let it get away. The best example came when a student at the University of Missouri–Kansas City was covering a beat in the city. She had chosen Northeast High School, one of the magnet schools in Kansas City's long and costly attempt to cure decades of ills.

Some of the best journalists in the country had taken on the complicated subject of magnet schools with their crosstown busing, incentives for suburban students and focused education like Northeast's concentration on law, the military and public service. Yet, after all the time, all the research and all the dollars, people still asked why some schools such as Northeast were such a mess. Why the low test scores, attendance problems and just plain lack of learning?

Sidebar 2

Don't Let the Big Story Overwhelm You

Big stories can overwhelm you. So can some reporters from major newspapers and networks who swoop down when the big story breaks. In those first hours or days there's no shortage of either talent or conceit at the scene of a story. And some will work hard to convince everyone, especially the newcomers, that they know everything there is to know about the current event before a single notebook is sullied.

They don't. If they think they do, they're already behind you, because you arrived knowing that you have a lot to learn.

Be open. Soak it up. If you feel like a wide-eyed cub reporter, use it. No matter how jaded your compatriots are, hold on to the joy that you're knee deep in history, that your eyes are seeing and your ears hearing for thousands or even millions who pay half a buck each morning for the best your mind, heart and soul can deliver.

An editor once called me Hoover after the vacuum cleaner. It was the nicest thing he ever said about me. For a good cub reporter, even an old cub, the problem is never what to write; it's always what to leave out. The night the Berlin Wall came down was a classic example. I wandered around the Brandenburg Gate for hours in a near panic. Not only did I have a notebook exploding with stories (an Aussie cowboy with Fosters beer in his hand and tears in his eyes; three Austrian school girls on the lam from their parents; an old Spanish couple, one blind and the other deaf; a London architect who had called in sick every morning for a week; and a teenage girl who lived 200 yards due east and was afraid to go home because the wall might close behind her), but,

because of the time difference, I had several long hours to stew about squeezing it all into a couple of columns of type.

The big story can also paralyze a good reporter, as it did one night in 1981 when a hanging skywalk collapsed at the Hyatt Hotel in Kansas City, leaving 114 dead and dying. Everything was chaos, on the streets and in the newsroom of the *Kansas City Star* and *Times*. Everyone who hadn't left town that Friday evening showed up in the newsroom to do whatever needed doing.

One of the paper's best young reporters was sent to the scene to gather information about the heroics of volunteers. Already there were stories floating around about doctors and nurses crawling under crumbling concrete, passers-by digging with bare and bloody hands before the dust even settled and a small army of construction workers who literally stole their bosses' heavy equipment, roared down clogged city streets from several directions and ripped lifesaving holes in the wreckage. It all turned out to be true. However, that night, his mind truly boggled by the awful enormity of the story, the young reporter couldn't see it. "No story," he told the desk editor.

When that word crossed the room, Mike Davies, the editor of both the *Kansas City Star* and *Times,* was speechless for about two seconds, then furious. "He's gone!" Davies hissed. "He's finished! I'm gonna fire him right now!"

Although the rest of the staff did a splendid job in covering that story and, in fact, won the Pulitzer Prize, the young reporter, who was actually not fired that night, is now doing something else.

The student, Cheray Fowler, reported two stories that shed more light than all the pros had managed. In one story, she wrote about a magnificent state-of-the-art library and media center—and about bright kids who fearfully smuggled out books under their shirts because the stigma and peer censure of reading, study and learning would get them beaten up or much worse. In another, she wrote about school security guards who used their refusal to arrest students as a tool to make kids behave. The reason? A rap sheet was a neighborhood status symbol; not being arrested hurt kids reputations with their friends. Arrest had become a reward, nonarrest a punishment. Tragic? Yes. But that story is incomprehensible no more.

Roadblocks often occur in covering important stories. For example, the American military told journalists it was often too difficult to hookup reporters with hometown soldiers in the war zone. The key to a good story often is finding a way around the restrictions.

Do What Is Necessary to Get the Story

Do what is necessary to get the story, not just what is expected of you by your bosses, your teachers or anybody else.

The big story can bring with it some heavy psychological baggage. For instance, why fly all that way to end up talking to somebody on the phone? But that's how I once got a great story in Houston about astronauts' families on the ground while a Skylab crew was circling above. In fact, it was the only way they'd talk, and I wasn't about to be a purist.

Michael Sneed, now a columnist for the *Chicago Sun-Times,* was a rookie at the *Chicago Tribune* years ago and one of the first to be sent out of town. Her story involved a dramatic hostage situation in Utah, and she wrote a dynamite story. When she returned, we all debriefed her, as was our custom then, to learn everything we could. She was reticent until the boss walked away. "The truth is," she then said, "I never left the hotel. I made a few phone calls, and everything began to click. I got a couple of people who really wanted to talk. They said they'd call me back. Then I couldn't leave. I'd have missed the story."

After all, the story is the important thing, and it doesn't need your footprints all over it to be good. It just needs telling.

Be Wary of Rules

Regard any rules (other than your own) with suspicion, and consider them only as suggestions if they get in the way of good journalism. On the big story, the rules are invariably made by people who do *not* have the interests of you, your paper or your readers at heart. Their rules will serve them but cripple you. And that doesn't apply just to government rule makers. During the Gulf War, the media grandees in Washington and New York cut self-serving deals with the military in order to protect their selfish interests at the expense of good journalism. And organized religion in America can be as closed to scrutiny as any mob in Las Vegas.

Thus, never mistake rules for laws or complex procedures for sound policy. Anytime anyone makes a rule designed to "protect" you, watch out.

Now and into the 21st century, it's all about access. Efforts to block the publication of information are so public and so inflammatory that they almost never happen in this country any more. Likewise, censorship, even in wartime, is clumsy and heavy-handed, and it leaves fingerprints all over the history books. But, for the rule makers, controlling access is a beautiful tool. It leaves no fingerprints, yet it dictates the news absolutely.

The Persian Gulf War warned us about this threat, especially after we understood the complicity of our major media. But that war also brought hints that American journalism had not yet entirely lost its stuff. One day on a bus in Kuwait City in a "restricted" area, where the military wanted us to listen to a general but not talk to the men and women who fought the war, a little rebellion broke out over the whole question of access. As things descended from rowdy to raucous, a Japanese reporter stepped forward, flanked by several of his countrymen, and tendered an elaborate apology to the military minders on board for our disgraceful conduct, adding that the Japanese reporters shouldn't be penalized for the Americans' misbehavior. As he spoke, many of us from the press corps took advantage of the unintentional Japanese screen to jump out the rear emergency door, disappear among the troops and go do our jobs.

Exercises

1. Find the most important story of the day in your newspaper. Compare that with a good but "less important" story. What is the same? What is different?

2. Look at one story that has won the Pulitzer Prize or a Columbia-DuPont broadcasting award. How is the story told? What are the essential elements of the story, using the previous examples of telling a story, researching a story and reporting a story?

3. Choose an example you think is good reporting. What makes it good in your estimation?

Suggested Readings

Kaplan, Robert D. *Balkan Ghosts*. New York: Vintage Books, 1994. Despite years of slaughter and hundreds of accounts from the front, the depth of the Balkan tragedy remains incomprehensible for many of us. It need not be. Kaplan's excellent book combines history, perspective, scholarship and the fresh smell of smoke. It's hardly the first draft of history; it's several steps down the road.

Kapuscinski, Ryszard. *The Soccer War*. New York: Vintage Books, 1992. Kapuscinski, a Polish journalist, is one of the finest reporters of this era. This book is a collection of his works, including his coverage of wars, famines, revolutions and most other major stories of the past 30 years.

Shirer, William. *Berlin Diary: The Journal of a Foreign Correspondent*. New York: Little, Brown & Co., 1988. If anyone has ever taken personal ownership of a really big story, it must be Shirer. His account of the runup to war in Hitler's capital stands as a model of keen observation and reporting excellence in all its aspects.

Smith, Hedrick. *The Media and the Gulf War: The Press and Democracy in Wartime*. Baltimore: Johns Hopkins Press, 1992. Smith, a former *New York Times* reporter, edits a masterful series of articles from the various players in the Gulf War from government spokesman to reporter and everything in between. He lets the documents and the individuals speak.

Waugh, Evelyn. *Scoop*. New York: Little, Brown & Co., 1977. Waugh's masterpiece is worth far more than laughs, which it has delivered aplenty since its original publication in 1938. Any seasoned correspondent recognizes the awful germ of truth in the political, diplomatic and media foul-ups that collide to change the course of one little country's history. Every reporter should read *Scoop* every few years, just to puncture our personal balloons of self-importance.

8 Writing the Story

Glen L. Bleske, Ph.D.
Assistant Professor, California State University, Chico
Daytona Beach (Fla.) *News-Journal,* Richmond (Ind.) *Palladium-Item*
and Melbourne (Fla.) *Times*

Chapter Outline

The lead

Organizing the story

Using quotes in your story

Ending a story

Finishing the story

   Improving

   Fixing

Sidebar 1 Reading to report

Sidebar 2 A checklist for fixing stories

Sidebar 3 Words that cause trouble

Sidebar 4 Do's and don'ts of quotes

Sidebar 5 The feature story

Sidebar 1

The writing of a news story begins long before the reporter sits in front of a computer and looks at the blank screen. As you've learned in previous chapters, writing begins with an idea.

From there, you report: Collect information from people, documents, data bases or your own observations. Most writers then rehearse what they're going to write. Rehearsal takes place in your head. You have to imagine your story and write it in your mind long before you put the first word on paper. Some journalists describe the process as "talking a story." You might even visualize the words in written form or hear the words in your head. Such rehearsal helps you realize what information is needed to tell the story. Rehearsal taps the creativity you'll need in developing the idea, gathering information and interviewing your sources.

Once you have the information you need, it's time to write. To help get your mind working, pretend you're telling the story to a friend or family member. Sometimes writers actually tell the story to their pets before they begin writing. This process helps writers to hear their words. Go ahead, move your lips; whisper the words to yourself. As you begin, one thing is important: Don't expect too much from your first efforts. Write fast and let the writing help you discover what you need to say next.

The Lead

The lead is the beginning of your story. Leads can be classified under dozens of different categories. Leads can describe something, tell a story, summarize an event, explain the effects of an action, ask a question or use a metaphor.

There is no single correct way to write a lead. Ten reporters might write 10 different leads for the same story. Most reporters spend lots of time writing their leads and you should, too. A good lead should be the hook into the story that grabs the reader and also helps a writer see what else needs to be written. As you think about beginning your story, let your imagination find your lead.

Following are some thoughts that will help you find a good launching point:

1. Remember that there are many good ways to write a lead. Good leads may be graceful or funny, cute or short. Good leads may vary by tone and content. But all good leads share some qualities: They sing; they tell a story; they are concise and clear; they are appropriate for the topic.

2. Ask yourself the following questions: What is the story about? What does the reader need to know from the story? It may help to list the four or five most important ideas in your story. Find the focus of the story by stripping it to the basics. It might be helpful to imagine that you're telling the story to a 5-year-old. What would you say first to the child?

3. What surprised you most in the story? By beginning with what you thought was interesting, you probably began with something that will interest your reader. And a good lead should hook a reader into the story. Pretend you're talking to your parents: "Hey, Mom, hey, Dad, listen to this. Did you know . . . ?"

4. Sometimes you can use words to paint a picture for your reader. If the picture captures the essence of the story, you have a great lead. For example, a story about a school board banning *Huckleberry Finn* could generate this lead: "High school students will not be rafting anymore with Huck Finn and Jim." Make sure, however, that your lead is not a cliché. Don't write about drug deals gone awry and bodies in pools of blood. Don't stretch too far to connect an image with your story.

5. Look for the conflict in your story. Drama can sell your story for you.

6. Meeting stories and government stories can be interesting if you begin by telling readers how the story will affect them. Don't say a new road will be built. Instead, tell readers they'll be able to get to the shopping mall in less time.

7. How can you summarize the story in one short sentence? If it all fits well, you might have a good lead. Ask yourself who did what to whom and why. In some cases, how something happened or where it happened is important.

8. Be concrete, not abstract. Don't tell readers about a problem in traffic control; tell them the city needs more stoplights. Use specific nouns. Don't call a library an educational facility.

9. Use action verbs in the active voice. Try to avoid intransitive verbs such as *is, are* and *were.* Have people doing something.

10. Don't pack too much information into your lead. Include the main details and save the secondary details for later.

11. Write more than one lead. Donald Murray, a Pulitzer Prize–winning journalist, says he often writes dozens of leads for his stories. Students' expectations are too high, and they often try to write the one perfect lead, struggling with each word, staring at the computer screen. It's much better to write many leads without much thought. Try to write five leads in five minutes. You can do it. Then choose one good lead from those five.

12. Learn from your failures. It's better to write 10 bad leads in 15 minutes than it is to write nothing. Be willing to take risks.

Sidebar 2

A Checklist for Fixing Stories

1. Before fixing your story, pause for at least two minutes. Look at something other than the computer screen. Clear your mind. Relax. Put some distance between yourself and the story, so you can see it with fresh eyes.

2. Double-check the spelling of all the proper names.

3. Begin at the end of the story and look at each word. Is it spelled correctly? Is it a homonym (*their, there, it's*)? Make sure you're using the right one.

4. Check each word for AP style problems: Numbers (time, dates, money, addresses); abbreviations and acronyms; titles. Justify each use of a capital letter.

5. Make sure that all quotes and paraphrases are punctuated correctly.

6. Have you used *said* and avoided *claimed, added* and *stated*?

7. Check your commas. Have a reason for using each one. Find the reason in the Punctuation Guide of the *AP Stylebook*.

8. Do all your pronouns clearly refer to nouns? Do they agree in number (singular pronoun with singular noun, for example)? Do all your subjects agree with their verbs?

Organizing the Story

Most reporters don't write an outline for their stories. Instead they use a process of "discovery" to tell their stories. During the idea stage and while they gathered information, their brains began organizing the story. Once they begin writing, they let what they have written suggest what comes next. The act of writing reveals what their brains have already accomplished.

You can use this process, too. One way is to write quickly and without notes. Just tell the story. Don't worry about spelling, punctuation or grammar. You can go back and fix your story later. Sometimes you might need more structure. Some reporters begin writing by transcribing their notes onto a computer screen. They choose the parts they think they're going to use. Then they move paragraphs. They add transitions and background. And, suddenly, the story takes shape and is nearly complete.

Reviewing your notes is a great way to start writing. Sometimes reporters list the facts in their notebooks, then number them in the order they want to use them. You can even rip the pages out of your notebook and arrange them in the order you'll use them. You can use different color highlighters to connect themes or ideas.

The key to good organization is to link each sentence to the next in a natural, logical flow of words. Following are five basic forms of organization that often appear in media writing. All the forms have a purpose, and they help the reporter tell the story.

1. Modified chronology. Rarely is a pure chronology used in media writing. Most news stories are told best if they begin with how the story ended or what is most important or interesting. But, once you tell the reader what a story's about, you can easily slip into the natural order of events. This method is often used in stories about crimes or accidents in which meaning comes from the sequence of events.

2. Inverted pyramid. This device requires ranking the facts of a story in descending order of importance. It's handy for fast writing of hard news: breaking news stories such as a plane crash or for a roundup of a natural disaster such as a hurricane. The inverted pyramid may tell readers what is most important, but in many news stories it doesn't work well. It can confuse readers and lead to choppy writing.

Sidebar 3

Words That Cause Trouble

Journalists need to understand words. Hundreds of words cause trouble for writers. A good grammar book written for journalists will help you keep track of the troublesome words. Following is a short list of words that give students problems:

1. *Affect, effect. Affect* is usually a verb. Generally, *effect* is a noun. "The effect of the program will be negative; the program will affect the college." *Effect* can be a verb that means to bring about. "The president sought to effect a change in attitude."

2. *All right. Alright* is never acceptable in professional writing.

3. *Compose, comprise.* This is a tricky one. See the *AP Stylebook* for more information. Remember that the parts COMPOSE the whole, whereas the whole COMPRISES its parts.

4. *Destroy.* You cannot "partially destroy" something. Therefore, "completely" or "totally destroyed" is redundant. "Almost completely destroyed" is nonsense.

5. *Hopefully.* This word is an adverb and describes how someone feels. "The student waited hopefully for the check to arrive." Don't use the word to mean "it is hoped." Don't write, "Hopefully, I will pass this class." Write, "I hope I will pass this class. If I use 'hopefully' improperly, I may not pass this class."

6. *Imply, infer.* A speaker implies, whereas a listener infers.

7. *It's, its. It's* means it is, whereas *its* is possessive.

8. *Its, their.* Remember that collective nouns take a singular possessive. "The faculty will hold its meeting."

9. *Lay, lie.* This is another tricky one because the past tense of *lie* is *lay.* *Lay (laying, laid)* is the action word and takes a direct object. "I will lay the book on the table; I laid the book on the table." *Lie (lying, lay)* refers to a state of being. "He will lie on the couch; he lay on the couch until he felt better."

10. *Less, fewer.* Use *less* when referring to a quantity that cannot be divided, *fewer* when writing about numbers. "There were fewer bottles of milk in the store today than yesterday." "My glass had less milk than his."

11. *Like, as.* Substitute *similar to* in the sentence. If it makes sense use *like.* Another way to tell the difference is that *as* or *as if* is usually followed by a phrase that has a verb. "Do as I do." "His house is like a garbage dump."

12. *Over, more than. Over* should be reserved for spatial relationships such as "flying over the city." With numbers, use *more than.* "He earned more than $8 an hour for the work." Unfortunately, many newsrooms use *over* as a substitute for *more than.*

13. *That, which.* Use *that* to introduce material that's needed to understand the word it modifies. In other words, use *which* when the material is an afterthought or could be deleted (put in parentheses). Remember: Use a comma to separate *which* from the word it modifies. "The river, which is polluted, runs by my office." "The city plans to clean up rivers that are polluted."

14. *Flout, flaunt.* You *flout* the law, but you *flaunt* your new sports car.

15. *Nouns.* Let nouns be nouns and verbs do the work. *Impact* is a noun, not a verb. Avoid nouns with "ize" tags: *finalize, prioritize* and *maximize. Use* is better than *utilize.*

16. *Anxious, eager.* You are anxious about passing this course, and you are eager to graduate. *Anxious* implies worry, not eagerness.

17. *Following, after. Following* is not a preposition. *After* is a shorter word. Use it.

18. *Before, prior to.* Again, *before,* the short word, is preferred. *Prior to* is stilted.

19. *Buy, purchase.* Again, use the common word *buy. Purchase* is pretentious. Avoid it.

3. Themes. Speeches and panel discussions are two types of stories that can be told well by dividing your notes according to main and secondary themes. Let your lead state the main idea of the speech. Develop the themes by introducing them and then developing what the speaker said. Variations of this method can be used in many stories.

4. Time contrast. Feature stories and profiles about people or programs can be organized according to the past, present and future. For example, a story about a change in the Social Security system could begin with a description of what the new law does. Then the story could contrast the new law with the old law. The story could then end with a look at what might happen to Social Security recipients in the future.

5. Traditional outline. Mapping a story according to topics and subtopics works for news stories. A written outline is especially helpful for long, in-depth articles.

Using Quotes in Your Story

News stories have three sources of information: What people say, what reporters observe and what is contained in documents. If you look at your local or school newspaper, you'll find that much of the story content comes from what people say. Good news stories effectively use what people say. It's a simple technique you need to learn.

There are three types of quotes:

1. Direct quotes. These are the exact words of the speaker.

   "Our nation is at a moral crossroads," Sen. Bob Jones said.

2. Indirect quotes. You can paraphrase a person's words by retaining the meaning of what was said while changing some of the words.

   The nation is at a moral crossroads, Sen. Bob Jones said.

3. Partial quotes. These sentences are a mixture of paraphrase and direct quote.

   The nation is at a "moral crossroads," Sen. Bob Jones said.

Readers want to know the source of your information. When attributing information, use the word *said.* If the information comes from a written document, use *according to.* In general, strong opinions need attribution. Statements of simple fact do not, unless those facts contain potentially libelous statements. For example, you would want to attribute to the police the crime details that follow an arrest.

Students often are uncomfortable with repeating words. However, there's no rule against repetition. You should also be aware that synonyms for the word *said* have specific meanings and can prejudice a reader. For example, *claimed* implies that you don't believe the speaker. And *added* should be used only to attribute a speaker's after-thoughts; all too often, poor writers use *added* when they mean *also said.* And don't be silly. People don't "laugh" or "cry" direct quotes.

Following are some typical examples of attribution. Note how each word is useful in some contexts but is troublesome in others.

- "O. J. Simpson claimed he was happy." Note how this sentence implies the opposite. In most journalism, such irony in writing makes an editorial comment and should be reserved for commentary. In a trial story, however, *claimed* might be a useful word when the validity of a statement is in dispute—for example, "The prosecutor claimed the witness was lying."

Look for the conflict when writing a story. Drama always interests readers. But be careful about oversimplifying conflict and overselling drama so the story does not cross the line into sensationalism.

- "Smith pointed out that religion is a crutch." In this case, *pointed out* implies that the information that follows is factual. The misuse of *pointed out* puts the reporter in the position of making a judgment about the validity of an opinion. But, in another context, when the facts aren't in dispute, the implication is fine: "Smith pointed out that freedom of religion is protected by the First Amendment."

- The Constitution guaranteed freedom of speech, Smith explained. It's unlikely that Smith has offered an explanation. The sentence is an example of inaccurate reporting. Reporters should not mindlessly mix *explained* and *added* into their stories as synonyms for *said*. Be an accurate reporter and use these words in the correct context—for example, "Smith explained that he was late because of a dentist appointment. As he left the room, Smith added that he would be late for the next meeting."

Words such as *stated* and *elucidated* sound stilted. And *maintained* implies that the speaker is being criticized or is defending a point of view. Your goal should be careful writing. Choose your words cautiously and remember that *said* is a neutral word, and is usually correct.

If the attribution is carefully placed, readers don't even notice the repetition of *said*. The general rule is to use *said* once per paragraph. Place it in the sentence that

Sidebar 4

Do's and Don'ts of Quotes

1. Don't over attribute. Usually one attribution per paragraph is adequate.

2. If you have multiple sources, be sure to clarify who is speaking. Sometimes it's best to write everything one speaker has to say before moving to the next source.

3. Be accurate and faithful to the words and meaning of the speaker when using quotes. Don't be sloppy when paraphrasing.

4. Don't add words to direct quotes. Avoid parentheses in direct quotes. If you need to explain a direct quote, perhaps a paraphrase would be better.

5. Make sure your direct quotes are special. They should say something in a better way than you can write. Think of direct quotes as exclamation points in your story.

6. Don't overuse direct quotes. Be picky. If you have too many, you dilute the effectiveness of your good quotes. Beware: Too many quotes are often the result of a disease exhibited by reporters who use tape recorders.

7. Beware of slang and dialect. They may be offensive. Don't embarrass the people you quote.

8. Do use language that makes the speaker sound special. If all your direct quotes sound like you, then you're not doing a good job.

9. Your direct quotes should not repeat information that was in a previous quote.

10. Avoid partial quotes. In most cases, partial quotes can be removed and not change the meaning. Reserve partial quotes for paraphrases that include a speaker's exact words that are strongly emotional or highly opinionated. Remember that a partial quote sometimes implies that the writer doesn't believe the words in the quotes are true: "He said he was 'happy.'"

contains the strongest opinion. In direct quotes with multiple sentences, place the attribution in the middle of the quote.

Sometimes reporters want to cut attribution. In long stories with only one source, that's easy to do. Skip the attribution on direct quotes as you move into the middle of the story. But be sure that it's clear who the speaker is. Other times, trying to eliminate attribution can be troublesome.

During interviews, journalists often ask their sources questions about what they think, believe or feel. The problem in reporting is that you don't know what someone is thinking, believing or feeling unless he or she tells you. The traditional method of attribution requires that reporters let readers know how they know someone's thoughts—for example, "Smith said he felt remorse for the crime" or "Jones said she believed in God."

Some critics say such constructions are unnecessarily wordy, especially in feature stories. They argue that a reader understands how reporters discover someone's thoughts. As with many things, there is no right or wrong answer. But the risk in eliminating the attribution can be high. For example, an in-depth story about a college's women's basketball team was heavily criticized by the players, who said the reporter had betrayed their trust. The most pointed criticism attacked the credibility of the whole article and fell on the writer's use of "she thought" without attribution. As one disgruntled player asked, "How did the reporter know what I thought?"

News stories effectively use what people say. Readers also want to know the source of the information a reporter uses.

Ending a Story

The ending of a news story should sound a note of finality. When a reader finishes your story, there should be a sense of completeness. One of the most popular ways to end a news story is with a quote. In a story about a speech, the quote might echo the theme of the speech. In a story filled with conflict, the quote might offer a hint for peace.

The following is an ending from a story a student wrote about the increase in cigar smoking among students. The story contrasts the views of local cigar shop owners with the harmful effects of cigar smoking. It ends with a quote from a representative of the American Lung Association.

"I hope these specialty shops that sell cigars are short-lived. Their sole purpose is a product that kills people," she said. "I don't think we need that. I'm sure they are nice people trying to earn a living, but they should find some other way."

Reporters should avoid commentary in their endings. Often such commentary sounds like the type of ending you'd see in an essay for an English class. Such endings violate the idea that journalists should keep personal biases out of their reporting. Sometimes such endings sound silly. Consider the following bad ending and compare it to the previous quote ending:

Obviously, cigar smoking is unhealthy. Students who smoke cigars are taking big risks just to be part of a trend that stinks. Let's keep our air and lungs clean.

Sidebar 5

The Feature Story
By Carol Schlagheck, Ph.D.

Assistant Professor of Journalism, Department of English Language and Literature, Eastern Michigan University

Once upon a time in a dark place far, far away from the modern newsroom, any story that read like fiction was deemed "fluff." If the end of the story wasn't in the lead, inverted-pyramid style, it was pushed aside for the day when the editor might need filler copy. Editors were clear about their priorities. No features or lifestyle stories appear on Page One. Most papers had "women's pages" for stories about cooking, society events, children and fashion, if they had to cover that sort of thing. More serious hobbies such as sports had their own pages.

Times have changed. In an increasingly competitive market, readers usually know the big stories long before they open their newspaper. How many heard about the Oklahoma City bombing by reading the newspaper? Most readers probably learned about it from television or the radio, then got additional detail from the paper. Today most news organizations understand that people care about the top stories, but they want more than "just the facts." They want insights into how something happened and why—and what it means. Of the traditional five "W"s and "H" of news, "why" and "how" are the least-often answered by the deadline-driven hard news story.

Feature stories can deliver this information. Commonly focusing on the people and emotions behind the issues, feature stories can bring the human element to events. Because these stories are not always written under deadline pressure, they can include greater insights into trends and social problems.

Although deadline writing can be difficult, feature stories should not be construed as "easier." In many ways, feature writing is the toughest of all, because it doesn't follow a formula. The writer has both the freedom and the challenge of crafting an interesting lead, explaining complex issues and writing pieces that usually are longer than the average hard news piece.

Some of the best feature writing techniques can be found in deadline writing, as reporters realize that details make their stories complete. What was the name of the cat lost in the hurricane? What cartoon character was on the crumpled lunch box found near the hit-and-run accident? Today, feature techniques—and feature stories—belong on Page One.

As you try your hand at feature writing, try incorporating the basic skills of newswriting with the compelling narrative style of fiction. Feature writing allows you (and requires you) to pay special attention to

Use of Description

Describe the person, the scene. Use your senses. What were the sights, sounds, smells? Use details to put your reader in the scene. What kind of sandwich did he order? What station was on the radio in her office? If her car is a pink Volkswagen convertible with a lime green roof, 12 cellular antennas and a license plate that calls her "EX-CON," don't just tell readers, "She drove off."

Show; don't tell. Give examples. Don't say it was a "modest" home, which can mean anything from a Swiss chalet to a cardboard box, depending on your life experience and perspective. Show the reader what you mean. Similarly, don't say, "She was wealthy." What does that tell your reader? That she pays her phone bill before the service is turned off? Or she just paid cash for a Mercedes? Like beauty, many descriptors hinge on the eye of the beholder; use detail to back up your observations. Never assume anything. You want accurate detail. Never make up something you can't remember, and never write more than you know. Say you're writing about your professor, who brings a coffee cup to class each day. You're tempted to describe her as a coffee drinker, but you want more detail. You think your readers would get a clearer picture of the professor if you could tell them whether her favorite coffee is regular, decaf, cappuccino, espresso or Marine-quality mud. So you ask. And you find out she drinks herbal tea from that cup all day. Does that change the story? Maybe. What if you find out she drinks hot chocolate all day everyday—even in July? More interesting, perhaps.

Correct Use of Quotations

Don't just quote someone because you have the quote in your notes: "Then the police were called," said the witness. If that's all he said, just report that a witness called police. Quote only something worth quoting: "I yelled, 'Martha, get on the horn and get some police out here before he kills us all,' " the witness recalled.

Sidebar 5 (continued)

Don't repeat yourself: The witness said the cars were drag racing. "I saw them drag racing," the witness said. However, do set up a quote that's not self-explanatory: "The witness said the cars were drag racing. They lined up on the yellow line and took off like a shot as soon as the light turned green," the witness said.

Banish the words *when asked* from your writing. "When asked about his plans, he said . . ." That only puts you between the reader and your subject. Just report what his plans are. You don't have to restate your questions. You can best demonstrate your interviewing skills by using the great quotes that you got in answer to great questions.

Again, use description even when quoting. How did she say that? Was her tone enthusiastic, angry, sarcastic? What was she doing when she said that? Was she gently stroking her poodle or throwing something across the room?

Lead and Ending

Your lead should make someone want to read your story. Freed from the constraints of the inverted pyramid, you have many options as you look for ways to entice a reader. You might draw a picture or set a scene. You might use a quote, if it's unusual enough. You might use mystery, irony or humor to invite the reader in. Be careful not to give the reader reasons to stay away: "Josh was a typical college student . . ." Then why should anyone want to read about him? Tell your readers why he's not typical—that is, why you're writing about him.

Does your ending "reward" the reader, making him or her glad he or she read to the end? Unlike newswriting, where inverted pyramid style dictates that only the least important information be used to end a story, feature writing calls for a pithy ending. Use a great quote, punctuate your story with someone's great insight, or find a creative way to return to the point introduced in your lead. Avoid editorializing as you end your story. Remember: You are not writing an essay.

Nut Graph

Why should anyone care about a story? The nut graph tells the reader near the top of the article why this story is different, or this information is vital. Your challenge is to tell the reader without breaking the flow of the story. For example, in your lead, you've established that Jonathan So-and-So is hard-working high school student who has earns straight A's, plays sports and holds down a part-time job. Then you say that Jonathan won't be graduating from high school on time. Next comes your nut graph in which you explain that Jonathan is only one of more than 7,000 students in the state who won't graduate because they failed proficiency exams in math. *This is why you're writing the story.* Jonathan is an example, not the main idea.

Transitions

Make your story flow. Think about where you're going with this story, and then go there. Use an outline, if necessary, or start writing and see if some natural patterns develop. At all costs, avoid choppy construction. Don't cut and paste paragraphs without paying attention to organization. Don't ramble. Instead, logically lead the reader through the story, paragraph by paragraph. Repeating key words sometimes helps. If you spend five paragraphs talking about someone's years as a championship sail boarder, don't just jump into "Her first job was at McDonald's." Make it flow. "She needed money to buy a better sail, so she found a job at McDonald's." or "Despite her heavy competition schedule, she still found time to work three nights a week at McDonald's. There, her first job taught her . . ." Make your story so tight that an editor would have trouble cutting it—and a reader couldn't put it down.

Finishing the Story

Journalists create all their stories under deadline pressure. Rarely does a writer feel that a story is as good as it could be. One more phone call, one more interview or one more hour of writing could always improve a story.

Even under deadline pressure, though, journalists need to revise their work carefully. You should do two types of revision: improving and fixing. (See Chapter 9.)

Improving

How much improvement you accomplish depends on how long you have to work on your story. Maybe you'll have time to call sources to get additional information or time to reorganize the material.

Following are some things to consider during revision:

1. Is your story easy to understand and read? Read it aloud. Do you stop anywhere or stumble? Make sure your paragraphs are short.

2. Do your sentences vary in length? Short sentences are best. If a sentence doesn't make sense or seems too complex, try rewriting it so it fits the form "subject-verb-object."

3. Make sure your subjects are next to their verbs and that modifiers are next to the words they explain.

4. Is your lead interesting?

5. Have you gotten rid of jargon, clichés and words that might be unfamiliar to readers?

6. Have you used good verbs?

7. Have you set up your direct quotes with a paraphrase?

8. Have you organized the story in a logical way? For example, does the second paragraph support the lead? Do quotes and paraphrases work together?

9. Have you eliminated all redundant information?

10. Are your sentences in the active voice? Have you used the past tense?

Fixing

A professional writer needs to understand the tools of written language. The tools help you complete the task. Writing is like carpentry, and the saw, hammer and nails of good writing are grammar, consistency of style, punctuation and spelling. It's also imperative that you ensure that all your information is accurate. A well-known maxim of journalism is that the three most important things are accuracy, accuracy and accuracy.

Exercises

1. Write a lead.

   Following is a list of information from an actual news story. While you're reading the facts, think about how you would tell this story to a friend.

   Where: a fast-food restaurant in Miami

   When: Sunday night

   Who: Gary Robinson

   What: Robinson told his wife he was going to buy some fried chicken. At the store, he was shot and killed.

   Why: When he arrived, the line was long and he pushed to the front. He was loud and drunk. The woman at the counter politely asked him to go to the end of the line, which he did. When his turn came, the woman told him she had run out of fried chicken and it was almost closing time. Robinson hit her and almost knocked her out.

How: A security guard shot Robinson three times.

On a piece of paper or at your computer, write a beginning for this story.

Following are some examples of leads written for the fried chicken story. Are any of them similar to what you wrote?

```
A security guard shot and killed a man at a fast-food
    restaurant on Sunday.
```

This basic lead is short and tells the most important facts but doesn't tell us the most interesting part of the story.

```
A man died after being shot Sunday night by a security
    guard at a fast-food restaurant.
```

Like the first lead, this one misses the most interesting part of the story. Notice that this lead is written in the passive voice and focuses on the man who was shot instead of the person who was doing the shooting.

```
After hitting a fast-food restaurant employee, a man was
    shot and killed by a security guard Sunday night.
```

Beginning a lead with a preposition is weak. The next one tries to fix that.

```
A man who hit a fast-food restaurant employee was shot
    and killed by a security guard Sunday night.
```

Here's one that has it all. What do you think?

```
A security guard at a fast-food restaurant shot and
    killed a man who hit an employee after he was told the
    restaurant was out of fried chicken Sunday night.
```

This lead has about 30 words. Note how packed it seems to be. Read it aloud. This lead may be too long.

Now here's the lead from Edna Buchanan, who won the Pulitzer Prize at the *Miami Herald* for her police beat reporting. Buchanan says she always tries to emphasize the human side of a story.

```
Gary Robinson died hungry.
```

Notice how this lead violates the rule of delaying identification in the lead. No one knows him. But this lead adds humanity to a senseless death. And it works. Rules are meant to be learned, applied and broken when appropriate.

2. Write a story from the following facts:

Who: I. M. Blasted, 18, a freshman at your school

What: found two sticks of dynamite

When: yesterday afternoon

Where: his dorm room

How: found them in a closet when he moved into his room

What: Campus police exploded the sticks at a field outside town.

Quotes:

Police Capt. Thomas Ridged: "We want to know who put the dynamite there. This was an extremely dangerous situation that could have hurt dozens of people."

Housing Director George Lumpy: "I don't know who owns the sticks. I am glad no one got hurt."

Freshman Blasted: "I hope my parents don't find out. It was, you know, bizarre. I can't believe it was real dynamite. I thought they were fake."

3. Write a news story from the following facts:

The U.S. Federal Aviation Administration has a unique device for testing the strength of windshields on airplanes. The device is a gun. It launches a dead chicken at a plane's windshield at approximately the speed the plane flies. The theory is that if the windshield doesn't crack from the carcass impact, the windshield will survive a collision with a bird during flight.

Recently the British became very interested in this and wanted to test a windshield on a new, speedy locomotive they're developing. They borrowed the FAA's chicken launcher, loaded the chicken and fired. The ballistic chicken shattered the windshield, went through the engineer's chair, broke an instrument panel and embedded itself in the back wall of the engine cab. The British were stunned and asked the FAA to recheck the test to see if everything was done correctly. The FAA reviewed the test thoroughly and had one recommendation. George Sampson, an FAA engineer, called the British and said, "Use a thawed chicken."

4. Write a story from the following material. Be sure to use at least three direct quotes in your story.

Where: George Mason University in Fairfax, Va. The orchestra level filled early and the overflow was directed to the balcony of the theater.

Who: Journalist David Halberstam, a Pulitzer Prize winner and *New York Times* reporter in Vietnam, spoke to more than 1,000 students and faculty.

Why: He appeared as part of a lecture on "The Power of the Media," sponsored by the university and held in the Center for the Arts theater.

When: yesterday

Paraphrase: Halberstam recalled the press during the 1960s and 1970s and the role reporters and editors played. Those days are over, he said. Halberstam said television and print diverged about the time of the Iran hostage crisis in late 1979. Until then, he said, newspapers set the daily news agenda, as most TV newscasts covered the stories appearing on the front page of the *New York Times,* the *Washington Post,* the *Los Angeles Times* and other metropolitan dailies. He blamed the media, especially television, for denying the public information about problems in society, and the result, he said, was a weakened nation. Halberstam complained about the dominance of TV as the chief source of news for many people and about the decline in values within television newsrooms, where, he said, image has become more important than substance. In TV's early days, reporters such as Walter Cronkite, David Brinkley and Chet Huntley had solid credentials as reporters. Now TV reporters, he said, are selected based on "star quality," then are under pressure to create an image.

Direct quotes:

"We have become an entertainment society. And TV is becoming ever more powerful. Television is driven by its own definition of reality, which reflects not the norms of journalism but of entertainment."

"Our democracy is seriously undernourished. If you don't believe it, look at this election season. It's not about what's really troubling people. And that is in some measure the fault of the media. It isn't giving people what they need to make judgments about their society."

"The greatest sin for a journalist in television is not to be inaccurate but to be boring. The only god out there is the ratings and the only ethics is the ratings."

"Since the success of TV comes from creating stars, the successful TV anchor or reporter becomes a star by being on television all the time, making it impossible to gain any experience reporting stories on the street. As a result, we have the journalist as VIP, talking only to other VIPs."

5. Write a personality profile of no more than 750 words. Find someone who interests you but is not just like you, someone who differs from you in terms of age, race, sex, national background and so on. The idea here is for you to see the world through someone else's eyes and to convey that vision to your readers. The key to an interesting person often is how interested that person is in something else—whether or not that seems to be interesting to you at first. Find someone who has a passion—from rock collecting to pipe fitting; then share that enthusiasm through your story.

    Think about the questions you're going to ask. You'll probably want to write at least some of them down before your interview, but don't let that list control you. Go with the flow of the interview. Don't rush it. Spend some time with the person, both one-on-one and in the person's natural environment—work, home, school. Talk to others who know the person. What do they think? Can they tell you any interesting stories? "She's the kind of friend who . . " "He's so funny that he once . . " "She's so good at her job that . . " As you write, remember your audience. What questions might they have about this person? Answer your own questions and you'll probably answer the readers' at the same time.

Suggested Readings

Grammar

Bernstein, Theodore M. *The Careful Writer: A Modern Guide to English Usage.* New York: Atheneum, 1986. This is Bernstein's most complete book on grammar. His common sense drives his discussions of knotty problems that challenge the traditional grammar rules. The book is well researched and easy to use, with entries listed alphabetically. It's a book every serious writer should own.

Kessler, Lauren, and Duncan McDonald. *When Words Collide: A Media Writers Guide to Grammar and Style,* Fourth edition. Belmont, Calif.: Wadsworth Publishing Co., 1996. This is one of the easiest-to-use grammar books written especially for journalists. It has easy-to-understand examples, and it covers the major problems journalists face. It also has an excellent list of words that cause trouble.

Good Journalism

Hersey, John. *Hiroshima.* New York: Bantam Books, 1985. This book is one of the great examples of literary journalism. It's a short, well-written and moving story about ordinary people who lived through the atomic bombing of the city. This book is a great teaching tool.

Good Writing

Murray, Donald M. *Writing for Your Readers.* (Out of print, but check your library). Written by a Pulitzer Prize winner, this book captures the essence of good journalistic writing. Murray, one of the leading experts in the teaching of writing, puts you into the minds of the best reporters and writers. He explains not only how to write better but also how to think like a journalist. This is an invaluable book for any reporter, regardless of experience.

Features

Camp, John. "Life on the Land: An American Farm Family." *St. Paul Pioneer Press and Dispatch.* 12 May 1985. This winner of the Pulitzer Prize for feature writing includes descriptive, compelling, wonderful narrative. The story is a prime example of a good feature writer taking the details of a seemingly "ordinary" life and making them read like fiction. Why should we care about the problems plaguing farmers? This story shows you.

Anything by the late Charles Kuralt. No one could introduce you to a person the way Kuralt could. His profiles glorified the "real people" of America. He made you care about people who build bridges and fix bicycles, people who have never been to New York or Los Angeles—people like those who live in most of the towns where young reporters work. For an education and inspiration, read any of his many books, watch any of his videos, catch cable reruns of his "Sunday Morning" program.

9 Editing the Written Word

Mark Paxton, Ph.D.
Southwest Missouri State University
Charleston (W.Va.) *Daily Mail, The Nashville* (Tenn.) *Banner* and
The Associated Press

Chapter Outline

Don't quit with the first draft

Double-check your facts

Check your spelling

Use only the number of words necessary

Make sure your subjects and verbs agree

Make sure your nouns and pronouns agree

Watch out for sentence fragments

Eliminate run-on sentences

Use parallel construction

Be active, not passive

Sidebar A craft or an art?

Many people—especially those who haven't written for publication—tend to see writing as an inspired act. Somehow the writer is visited by "the muse," and through an unexplainable force the words magically speed their way through the writer's body and onto the page. Thus are born great works of art.

Those who have written extensively for publication, however, know that writing is not an act but a process that requires writing, revision and rewriting. Rarely are the words that first appear on the page the same words that are on the page at the end of the process. Legendary novelist Jack Kerouac, whose "beat" generation works include the classic *On the Road,* is said to have inserted the end of a large roll of newsprint into his typewriter and started writing in a sort of stream of consciousness with his first draft his only draft. As the paper rolled through the typewriter, it piled up on the floor, a finished work. That's probably something of a myth. Even Kerouac had to rewrite some of his work.

Deciding what stories to write and how to gather the information to write those stories are the subjects of other chapters in this textbook. This chapter looks at the writing process once you've gathered the information, and it also gives some concrete, easy to implement tips for ways you can improve your own writing to guarantee that your finished product is as polished as it can be.

Don't Quit with the First Draft

The most common mistake beginning writers make is to think that their work doesn't need revision. A talented writer assigned to write a basic news story can usually come up with an acceptable who-what-when-where-why-how lead that covers all the bases. But the best writers know that those first words are just a beginning. For instance, consider the beginning reporter assigned to write a newspaper lead based on the following information:

There was a house fire Thursday (today). The house is in Springfield at 1545 West Walnut Lawn St. A woman was killed in the fire. She owned the house. Her name was Jane Anderson. She was 88 years old. She died of smoke inhalation. The fire started at 4:40 a.m. She was pronounced dead at Cox Medical Center-South. The house was destroyed by the fire. This information comes from Springfield Fire Department Capt. Sam Wellman.

A beginning reporter wrote the following lead, without revision:

```
An 88-year-old Springfield woman died of smoke inhalation
early Thursday after her house on Walnut Lawn Street
caught on fire.
```

Despite some wordiness (that is, *burned* is one word that does the work of the three words *caught on fire*), the student's lead was basically acceptable. But by revising and fine tuning the same information, the student could have come up with a lead that told the same story in a more interesting fashion:

```
An 88-year-old woman died when fire raced through her
Southwest Springfield home before dawn Thursday, a Fire
Department captain said.
```

Both leads convey the same information (a woman died when her house burned) and have the same number of words (22). But, through rewording and fine tuning, the revised lead makes for a more interesting story.

Beginning writers often think that their work doesn't need revision. A good writer often rewrites an uncomplicated story about a fire to determine the best way to inform the reader or listener.

Don't be afraid to tinker with your writing; it isn't written in stone. If you revise it and don't like the changes, you can always go back to the original. If you do go back, however, you'll be making a conscious decision rather than blindly sticking with the first words that appeared on your page.

Double-Check Your Facts

It's surprisingly easy for factual errors to creep into your copy. One of my favorite stories about my own newswriting skills occurred when I was a reporter covering state government and the state legislature. One morning I came into work and one of the other reporters, who had been covering the statehouse for more years than I had been alive, looked at me with a sly grin and said, "You're a jazz fan, aren't you?" "Yes," I replied. "How did you know?" He then showed me a copy of the story I had written the day before about an appearance before a legislative committee by a state official named Miles Dean. The problem was that I had called him Miles Davis, the jazz musician.

Sometimes our minds slip into neutral, and strange little demons go to work on our copy. A prosecutor named Monty Brown mysteriously turns into Monty Hall (the "Let's Make a Deal" game show host). A story about John Jones refers to him later as Johns instead of Jones.

Writers should always double-check their information before turning in their final drafts. A good tip is to have someone you trust read your piece; others can spot errors you may have missed.

If the material you're writing mentions six people, make sure it names six and not five or seven. If what you're writing includes a telephone number, double-check

Contestants in the National Spelling Bee compete for a variety of scholarships and prizes. Writers won't win any prizes for spelling, grammar and punctuation, but they do earn high marks from editors.

the digits. If you include a date, check the calendar to make certain you have the right day and date.

Whether you're writing a news story, a press release or a documentary film script, there's no substitute for getting the facts right.

Check Your Spelling

Nothing sticks out like a misspelled word. And, with the proliferation of computer spell-checker programs, most of those incorrect spellings can be corrected easily. But every spelling error won't be caught by your computer, no matter how consistent you are about running the spell-checker.

```
Ewe must no the rite spellings of many words, or Yule
misspell sum words even if the computer says their OK.
```

After I wrote the preceding sentence, I ran my computer spell-checker program. According to it, every word in that sentence is correct. Obviously, though, some words are spelled incorrectly, which points out the problem in relying on your computer to do your spelling. A computer spell-checker can't tell the difference between words that sound the same but have different meanings and spellings. For instance, *to, too* and *two* are all legitimate spellings according to the spell-checker, but they obviously aren't interchangeable.

You learn to spell through practice and memorization. Virtually every grammar book contains lists of commonly misspelled words (a list of basic grammar books follows at the end of this chapter). The following, is a short list to get you thinking about spelling. Which of the following words are spelled incorrectly?

accommodate

battalion

canceled

desperate

embarrass

harassment

hemorrhage

inoculate

judgment

likable

manageable

occurred

questionnaire

separate

weird

The only way to learn most of these words is to memorize them. You have to remember that *accommodate* has two *c*'s and two *m*'s, that *harassment* has one *r* and two *s*'s, that *occur* has one *r* but *occurred* has two. Oh yes, in case you haven't figured it out yet, all 15 words in the list are spelled correctly. The only way to know that for sure is to learn to spell them yourself.

Use Only the Number of Words Necessary

Nothing robs a sentence of its power faster than extra words. This is especially true in the various mass communication fields. A newspaper or magazine story that's too long can't physically fit on the page; it's hard to imagine type running off the bottom of the page and hanging there by itself. A broadcaster whose script is too long will still be speaking when the next commercial begins. And an advertiser whose copy doesn't fit in the space (in the print media) or is too long (in the broadcast media) will see his or her message cut off before the end. In all areas of media, tight writing is essential.

At one time, freelance writers—those who were not on a writing staff but were paid story-by-story—were paid by the word. As a result, writers tended to pad their articles with extra words to make more money. Today, most freelancers are paid by the article, not the word, so there's no financial incentive to use extra verbiage. There's an important lesson to be learned here, though. When you're writing, imagine not that you're being paid by the word, but that you're paying someone else—your teacher or editor, for instance—for each word you use. To save yourself money, use as few words as possible.

It's easy to allow extra words to creep into your writing. Easter becomes Easter Sunday (as if Easter ever falls on any other day of the week). Something falls down, rather than just falls (when was the last time something fell up?). Something is totally unique (*unique* means one-of-a-kind and, if it's one-of-a-kind, it is total).

When you're revising your writing, watch for words that eat space without adding meaning. Watch for redundancies such as 12 noon (if it's noon, it has to be 12). Watch for sentence constructions that can be made simpler without changing the meaning ("the sheriff of Greene County" can just as easily be written "the

Greene County sheriff"; you're saving only one word, but, if you do that 10 times in one story, you save an entire sentence). Above all, be concise.

Make Sure Your Subjects and Verbs Agree

Most of us can remember studying grammar in elementary school or middle school. Some of us can remember diagramming sentences. By the time we reached high school, studying grammar took a back seat to studying literature. In English composition classes in college, we probably spent more time learning how to document sources and write thesis statements than we did learning grammar.

Some common grammatical errors can be fixed simply and easily. The first of these is subject-verb agreement. In most sentences, it's easy to figure out the subject and verb. In the sentence "Joe hit the ball," "Joe" is the subject and "hit" is the verb. The trouble comes when the subject isn't so easy to identify.

Take the sentence "Beneath the sea lie/lies adventure and danger." What's the subject? It's not "Beneath," although that comes before the verb; rather, it's "adventure and danger." And, as we all remember from our grammar lessons, a compound subject takes a plural verb. In this case, therefore, the sentence should read "Beneath the sea lie adventure and danger."

Now examine this sentence: "Neither Joe nor the twins is/are going to the fair tonight." The subjects are "Joe" and "the twins," so obviously the verb is the plural "are." Correct? Yes. But now turn the sentence around: "Neither the twins nor Joe is/are going to the fair tonight." Now, surprisingly, the verb turns into the singular "is." Why? Whenever you have the construction "either . . . or" or "neither . . . nor," and the subject consists of a singular (such as "Joe") and a plural (such as "the twins"), the number of the verb—that is, whether it's singular or plural—is determined by the subject that's closer to the verb. It's the only instance in the English language that the position of the subject determines whether the verb is singular or plural. Here are some more subject-verb agreement tips.

- In the construction "There is . . ." or "There are . . ." the subject is *not* the word *there.* The subject follows the linking verb "is" or "are." Examples: "There is one man," but "There are a boy and girl."

- The construction "as well as" is not part of the subject. Example: John, as well as Bill and Ted, is going to the store. "John" is the subject and requires a singular verb.

- The following words, when used as a subject, *always* take a singular verb: *each, either, anyone, everyone, much, no one, nothing* and *someone.*

- When *each, either, every* or *neither* is used as an adjective, the noun it modifies always takes a singular verb. Examples: Every cask of wine was spoiled. "Every" modifies "cask," which is the subject. "Cask," therefore, takes a singular verb.

- *Number* can be singular or plural. Use "the number is" but "a number are." The same rule holds true for the words *majority* and *percentage.*

- *None* is almost always singular. Think of it as "not one." Example: None of the boys is ready to play.

Make Sure Your Nouns and Pronouns Agree

Not only must your subjects and verbs agree, but your pronouns and the nouns they refer to also must agree. We all know that verbs come in singular (*is*) and plural (*are*). The same is true for pronouns. There are singular pronouns (*he, she, it, his, her, its*) and plural pronouns (*they, their*). The trick is making sure you use a singular pronoun when the noun it refers to is singular and a plural pronoun when the noun is plural.

The trickiest time to do this is when your noun is a "collective" noun. For example, consider the word *team* in the sentence "The team won its/their third game of the season." Is *its* or *their* correct? To answer this, determine what the noun is. In this case, it's *team.* How many teams are in this sentence. Just one? If so, then *team* is singular, and the word requires the singular pronoun *its:* "The team won its third game of the season."

But what if, instead of the word *team,* the sentence used the team's nickname? "The Bears won its/their third game of the season." In this case, how many Bears are there? Isn't each member of the team a Bear, and together they make up the Bears? If so, Bears is plural and requires the plural pronoun: "The Bears won their third game of the season."

It gets trickier still. What if the team is the Marshall University Thundering Herd? How many Thundering Herds are there? Just one. Each member is not an individual Thundering Herd, so the team nickname is still singular: "The Thundering Herd won its third game of the season."

One way to check for noun-pronoun agreement is to read back through your work and identify each pronoun; then find the noun that the pronoun refers to (called the antecedent). If you have trouble finding the antecedent, that means your sentence is probably unclear and needs to be rewritten. If you can easily find the antecedent, though, double-check to make sure it and the pronoun are in agreement.

Watch Out for Sentence Fragments

A sentence fragment is an incomplete sentence that lacks either a verb or a subject and that cannot stand on its own. This is a fragment: "A big gray cat with sharp claws."

Sometimes sentence fragments are stylistic tools. What causes problems, though, is when writers use fragments unintentionally. Until you're a skilled, practiced writer who understands grammar thoroughly, it's probably best to stay away from fragments. Unfortunately, writers use so many fragments as stylistic devices that many of us have become immune to them. Unless they're pointed out, we don't recognize that they're fragments.

So how do you spot sentence fragments in your own writing? Margaret Weaver, director of the Writing Center at Southwest Missouri State University, came up with an interesting way to spot fragments. When you proofread your paper, read it backwards. Start with the last sentence and read it. Does it make sense? Can it stand alone? If so, read the sentence immediately before the last sentence. Does it stand alone? Read the entire paper backwards, a sentence at a time. If you do this, fragments will leap out at you, and you can fix them before you turn in your paper.

Eliminate Run-On Sentences

When I teach beginning news writing, I have my students write one-sentence who-what-when-where-why-how leads, known as summary leads or spot news leads. Beginning writers—especially beginning news writers—tend to try to cram as much information into that one sentence as they can. The result is that they string together two or more sentences connected with a comma:

```
The administration, namely John Kriebs, was stuck with
finding someone to coach the team, the men's coach,
Richard Clark, was forced to take time out to help coach
the women until a new coach was named.
```

That's called a comma splice, and it's one of the fundamental errors of writing. If you look at the example carefully, you'll see it has two subjects ("administration" and "coach" and two verbs "was struck" and "was forced"). Each subject and verb combination makes up a complete sentence. "The administration, namely John Kriebs, was stuck with finding someone to coach the team" is the first sentence; it can stand alone. "The men's coach, Richard Clark, was forced to take time out to help coach the women until a new coach was named" is the second sentence; it, too, can stand alone. The problem is that the writer has combined two sentences, both of which can stand alone, with a comma. A comma isn't strong enough to combine two sentences.

There are three simple ways to fix a comma splice. The simplest is to break the spliced sentence into two sentences separated by a period:

```
The administration, namely John Kriebs, was stuck with
finding someone to coach the team. The men's coach,
Richard Clark, was forced to take time out to help coach
the women until a new coach was named.
```

The second way of fixing a comma splice is to separate the two sentences with a comma, and insert what's called a coordinating conjunction. There are seven coordinating conjunctions, and you can memorize them with a little rhyme: *and, but, for, while, or, yet, nor.*

```
The administration, namely John Kriebs, was stuck with
finding someone to coach the team, and the men's coach,
Richard Clark, was forced to take time out to help coach
the women until a new coach was named.
```

The third way of fixing a comma splice is to use a semicolon instead of a comma. Think of the comma as a weak pause in the sentence, and the semicolon as a bulked up comma on steroids. A semicolon is halfway between a comma and a period; unlike a comma, it's strong enough to separate two sentences:

```
The administration, namely John Kriebs, was stuck with
finding someone to coach the team; the men's coach,
Richard Clark, was forced to take time out to help coach
the women until a new coach was named.
```

Whichever method you use—splitting into two sentences, using a comma and a coordinating conjunction, or inserting a semicolon—the goal is to make sure each sentence stands on its own without being weighed down by another sentence grafted onto the end of it.

Use Parallel Construction

When ideas are not expressed in a parallel manner, the rhythm of the sentence is thrown off and logical relationships are made less clear. Simply put, parallel construction means that in a series all items should be alike, whether all are nouns, gerunds, infinitives, phrases or clauses. For example, the following sentences, written by students in a reporting class, have problems with parallel construction:

```
The university has had a local chapter for only two years
but already has succeeded in sponsoring trash pick-ups,
ozone awareness seminars and has increased recycling
efforts in the Springfield area.
```

```
The three most common answers were persistence, hard
work and becoming familiar with Branson entertainment.
```

```
Students have the opportunity to work in the lab doing
fingerprinting, take mug shots for the jail, develop
film, help at the substation in the mall and participate
in crime analysis.
```

In each case, the sentence is weakened because the items in the series are not the same part of speech. Consider the first sentence. The phrases "sponsoring trash pick-ups," "ozone awareness seminars" and "has increased recycling efforts" are clearly not the same.

But parallel construction is almost always easy to fix. In the first sentence listed, by turning all three phrases into verbs and objects, you can create a parallel sentence:

```
The university has had a local chapter for only two years
but already has sponsored trash pick-ups, has conducted
ozone awareness seminars, and has increased recycling
efforts in the Springfield area.
```

In the second sentence listed, "The three most common answers were persistence, hard work and becoming familiar with Branson entertainment," the problem lies in the phrases "persistence, hard work, and becoming familiar with the Branson area." How can it be fixed? Make "becoming familiar with Branson entertainment" into a noun and prepositional phrase. The sentence then becomes:

```
The three most common answers were persistence, hard
work and familiarity with Branson entertainment.
```

The third sentence listed has a problem with parallel verb use: "Students have the opportunity to work in the lab doing fingerprinting, take mug shots for the jail, develop film, help at the substation in the mall and participate in crime analysis." Can you fix it? How about turning the verbs in the series into gerunds:

```
Students have the opportunity to work in the lab doing
fingerprinting, taking mug shots for the jail, developing
film, helping at the substation in the mall and
participating in crime analysis.
```

By making sure your sentences have parallel construction, you'll be avoiding one of the most common grammatical errors.

Be Active, Not Passive

The final tip is to make your sentences active rather than passive. In other words, have the subject of your sentence doing something rather than having something done to your subject.

In an active sentence, the subject of the verb acts. In a passive sentence, either the verb acts on the subject or the verb is acting on an unspecified thing. "The governor vetoed the bill" is active. "Governor" is the subject and "vetoed" is the verb. The subject is acting. The same sentence can be written passively; "The bill was vetoed by the governor" is passive. Who is acting? Note the subject of that sentence, which is "bill."

Another way of writing the same sentence passively is to leave out entirely who or what is doing the acting: "The bill was vetoed." Who vetoed the bill? We can't tell. And that's often the problem with passive sentences—they're not only weak, but they're unclear.

People often think they can identify a passive verb because it uses a form of the verb "to be." Although passive voice often does use the "to be" form, not all "to be" verbs are passive: "She was managing the department" is active. "The department was managed by her" is passive.

Don't try to identify the passive voice by the tense of the verb. Instead, find the verb and ask yourself who or what is performing the action? If the actor is missing, or if the actor is having the action performed on it rather than directly taking the action, then the sentence is passive.

Sometimes, however, the passive voice is OK, particularly in news writing. If the recipient of the action is more important than the actor, the passive voice may be appropriate, as in the following sentence:

```
The four injured miners were rushed to the hospital by
rescue workers.
```

The most important information is that the injured miners were taken to the hospital. Who took them there is less important.

In addition, sometimes the actor is unknown: "The cargo was damaged during shipment." Who or what damaged the cargo? No one knows.

In general, though, avoid the passive voice. Keep your sentences active, and they'll be both clearer and more exciting.

Exercises

1. Rewrite the following sentences to eliminate comma splices, run-on sentences and sentence fragments.

    "I'm kind of a little disappointed, I always felt it was a fairly good thing to do."

    On Saturday, the university will introduce its new state-of-the-art classroom. Only the second of its kind on campus.

    He feels a natural feeling of it being his fault and what if he had done something different.

    As you can see, Mike's life pretty well revolves around his duties at school, which should make him a wonderful candidate for my topic because he should be well aware of what is lacking in the Buffalo School District and hopefully I will be able to tie that in to the big picture of school desegregation.

Sidebar

A Craft or an Art?

I've often heard writing compared to a craft, a comment that's always created in my mind the image of people doing amateur woodwork in their workshops in the back of their homes. Personally, I believe good writing is as much art as it is craft. But the metaphor of writing as a craft does have its good points.

Imagine, if you will, a carpenter building a home. Rather than working from a detailed plan, the carpenter pounds nails and saws wood at random, hoping the pieces fit together. Occasionally, this carpenter puts a nail in the wrong place but rather than pulling the nail out and trying again just leaves the nail where it went the first time. Further, imagine that this carpenter doesn't know how a power drill works and uses the drill bit in an attempt to cut a 2-by-4 in half.

I don't know about you, but I wouldn't want this carpenter building anything I would plan to inhabit. Like the carpenter who works without planning, revision and knowledge of how the tools work, writers who put words on paper (or on a computer screen) without double-checking their work without writing and revising and without knowing the basic rules of grammar are destined to construct something that no one wants to read. And, after all, writing so that someone else will read it is what we're all trying to do.

Finally, if you have more questions about grammar, you might want to check one of the several excellent grammar books geared toward media writers.

Johnny on the outside looks very healthy he weighs 196 pounds, and has never lost more than 5 pounds at a time.

She got married soon after coming to Springfield. With her daughter arriving in a few years.

This may seem like Greg has established one of his goals, however he is not completely content.

She explained that it just happened, however she is very happy with her career.

She states that while she was married to her first husband, he beat her so badly that she was unable to have children, and that her two daughters are adopted. Adopted from a friend (at that time) who was an alcoholic and a drug addict, and could no longer take care of her children.

The topic I chose is unemployment. In particular unemployment as it relates to recent college graduates.

Smith's apartment is a very simple one there is not much furniture.

Volunteers work in over 500 constituent chapters, subchapters, branches, support groups and international associated groups in 37 countries worldwide, provide the majority of services which link the Lupus Foundation to thousands of lupus patients and their families.

2. Rewrite the following sentences to eliminate agreement problems.

Jones declined to comment on how much a coach can make above their salary with endorsements.

And just like cancer or AIDS, alcoholism can destroy a person's life and the lives of all the people around them.

Each student progresses through the lessons at their own pace.

Each teacher chose one student from each class to read their speech or poem to the audience at their assembly.

Dr. Ralph Adams, director of the gerontology program, said that a student interested in this program must be diversified in their studies.

Anderson said she enjoys the high-tempo environment, tips, and added that their uniforms were "no less than what you would see in a gym."

A person may call a 1-800 number that connects them with an operator.

If his accusations are in fact true, I would like to find out what measures Greene County is taking to protect their children.

Heidi says her main goal is to make sure the Literacy Council receives enough money to keep their current students and to help the program grow.

Furthermore, someone with a specialized education may see their field of study obsolete in just a few years.

Last year's freshman class will, on the average, leave the college that they are attending for four years with a $13,600 debt.

A group of downtown business owners have even started a committee to lobby for improvements.

3. Rewrite the following sentences to turn passive sentences into active sentences and to fix problems with parallel construction.

The first two events in Springfield's Right from Wrong Campaign were a challenge to church staff members to stand for Christian values in a world with relative standard and McDowell addressed parents and adults on the basis of values.

Hendricks said this is probably due to normal use, worm holes and parts of it appear to have been burned.

Family members had taken turns caring for her in their homes, but soon another alternative was sought.

Wilson Keiser, special projects assistant to the vice president of administrative services, says that this program has not been as successful as they had hoped it would be.

What this means, Scott said, is ethics, proper behavior and what's expected of individuals as a group in the community.

The computers in each truck will also contain ownership information, hazardous material information and where to shut off gas and electricity.

The piano is also quite well played by his sister, and his brother can drum as well.

Leadership is a quality that emanates from Cadet Wentz.

At first sight Leo will appear to you as a shy and reserved person.

One of the biggest effects breast cancer has on women is emotional, psychological reports say.

Renovation of the student union and a new computer class that is to be offered were two issues that were dealt with at the Student Government Association meeting Tuesday night.

Suggested Readings

The Associated Press Stylebook. New York: The Associated Press, 1996. Not only does the stylebook tell you when to capitalize and abbreviate, it also has the best punctuation guideline section I've seen. It also provides word usage tips.

Brooks, Brian S. et al. *Working with Words: A Concise Handbook for Media Writers and Editors,* Third Edition. New York: St. Martin's Press, 1997. This is an excellent grammar book for media writers and includes an extensive section (and appendix) on troublesome spelling words.

Cappon, Rene J. *The Word: An Associated Press Guide to Good News Writing.* New York: The Associated Press, 1982. This book, written by a veteran AP writer and editor, provides detailed examples of actual AP copy illustrating how to improve your writing style.

Clouse, Barbara Fine. *Working It Out: A Troubleshooting Guide for Writers,* Second Edition. New York: McGraw-Hill, 1997. This book is aimed at all writers, and it includes helpful sections on the writing process such as coming up with ideas, writing drafts and revising.

10 Photographing the Story

James H. Kenney Jr.
Photojournalist-in-residence, Western Kentucky University
Las Vegas Review-Journal, Las Vegas Sun, Reno Gazette-Journal and
Hanford (Cal.) Sentinel

Chapter Outline

The craft of photojournalism

News

Sports

Features

Picture essays and picture stories

Tools

Technique: Light, composition and color

The moment

The caption: Getting words

Being an idea person

Digital photography

Sidebar Tips for photographers

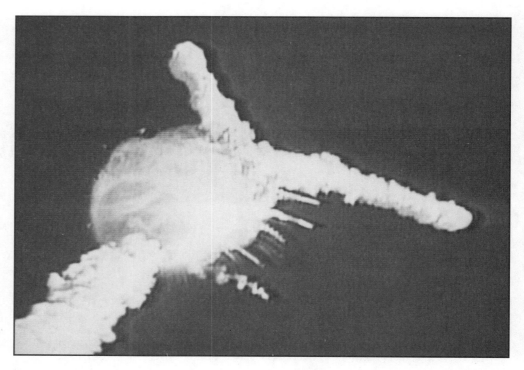

Photos often capture historic events such as the explosion of the Challenger. These photographs have become visual icons of pain, triumph, tragedy and courage.

Much of what we learn comes from what we see. Numerous studies have concluded that if you want to make an immediate or a lasting impact, do it visually. Newspapers and magazines began to figure this out in the 1920s. Publishers discovered that if they ran a lot of pictures and ran them big, they could sell newspapers. As a result, the photograph emerged as a powerful tool to inform, educate and influence. It called people to right a wrong, to change their minds about a war and to remember.

Consider these historical events caught on film: American troops raising the flag at Iwo Jima, a virtually unknown island in the Pacific captured by the Allies; the kiss of a sailor and a woman in New York City's Times Square when World War II ended; the execution of a suspected Viet Cong supporter; the shooting of Vietnam protesters at Kent State University; the lone protester in front of a line of Chinese Army tanks in the Tiananmen Square; and the body of an American soldier dragged through the streets of Mogadishu, Somalia.

Still and video photographers from television captured the images of the U.S. hostages at the American embassy in Iran, the sadness of the Marines after 241 of their fellow soldiers died in Beirut, the power and grace of Muhammed Ali, the explosion of the space shuttle *Challenger* and the joy of veterans returning from the Gulf War. These moments are more than just a visual history of events. The images have transcended the events themselves to become visual icons of pain, triumph, tragedy and courage—timeless and timely recordings.

Pictures, however, aren't solely responsible for people's memories and impressions of events. Words and pictures combine to create journalism's power. But often it's the picture that draws a reader into a story. In many news events, the picture is the first thing you notice and the last thing you remember.

The Craft of Photojournalism

Many people's impressions of photography are based on their own experience with a camera: Push button, develop film, get pictures. How is the photojournalist's job any different? Using essentially the same technology as the weekend photographer, photojournalists must go beyond just recording the fact that they were at the scene of a news event. The challenge is to make a photograph that brings thousands, or perhaps millions, of readers to the scene as well. But even this isn't enough. The real challenge for the photojournalist is to take a photograph that makes the readers want to be there.

What do photographers do? Photojournalists take pictures that tell stories about *people,* not about dogs or about rocks—about people. This isn't to say that a dog or rock can't be a significant part of a story. But at its root the photograph must have the human element. For instance, consider a story about a family dog that gets lost for two weeks, then makes its way home. A major element of this story certainly is the dog. But the picture the photojournalist looks for is the reunion between the dog and its owner. As humans, we respond to this relationship between dog and owner more than to the dog being lost.

Perhaps one of the easiest ways to define photojournalism is to describe the kinds of pictures a photojournalist takes. At a basic level, photojournalism can be divided into four categories—news, sports, features and picture stories—though the distinction between the categories is often blurred. Following is a look at what's contained within these categories.

News

News can be separated into two subcategories: general news and spot news. General news is a planned event such as a city council meeting. Spot news is an event for which planning is impossible. A house fire, a drowning and a tornado are spot news events.

Spot news photographs are perhaps the more difficult and dangerous to capture on film. You're often caught on the front lines of sensitive situations. For instance, at the scene of a house fire, you first need to convince the police or fire officials that you must get closer to the event than what is safe just to make a photograph that tells a story. The police and fire teams really don't want you there. And the fire victims may look at you as a vulture, invading their very private moment. *You* probably wish you were somewhere else, too. It's difficult to explain to a grieving, often angry victim that you're there because of your job. The victim often sees you as an intruder. In some respects, those victims have a point.

However, some of the most memorable historical news events have been preserved by photographers. Consider the horrible pictures from the Nazi concentration camps at the end of World War II. These pictures are not easy to view. One could say they're too invasive, too degrading to the individuals. But without them what would be our memory? What would be our reminder?

Sometimes a photograph of a local tragedy can make a community more aware of a problem. In Las Vegas, I had to photograph the funeral of a little boy killed by a drunk driver. I didn't want to be there. Funerals can be the worst examples of invading someone's most private moments. After the funeral, the boy's father came up to me. I thought, "Oh no, here it comes." Instead, the father told me how much he appreciated my being there. He felt that if people saw his son's picture and his death's effect on the family, they might think twice before drinking and driving. Even in the worst moments, a photograph has the potential for a positive impact.

Sports

I've always had a love-hate relationship with the sports assignment. I've loved to shoot sports, but I could tell you too many stories of the great picture that got away. One semester in college, I got so tired of going to sports assignments and coming back with nothing in focus that I resolved to shoot sports daily until I got it right. I shot about every game that semester. When there wasn't a college game available, I'd shoot high school sports—anything with a ball and action. This experience made me a consistent sports photographer, and it remains my best advice for those struggling with shooting a moving target. Shoot often.

Good sports photography requires a thorough understanding of the game, strategic positioning, quick reflexes and a little luck. You can often make your own luck with a combination of the first three. Understanding the game allows you to anticipate what's going to happen on the next play. It also helps you determine what position to take to get the best angle for the picture. Quick reflexes allow you to follow a baseball traveling 90 mph and to get out of the way of a 300-pound lineman.

However, the most important aspect of the sports assignment can be those who react to the action. If you photograph a state high school basketball final and shoot only the action on the court, you'll miss the image of the players on the bench leaping for joy when a player sinks a winning basket at the buzzer. You'll miss the coach trying to console his players at the end of the game after a loss. You'll miss the fans mobbing the hero of the game. When shooting the big game, don't forget to turn around to see the rest of the story.

Features

The successful feature photographer finds prominent characteristics in what others consider the most mundane of circumstances. For instance, newspaper subscribers might pass a street corner where kids are selling lemonade and not give it a second thought until seeing a picture of them in the newspaper. A feature photographer takes that rather typical scene and grabs the reader's attention. It may bring back a childhood memory or produce a smile. In some way, the reader is moved by the photograph.

Like news pictures, features can be either planned or unplanned. An example of a planned feature is a photograph of a dance-'till you-drop competition advertised in a community newspaper. An unplanned feature, better known as "enterprise art" or "wild art," can best be captured by having your camera with you at all times.

Many times, you'll get a request from the newsroom to go find a feature for the front page or local news section. This is what photojournalist and educator Dave LaBelle calls "the great picture hunt" in his book by the same name. One of the feature photographer's greatest qualities is the ability to be able to consistently find interesting slices of life while "hunting" in the community.

One of the best ways to find features is to watch for them when you're on other assignments. One of the best examples of this is a picture a photographer made at a city council meeting. The meeting itself held little visual interest—a bunch of council members sitting around talking. But the son of one council member had come to the meeting and had fallen asleep on the floor of the council chambers.

An unplanned feature is known as *enterprise* art or *wild* art. Author James Kenney captured this photograph of children in Las Vegas, Nev., experiencing a rare snowstorm.

This humorous feature photo certainly held the readers' interest more than a photograph of the council proceedings.

Portraits and illustrations are often loosely grouped into the feature category, although they could easily be put in categories of their own. A good portrait shows what a person looks like and reveals a part of his or her character. A portrait photograph might consist of a close-up of the subject's face or a picture of the subject in his or her environment.

For example, you might be assigned to photograph a local artist. You could shoot a close-up of just her face or move back and shoot her in her studio, showing her paintings in the picture as well. Which one reveals more about the story? If the story is about the fact that she's an artist, then the portrait in the studio would reveal more to the reader. If the story is about her living 50 years in the same town, then perhaps a tight frame emphasizing her face would work better. When in doubt, shoot both pictures. Give your editor a choice.

In both cases, the emphasis should be on what your subject looks like and not on what he or she is doing. This is why a typical portrait usually has the subject looking directly into the camera. Readers should see the subject in much the same way as if they met the individual in person. If the subject turns away from the camera, the reader concentrates on what activity is being done. At this point the photograph becomes more of a feature picture than a portrait.

Illustrations often resemble commercial or advertising photography rather than documentary photojournalism. Most of what a documentary photojournalist covers is news, sports or feature events where what the subjects do are out of the photographer's control. With food or fashion illustrations, the photographer maintains complete control of the picture from concept to finished product. The

A good portrait shows what a person looks like and reveals a part of his or her character. A portrait can be a close-up of the subject's face or a picture of the subject in his or her environment.

photograph is then used to illustrate a story on strawberries or back-to-school fashion that would run in a newspaper's food or fashion sections.

Picture Essays and Picture Stories

If individual news, sports and feature photographs could be compared to a sentence, the picture essay or picture story would be a paragraph. Both sentences and paragraphs make a complete statement, but the paragraph allows you to dig deeper into your subject. A picture essay or picture story uses several photographs, usually five or more to communicate a story.

Although the picture essay and picture story both involve multiple pictures, they take different approaches to the same subject matter. For instance, let's say that you decide to photograph a health issue such as cancer. If you take the essay approach, you might photograph several people in varying stages of the disease. You might photograph someone winning the battle against cancer and someone losing it. You could explore people going to different countries, seeking alternative treatments, or you could photograph a pioneering researcher in the cancer treatment field.

If you covered cancer as a picture story, you would concentrate on one person's struggle with cancer or one doctor's attempt to cure the disease. You tell the story about cancer from the perspective of how a particular individual deals with it.

An essay will take more time and resources than a story, but as a result you often end up with a more comprehensive report on the disease. However, many readers can better understand cancer when told from an individual's perspective.

A picture essay or picture story can be compared to a jigsaw puzzle. Each picture should be strong and make a unique statement about the subject, but no one picture works as well as when all the pictures are put together as a whole. The extra time involved in shooting a picture essay or picture story allows you the luxury of establishing a closer relationship with the subject. With this closer relationship comes a deeper understanding of the issue and the people involved in it. As a result, the photographs pass on that deeper understanding to the reader.

Tools

So you're out in the field with camera in hand, looking at a perfect picture opportunity. Now what? You've got to translate that opportunity into an image on film. This is a two-step process. The first thing you need to do is master your camera controls. The second step is to master the three primary technical elements available to photojournalists—light, composition and color.

First, let's look at the camera. You'll need a 35mm single lens reflex camera. The 35mm refers to the size of film. The 35mm film is the same most amateur cameras use. Single lens reflex, also known as SLR, refers to the feature that allows you to look into the viewfinder of the camera and see what the lens sees.

You'll also need some lenses. Lenses are also measured in millimeters. Lenses between 50 and 60mm are called normal lenses because they approximate the view of the human eye. Lenses longer than 60mm, called telephoto lenses, magnify the image. Telephoto lenses are often used on sports assignments when a photographer can't get close to a subject but still needs a tight shot of the action. Lenses shorter than 50mm are referred to as wide-angle lenses because they take in a wider view than the human eye.

A picture story or essay uses several photographs, usually five or more, to communicate the story instead of just one. Here, author James Kenney focuses on a homeless family.

The kind of equipment you need depends on the assignments you shoot. A good selection of equipment includes two camera bodies and four or five lenses. Have a range of lenses, including a standard lens (50 to 60mm), a wide angle (24 and 35mm), a short telephoto (85 to 100mm), a medium telephoto (135 or 180mm) and a long telephoto (300 or 400mm). An alternative is to use a zoom lens, which is not limited to one lens length. For example, a good zoom lens to carry is an 80 to 200mm lens.

Along with cameras and lenses, you'll also need a flash unit when there isn't enough light to expose the film properly or when you want to create a special lighting effect.

This is only a basic list of equipment. Some photographers use more; some use less. In any case, it's easy to get caught up in an equipment frenzy. Don't. A camera is like any tool. That same tool placed in two different hands can produce different results. It can't make you a great photographer; it just helps you get an image on film. The success of that image depends on you—your head and your heart.

Technique: Light, Composition and Color

Photojournalists are constantly looking at pictures. When you come across a good one, take it apart and analyze it. What makes this picture effective? In terms of technique, the answer always comes down to three major elements—light, composition and color. Each contributes to the final product. Without light there could be no photograph. But light is not enough. How you use light in your photograph often means the difference between a great picture and a mediocre one. Effective light draws your viewer into the photograph.

In his book *Photojournalism: Content and Technique,* Greg Lewis notes: "Light is to the photographer what words are to the writer. Light illuminates, but light is also darkness; shadows are as important as highlights. Light isolates, blends, emphasizes, de-emphasizes, reveals or reduces shape, enhances or hides texture, creates atmosphere and mood and can direct or distract the viewer."

Light should be one of the first things you look at when you arrive at an assignment. First, look at the intensity of the light. How bright or dim is it? This will determine how you'll expose your film. Second, look at the quality of the light. Is it soft light with minimal shadows or hard light with harsh shadows? You'll find the soft light early and late in the day when the sun is low on the horizon. Hard light exists in the middle of the day when the sun is high and at its most intense. Neither quality of light is better; each creates different moods in the photograph. Third, ask yourself, what direction is the light coming from—the front, side or back? Try this: Take three photographs of the same subject, using the three directions of light. Changing the direction completely alters the appearance of your subject and the meaning of the photograph. Because of the lack of shadows in the front-lit picture, your subject will lack form and texture in the face. Your side-lit picture will highlight one side of the face and provide a shadow on the other. This will give the face form and texture, producing the illusion of three-dimensional depth in the photograph. That same subject with light coming from behind will put the face in total shadow, producing an effect called silhouette. Three different directions, three different results, three very different interpretations of the same subject. Make light your priority. It will make the single greatest impact on your photographs and those who look at them.

To create good composition, pay special attention to organizing your frame through the viewfinder of your camera. Most beginning photographers stand too far

Light is to photographer what words are to the writer. Light can illuminate, but shadows are as important as highlight. Light creates atmosphere and mood and can direct or distract the viewer.

A good photograph enables the viewer's eye to move easily from one element in the picture to another. The use of lines, as in this fire photograph, leads the viewer to the focal point of the picture.

from a subject when they take the picture. Too many holidays photographing Aunt Mabel and her 15 grandchildren have conditioned us to stand back about 10 to 15 feet when making a photograph. This is too far away to highlight any particular element in your frame. Remember that you're trying to lead the viewer from one element to the next. When you're too far away, everything gets the same emphasis. The eye doesn't know where to go first, let alone know where to go next.

To prevent this visual confusion, you need to establish a focal point in your photograph, a place where the eye goes first. Establish a focal point by following this principle: Fill the frame. Move in as close as possible to your subject without losing the meaning of the story. If you're photographing a story about a Baptist minister and you want to show him preaching to a crowd, include only part of the crowd to tell your story. If you want to emphasize the expression on his face while he preaches, move in as tight as possible.

Use a guideline borrowed from artists called the rule of thirds (see illustration). To understand this rule, draw a rectangle with dimensions similar to the 35mm camera viewfinder (about 1.5 inches wide by 1-inch deep). Then draw lines inside of the rectangle like a tic tac toe grid. Now circle the intersecting points of the lines. These points are where you should try to place your focal point in the viewfinder. This avoids placing your focal point in the center of the frame, which usually creates an uninteresting photograph. Placing your subject off-center allows the viewer to move from the focal point to other related elements in the photograph. Keep in mind that, even though the rule of thirds suggests that the *rule* should never be broken, I consider it more of a guideline. However, carefully following the guideline provides valuable insight into when it's best to break the rule.

A photojournalist has the ability to know where to stand when the moment presents itself, the patience to wait until the storytelling moment fills the veiwfinder and the instincts and the reflexes to push the button at just the right moment.

Sidebar

Tips for Photographers

1. Connect with your subject as a person first and a story subject second.

2. Master your equipment and your technique so you can concentrate on the moment when you're on assignment.

3. Take a genuine interest in your community. Be curious.

4. Take your writing seriously. It will make you more marketable, and it's your responsibility as a photojournalist.

5. Know the difference between photographing what people do and what they feel about what they do. Photograph the reaction to the action.

6. When on assignment, go early and stay late. You never know when the moment that best tells the story will happen. But don't miss deadline.

7. Find the unusual within the usual circumstances.

8. Lead the way in your profession: Be an idea person.

9. Embrace the new technological tools, but do not expect these tools to make bad pictures good. Remember: Garbage in, garbage out.

10. Be prepared. Be resourceful. Be flexible.

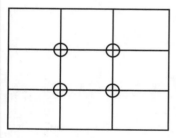

The rule of thirds provides a guideline for positioning subjects in a photograph. Placing your focal point in the center usually creates an uninteresting photograph, while putting the subject off center allows the viewer to move from the focal point to the other related elements in the photograph.

The rule of thirds, combined with selective focus, creates movement and direction in a photograph. Selective focus means that a lens can focus critically on only one plane in the photograph. If you focus on someone's eyes, nothing in front of and behind the person will be quite as sharply focused. Since a viewer's eyes usually go to the sharpest point in a photograph, you can use selective focus to first draw your viewers to that point and then allow their eyes to move to the other elements in the frame.

A photographer can use many other devices to give the photograph more impact. As you look at a good photograph, your eye should move easily from one element in the picture to another. This is no accident. The photographer has used several compositional techniques to lead you through it. For instance, straight and curved lines can lead the viewer to the focal point of the picture. If you were taking a picture of a marathon runner running along a road, you could use the road as a line leading to the runner, the focal point. The road also gets narrower as it runs from the foreground to the background of the picture, giving an illusion of depth in the photograph.

One other major compositional element is the use of framing to highlight the focal point in the photograph. Usually, a frame is in the foreground of the photograph. It acts just like a picture frame so that the eye is drawn into the frame and concentrates on whatever is contained within it. If you want to emphasize your focal point, place it within the frame. When you realize the power of the frame, you'll begin to see the possibilities everywhere you look. Trees, fences, a hole in the wall, columns in a building and even humans qualify.

The best way to look at how color affects a photograph is to look at the same image in black-and-white. Colors become tones of gray, and similar colors look the same. Color in that same picture adds a new dimension. First, it's more familiar to us since we see in color. Second, we respond emotionally to certain colors. Colors such as yellows and oranges give many people a feeling of warmth, whereas blues and greens create a cool feeling. Reds and yellows stand out to the viewer; blues and greens seem to fade into the background.

Color also can hurt your delivery of information in the photograph. Let's say you take a portrait of a man at a park. You want to emphasize his face. You also want to show that he's in the park, so you include some of the park in the background. Your final photograph shows someone in the background with a red jacket on. Even if red is a small element in the background, it can dominate the photograph.

Try your own experiment with color. Look at a photograph and determine what color you notice first. Then see if the color is a significant part of the frame. If it is, then the color is working for the photographer to lead you to the focal point. If not, the color is nothing more than a distraction.

The Moment

Why is it that two photographers, given the same tools and techniques, can cover the same assignment and one will come back with a better photograph? If tools and technique were the only necessary elements for a good photograph, photojournalism would be a lot more predictable and boring. The element in the photograph that gives a picture its storytelling quality is called a moment.

A moment is determined primarily by place, time and timing. As a photojournalist, you must develop the instincts to anticipate where you need to be standing when the moment presents itself. Once you find the place and angle, you need the patience to wait until the moment that tells the story best fills your viewfinder. Finally, you need the instincts and reflexes to push the button at just the right moment.

Henri Cartier-Bresson, one of the great documentary photographers of the 20th century, is best known for his photographs embodying what is described as the decisive moment. He uses light, composition and camera angle to set the stage. Then he uses facial expression, gesture, body language, interaction between his subjects and a suggestion of motion to provoke an emotional response from the viewer. Often, this moment is caught in a split second—an instant *before* the moment didn't exist, an instant *after* the moment is gone. If your subject reacts to a question with surprise, that expression will last only an instant. If you aren't anticipating it, the moment will pass before you lift your camera to your face.

A moment is perhaps the greatest difference between the moving picture on television and the still picture. Moving pictures use the same light, composition and techniques as the still picture. But moving pictures rely on time, motion, sound and color the image to evoke emotion from the viewer. The still picture can rely only on the moment that's captured in the single image. The image must suggest sound, motion and emotion captured in less than a second.

The moment must contain not only the facts of the story but the photojournalist's interpretation of the event. Remember the historical photographs mentioned at the beginning of this chapter: Raising the flag at Iwo Jima, the kiss of a sailor and a woman when World War II ended, the execution of a suspected Viet Cong supporter and the lone protester in front of a line of Chinese Army tanks. They do more than just document that the event took place. They provoke an emotional response to the event.

Your success as a photojournalist depends on your ability to find moments in everyday events. For example, if you photograph a teacher and shoot only what the teacher does, you'll end up with a teacher standing in front of a class and other insignificant moments. The pictures provide information but fail to provide any insight about the interaction between the teacher and the students. A wonderful moment would be a photograph of the teacher yawning while grading papers after a long day. Moments often make the difference between the viewer reading the story or turning the page. Finding these moments begins by taking a genuine interest and curiosity in people. Slow down and notice details others fail to see. By doing so you tell stories others can't.

The Caption: Getting Words

The word *photojournalist* implies two meanings. One, you're a photographer. Two, you're a journalist. Essentially, you're a reporter with a camera. But pictures don't work in a vacuum. Carefully written words can add tremendous impact to the pictures. As a photojournalist, you need to be responsible for not only what is in the picture but also for the words that are attached to it.

Writing captions is a great way to get the respect in the newsroom that photojournalists have long wanted. The caption seems an unlikely way to get that respect. After all, good shooting should do the trick. But a quality caption reaches writers and editors in territory they know best: the written word. You provide an example of being a complete journalist—one who brings words and pictures back to the newspaper in circumstances where you're the only one present at the scene.

Writing a good caption is an easy process, as long as you gather your information correctly. The first key task is to make sure the caption doesn't become an afterthought. A good caption is made while the photojournalist is still out in the field. If you wait until you get back to the newsroom to start writing, it's too late. You'll have inadequate information, leading to a dull, generic and cliché-ridden caption hastily written on deadline.

While in the field, make sure to collect the important information. The caption should answer the following questions:

Who's in the picture?

What's the story about?

Where was the story located ?

When did the story happen?

Why did the story happen?

How did the story happen?

While collecting this information, listen for great quotes. Just as you should be looking for great moments in your pictures, listen for those same kinds of moments while a person tells you his or her story. A quote avoids one of the worst sins of caption writing—putting words in your subject's mouth. Phrases such as "John Smith *seems* to be enjoying the sunny day at the beach" and "It *looks as if* Mary Jones is not happy with the results of the election" wouldn't be tolerated within a story, so why should they be acceptable in a caption?

Once you're back in the newsroom with information and quality quotes in hand, it's time to start writing. This seems to intimidate many photographers. Perhaps it's because they weren't trained as writers. A photojournalist needs only a little confidence, some basic writing skills and a good dictionary. Write clearly and don't misspell words. Don't repeat what's already obvious in the photograph. If you have a picture of a girl jumping into a pool on a hot summer day, don't waste valuable newsprint by repeating that fact in the caption, "Jane Smith jumps into a pool to cool off." Instead, use a quote from Jane that tells your reader how she *feels* about jumping into a pool on a hot summer day.

Bringing back a picture without a caption is like a reporter writing a story without including critical facts. You aren't doing your job as a journalist if you're not accompanying your pictures with relevant and interesting words.

Being an Idea Person

Bob Gilka, former director of photography for *National Geographic,* makes a distinction between picture-taking photographers and idea-making photojournalists. "We are up to our armpits in photographers and up to our ankles in ideas," he says. If you can combine good photography and writing skills with good ideas, employers will pursue you as much as you're pursuing them.

How do you generate good ideas? Here's a start. If you aren't already, become a news hound. Read newspapers, magazines, billboards, the yellow pages, flyers, brochures and books. Visit the library. Search the Internet. Use the subject of the story you're working on as a resource. Subjects often know other people with good stories to tell. Establishing yourself as an idea person makes you a valuable resource in the newsroom instead of merely a recipient of assignment orders.

Digital Photography

When you consider that photography has been around only since the 19th century, the monumental changes in technology shouldn't be that surprising. Photojournalism's latest stage is digital photography. The 100-year standard of silver-based film developed in chemicals is quickly being replaced by images recorded digitally on computer disk drives built into camera bodies. At many newspapers, the traditional darkroom with chemical washes and baths is being replaced with computers that process images digitally.

Although traditional photography processes are not obsolete, some publications and picture agencies have gone completely digital. This means that photographers are shooting with a digital camera, then downloading (the "techno" term for the word *moving*) those images into a computer hard drive. Using imaging software such as Adobe Photoshop, the photographer can adjust exposure, contrast and color balance on the computer monitor rather than in the darkroom.

Until recently, the poor quality of digital cameras limited them from mainstream use. Today, however, some photographers use nothing but digital cameras because of recent improvements in quality. Mark Humphrey, an Associated Press photographer based in Nashville, Tenn., used a digital camera to photograph the 1996 Super Bowl and has not used a film camera since. He found one of the major advantages to the digital camera is that he didn't have to leave his location to process or transmit photographs. With a digital camera, a computer and a phone line, you can send pictures electronically from your location anytime you want. Computer technology has literally taken the photographer out of the dark and into the light of the newsroom. The closer relationship among the newsroom, the photography department and the press room has resulted in a better understanding of what each department does.

Although the technology has changed, the traditional role of photography remains intact. No amount of hardware or software can turn a bad picture into a good one, a mediocre moment into a meaningful one. The computer can't generate ideas. The computer and digital camera are only tools to make a photojournalist's job easier and more efficient. The photojournalist creates the ideas and makes the pictures to tell the story.

Exercises

1. Find a subject—a building or a statute—you can return to several times during the day and evening. The subject should be in contact with the sunlight throughout the day. Make six photographs of your subject: one each at sunrise, midmorning, noon, midafternoon, sunset and just after sunset. Notice how light affects the appearance of your subject and the mood of the photograph.

2. Go to a small town and make two portraits of its oldest resident. One photograph should be a close-up of just the subject's face. The other should be an environmental portrait. Make sure the environment you include contributes relevant and interesting information about your subject. Call the town's Chamber of Commerce. Talk to the town historian. Visit a local hangout, usually a coffee shop or diner, and strike up a conversation with the locals. You'll meet some interesting people, you'll find your subject and, if you listen carefully, you'll discover several other picture opportunities.

3. Choose a human interest issue that's important to you. This could be social, health-related or any other kind of current news story. If you have a difficult time coming up with an idea, go to the library and read several newspapers and periodicals. Keep an eye on television news programs. Once you find an issue, do some research on it. Does the story have visual potential? Is it an issue that lends itself to a local angle? Is there an expert in the area who can give you current information and provide leads for a possible story subject? Can you get the access necessary to tell a complete story? Next, find a person involved with the issue who's willing to tell the story. This will identify an issue with a specific person who's affected by it. Then photograph your subject, keeping in mind the techniques involved in shooting an effective story discussed in this chapter.

Suggested Readings

Chapnick, Howard. *Truth Needs No Ally: Inside Photojournalism.* Columbia, Mo.: University of Missouri Press, 1994. The late Howard Chapnick, an icon in the photojournalism field, recounts his experiences with photographers during his years as head of Black Star photo agency. He also provides valuable insight into his philosophy of photojournalism and some sound advice for those trying to break into the business.

Kobré, Kenneth. *Photojournalism: The Professionals' Approach,* Third Edition. New York: Focal Press, 1996. This book is another good photojournalism resource book. It includes excellent visual examples of features, spot news, general news, portraits, illustrations, sports and pictures stories. The book also includes a chapter on photo editing.

Lewis, Greg. *Photojournalism: Content and Technique,* Second Edition. Madison, Wis.: Brown & Benchmark Publishers, 1995. Lewis's book provides an excellent overview of photojournalism, including shooting, lighting, composition and darkroom techniques. It also includes chapters on digital photography, the law, ethics, history and color. Perhaps the most valuable chapter is the one on getting a job in photojournalism, including how to put together a portfolio.

Broadcast Writing and Reporting

Christopher Harper
Professor, Ithaca College
Idaho Statesman, Associated Press, *Newsweek,* ABC News and
   "ABC 20/20"

Chapter Outline

Script preparation

What is news?

Finding what's important

On location

Getting pictures

Editing the story

Sidebar 1 A radio host's view

Sidebar 2 A view from a television anchor

Sidebar 3 Videotape log

Sidebar 4 Television scripts

Sidebar 5 Doing longer television stories

Local and network broadcasts occur all the time, and they have a news hole to fill. Some days it's fun. Some days it's hell. It's never dull.

Let me tell you how I got into broadcasting. For eight years, I worked for the Associated Press in Chicago and *Newsweek* in Chicago, Washington and Beirut, Lebanon. As a print journalist, I thought television was the last medium for which I ever wanted to work. That's because I didn't know much about broadcasting. You know the clichés—blow-dried hair; the lights are on, but nobody's home. The athletic hunk or the blond bimbo were the only ones who did television. Ignorance is useful for bliss and intolerance. One day, I was talking with a friend from ABC News, and I asked him how much he was paid. He told me, and I then asked how one got into television. He said I could meet with the director of foreign news, who happened to be coming to Beirut the next day. ABC was having some trouble convincing someone to go to Cairo, Egypt. I volunteered, and ABC hired me.

I knew little about broadcast writing style—writing for the ear of the listener rather than the eye of the reader. Telling broadcast stories is much more informal and conversational than writing for newspapers and magazines. That's because a broadcaster speaks the words of a story to the listener. In addition, the broadcaster usually gets only one chance to pass on the information. Readers can go back to the previous paragraph if they don't understand something in a newspaper. Unless listeners or viewers are recording everything they hear, the broadcaster has one chance to get it right. After 15 years in the broadcast business—in front of the camera and behind it as a producer at ABC News and "ABC 20/20," here is what I learned, mainly the hard way.

There's never a day when nothing happens. Local and network broadcasts occur all the time, and they have a news hole to fill. Some days you feed the beast well. Other days the beast can eat you alive. Some days it's fun, but some days it's hell. It's never dull.

What's the difference between writing a sentence in newspaper style versus writing in broadcast style? Here's how a newspaper might use a quotation from Wall Street after the Dow Jones tumbled 60 points the previous day:

```
"It's very tense. I'm waiting to see what happens. I'm
very nervous," said Arthur S. Simon, a stock broker with
Merrill Lynch as he waited for today's market opening to
see if stocks would plunge further than they did last
Friday.
```

Read it out loud, as though it were for a broadcast:

```
QUOTE It's very tense. I'm waiting to see what happens.
I'm very nervous UNQUOTE said Arthur S. Simon a stock
broker with Merrill Lynch as he waited for today's market
opening to see if stocks would plunge further than they
did last Friday.
```

When did you run out of breath? Did it make any sense? Of course, it didn't. Let's assume that there's no audiotape of the conversation with the stock broker. All the broadcast writer has is the information. What's the most important point? The stock broker is nervous that the market might go down. What else is important? Maybe his company. Maybe his name. That's about it.

```
Stock broker Arthur Simon of Merrill Lynch says he's
nervous that the market may drop further today.
```

Following are some of the differences between writing for broadcast and writing for the print:

1. The source of a broadcast story usually starts a sentence unlike the source in a print story.

2. In a broadcast story, middle initials are usually edited out.

3. In a broadcast story, the quote gets shortened.

4. In a broadcast story, the verb is often in the present tense rather than the past tense.

Consider another example of how sentence would be written in a newspaper versus for a broadcast outlet:

Newspaper version:

```
Alfred S. Walker, 18, was charged with attempted murder
after he shot the owner of a liquor store during a
holdup, police said.
```

Broadcast version:

```
Police say an 18-year-old man is being charged this
afternoon with shooting the owner of a liquor store
during a holdup.
```

Differences:

1. The attribution goes at the beginning of the sentence: "the police."

2. The man's name is less important in the broadcast version. It could be used in the next sentence such as "Police identified the man as Alfred Walker." Again, the middle initial should not be used unless there's a common practice otherwise: "the late President John F. Kennedy."

Following are a few more examples. Numbers are often difficult to understand from a broadcast.

Newspaper version:

```
The head of the concession said 4,987 hot dogs were sold
during last weekend's game.
```

Broadcast version:

```
The head of the concession says nearly 5,000 (or five
thousand) hot dogs were sold during last weekend's game.
```

Newspaper version:

```
The Dow Jones Industrial Average gained 7.1 points.
```

Broadcast version:

```
The Dow Jones Industrial Average gained more than seven
points.
```

Newspaper version:

```
The lottery is worth $14.5 million.
```

Broadcast version:

```
The lottery is worth 14 and one-half million dollars. (or
14-point-5 million dollars.)
```

Script Preparation

The manner in which scripts are handled differs from broadcast outlet to broadcast outlet. Some broadcasters use only capital letters. Others use capital and lowercase letters. However, all copy should be double- or triple-spaced to allow for corrections. In the upper left-hand corner, the following information should appear:

Today's date. Some broadcasters use 1/22/98. Others use 1/22 or Jan. 22, 1998.

The slug. Make the slug consistent and keep it the same throughout any updates.

Your last name

The approximate time of the copy after you've actually read it and timed it

The name of the broadcast

All this information enables the team to know the date the story was written, what it's about, who wrote it, the story's length and the place it will be used. Broadcasts have been compared to wars without weapons: Logistics and command structures

Television journalism in the field usually involves a team—sometimes as large as a producer, reporter, camera operator and sound technician. That team has to work together to create an effective television story.

are important to a successful broadcast. Everyone literally has to be on the same page. Remember that times are important. Read your scripts out loud and time them precisely.

What Is News?

Identifying the news is virtually the same for all media. For example, take a look at the following information a newsroom received about the mayor's news conference. Write a lead and a second paragraph for what's known as a "reader," where you or the broadcast anchor reads the news. Slug the story "Mayor."

News conference in the Blue Room at City Hall

2 p.m. today

About 50 reporters are on hand. Pretty full room. Mayor Rudolph Giuliani walks across the room to the podium. He says: "I have an important announcement to make. Because of an anticipated budget shortfall much more serious than we expected, I am taking some drastic action. First, I am ordering an across-the-board job freeze. There are more than three thousand jobs to be filled. They will not be filled. I am also instructing all department heads to reduce by 20 percent the moneys they had planned to spend on supplies and equipment during the next 90 days. This is a painful decision for me. I know it may cost me politically, but I must protect the fiscal integrity of this city."

```
The anticipated shortfall between now and the end of the
fiscal year, June 30, is $365 million.
```

First, list the facts at hand. Number what you think are the most important facts with 1 being the most important and 5 being the least important:

_____ News conference in the Blue Room at City Hall at 2 p.m. today. The mayor looks grim. No smiles.

_____ Department heads instructed to reduce by 20 percent the money they had planned to spend in the next 90 days.

_____ Mayor describes the decision as "painful."

_____ Mayor says, "I know it may cost me politically, but I must protect the fiscal integrity of this city."

_____ The shortfall between now and June 30 is $365 million.

Finding What's Important

There are many ways to write a broadcast story, but here is a simplified way to tell your listeners what happened. Determine what's important. The mayor is important because he said it. So let's start the story with "The mayor."

What did the mayor do? He "announced."

When did he do it? "today"

Where did he do it? "at a City Hall news conference"

What did he say? How will the plan be implemented? "that he has told all department heads to cut expenditures by 20 percent during the next 90 days"

Why did he say it? "because the city faces a 365 million dollar budget deficit"

The lead becomes

```
The mayor announced today at a City Hall news conference
that he has told all department heads to cut expenditures
by 20 percent during the next 90 days because the city
faces a 365 million dollar budget deficit.
```

There are many alternatives:

```
Describing the action as painful, the mayor announced
today at a news conference that city agencies face severe
budget cuts. City agencies face cuts of 20 percent
because of a 365 million dollar shortfall in the budget.
That's what the mayor told reporters today at a news
conference.
```

```
Acknowledging that he may face political fallout from his
decision, the mayor told a news conference today that
city budgets are being cut by 20 percent over the next 90
days.
```

Let's try the second paragraph after the lead. What's the second important news item after the information in the first lead? It's important to determine what was not in the lead. Let's look again at lead No. 1:

```
The mayor announced today at a City Hall news conference
that he has told all department heads to cut expenditures
by 20 percent during the next 90 days because the city
faces a 365 million dollar budget deficit.
```

Is the Blue Room important? Probably not, because the lead already includes the location at City Hall. Emotion attracts listeners. In lead No. 1, there's no pain, no political fallout, no grim face. Let's try to choose the words carefully and insert some emotion into the story.

Description: "A grim-faced mayor"

Verb: "acknowledged that"

What did he acknowledge?

```
He may face some political fallout from what he describes
as a painful decision. But he insists the measures are
necessary to protect what he calls the financial
integrity of the city.
```

It's important to get the job freeze into the story. It's possible to put the job freeze into the lead, but it has no apparent effect immediately because the jobs are unfilled so far. Unless it's known that the 3,000 jobs are 10 percent of the police force or fire department, it's difficult to determine exactly how important this fact is. For a later broadcast, this information should be obtained to update the story.

```
The mayor also ordered an immediate freeze on new hiring,
leaving three thousand jobs unfilled.
```

Let's look at what additional information is needed for Lead No. 2:

```
Describing the action as painful, the mayor announced
today at a news conference that city agencies face severe
budget cuts.
```

There were no facts or figures, so try to write that information into the second paragraph.

Following are leads No. 3 and No. 4 in broadcast style:

```
City agencies face cuts of 20 percent because of a 365
million dollar shortfall in the budget. That's what the
mayor told reporters today at a news conference.
```

```
Acknowledging that he may face political fallout from his
decision, the mayor told a news conference today that city
budgets are being cut by 20 percent over the next 90 days.
```

What information should be included in the second paragraph in these stories?

There are many correct ways to write a lead and the following paragraphs. In broadcast writing, you have a limited number of words to use. Use strong verbs. Use the active voice, if possible, and avoid the verb "to be." Write clearly and concisely. In most broadcasts, a writer has only 150 to 200 words for a story. Choose those words well.

Let's try to figure out a whole story from a police report.

September 7, 1996

Las Vegas, Nevada

11:15 p.m.

One vehicle, a BMW, was leaving the fight of Mike Tyson.

Driver: Marion Knight, 31, aka (also known as) "Suge."

Business: CEO, Death Row Records

Criminal record: Assault with deadly weapon; conspiracy
to obtain guns illegally (took delivery of two Glock
machine pistols); robbery and assault (sentenced to nine
years, suspended, 1994).

Victim: Tupac Shakur, 25, born in New York.

Criminal record: Bail pending appeal against conviction
for sexually abusing a woman fan in a hotel room; in
1993, pleaded guilty to felony weapons charges; charges
in shooting of two off-duty police officers in Atlanta
dropped; sued by limousine chauffeur for an alleged
beating.

Witnesses say a white Cadillac pulled up next to the BMW.
Two men stepped out and started shooting. Passenger
Shakur was shot four times as he tried to scramble into
the back seat. Driver Knight's head was grazed by a
bullet. Others returned fire.

That's what a police report gives a reporter. There may be a sketch of the death scene, but you don't have that much to go on. Who is Tupac Shakur? Who is Marion Knight? There are no stupid questions in this craft—only those that go unasked. If I were to receive the police report about Tupac Shakur, I would have no idea who these subjects were. But I would find out pretty fast. Tupac Shakur was one of the hottest rappers until he was gunned down in Las Vegas on Sept. 7, 1996, by unknown assailants after the singer attended a Mike Tyson heavyweight fight. You need to write copy immediately for broadcast in three minutes. You don't know who Tupac Shakur is. Report only what you know:

Police say a 25-year-old man has been seriously wounded
tonight in a drive-by shooting after the heavyweight
title fight. Police identified the victim as Tupac Shakur
of New York City.

Witnesses say a white Cadillac pulled up next to the BMW
in which Shakur was a passenger. Two men stepped out and
started shooting. Shakur was shot four times as he tried
to scramble into the back seat. Police say record
producer Marion Knight—who was driving the car—was
slightly wounded in the head.

Now it's time to do some research and make some telephone calls:

Again, who is Tupac Shakur?

Who is Marion Knight?

Sidebar 1

A Radio Host's View

Rush Limbaugh, radio talk show host

1. The most important thing I learned early on is that there are a lot of people students will meet who have failed and who will advise them it's a cutthroat business, a bunch of egos—they'll chew you up and spit you out. I was influenced by those people way too much early on. I really got lucky by meeting some people who were really successful. It's much better to be inspired by people who have been successful in the business than by those who have failed.

Radio talk show Rush Limbaugh recommends that journalists should treat their audiences with respect and never underestimate the intelligence of the listeners.

2. Journalism is changing and don't be fooled by the superstar status on heretofore unknown journalists. There's a growing public distrust, distaste and skepticism about the press in general. The market is going to be wide open for people who can fulfill the original purpose of journalism—the who, what, when, where and why. See something and report it with as little judgment as possible.

3. Understand that objectivity is a difficult thing for a thinking individual to do. You're going to have an opinion about what you see. But there is a burgeoning market for those who can objectively report the events they see.

4. Fairness is a bogus objective because I defy anybody to define fair that is universal. Fair to Peter Jennings may be totally different from what is fair to me.

5. You can go out and destroy somebody's life on the hope that the *New York Times,* the *Washington Post,* ABC, CBS or NBC will spot you and hire you.

6. Don't go into journalism if you want to change the world. Don't go into journalism and correct the injustices of the world. Don't got into journalism if your objective is to spot the inequities in life and reverse them. That's not journalism. If that's what you want to do, you should run for political office or go to work for someone who is in office.

7. Never underestimate the intelligence of the audience. Most journalists think people are blithering idiots who would not be able to drive to work were it not for the 11 o'clock report on how to stop at a stop sign. Treat your audience with respect.

What hospital is treating them?

What is the condition of each man?

What do the police think happened?

By the next hour, you'd better be able to report about one of the top rappers in the United States and what happened:

```
Rap singer Tupac Shakur is in critical condition tonight
after being wounded four times in a drive-by shooting.
```

Hospital officials report that the 25-year-old victim—
known for his lyrics about killing on the streets—
suffered serious wounds to the chest. He was listed in
critical condition and was not expected to live.

Witnesses say a white Cadillac pulled up next to the BMW
in which Shakur was a passenger. Two men stepped out and
started shooting. Shakur was shot as he tried to scramble
into the back seat. Police say record producer Marion
Knight—who was driving the car—was slightly wounded in
the head. He is listed in fair condition.

Knight is the chief executive officer of Death Row
Records, the label for several prominent rappers,
including Shakur. Police say no arrests have been made.

On Location

Radio reporters often work alone. Their tape recorders become notebooks. Let's say you've been sent out to cover a fire. Remember the following tips:

- Look for the person in charge.
- Find out the time the fire started.
- Get the location.
- Find out the number of victims, including their names, ages and addresses.
- Find out the possible causes.
- Get reactions from survivors and eyewitnesses.
- Find out the monetary amount of the damages.
- Get physical details and descriptions.
- Provide historical context and the significance of the fire.

In writing a broadcast story, you need to describe with your voice what a newspaper reporter would write. You have fewer words. More important, you need to ask questions that start with "how," "what," "describe," "tell me about" and "why did this happen?" You want to make certain that you ask open-ended questions, which can't be answered with yes or no. (See Chapter 5).

> Was it a big fire? The eyewitness who has probably seen only one or two fires will answer yes.

> Can you *describe* what the fire looked like? "I've never seen anything like it before. It took seconds and the house was gone. I'd lived there all my life."

> Were you afraid? "Yes."

> *Describe* how you felt. "I was so frightened. I almost didn't get out alive."

The same interviewing approach should be used for television interviews. The only "stupid" question is to ask a mother of four how she feels after all her children have died. It's insensitive and bordering on immoral. Sometimes, however, family members do want to talk about their loss. A better question, if appropriate, is "Describe what you want people to know about your children."

Sidebar 2

A View from a Television Anchor

Peter Jennings, anchor of the "ABC Evening News"

1. This craft never changes. We have this great opportunity to convey to the public what is happening. We want reporters who are hungry to know what's happening.

2. When we're looking for reporters, it's hard to find good ones.

3. We in journalism need specialists. But we also need people who are curious and capitalize on the *N*, not the *T*, in television news. If you come with the idea of being on television, you'll be disappointed, and we'll be disappointed with you.

4. There's a danger in wanting to be a star. Kids come into my office and say I'd love your job. And I say, "It took 30 years."

5. I want people who report their own stuff and believe in the value of writing.

6. You have to be prepared for less freedom. The networks keep people on a tight lead because of budgetary restraints, and technology allows the networks to do that.

ABC News anchor Peter Jennings says that news organizations are looking for reporters who are hungry to know what's happening.

7. Journalists should be people who, when they leave at night, have nothing to do with the media. They should hang out with boxers and ballet dancers.

Covering a television story is much more complicated than reporting for print publications. You have to work as a team with a photographer. If you don't have pictures, you don't have a good television story.

Sometimes there's a sound technician in the field who can capture the crackle of the fire, the sound of the sirens or the irrelevant sound of reporters cracking bad jokes. Sometimes you'll work with an on-scene producer. You need to work together. With one weak link, the chain is damaged. That weak chain may break, and it will reflect poorly on all of you. You may have a wonderful relationship with some of the team and dislike working with one member. That can get in the way of reporting a television story. You depend on one another, and without everyone doing his or her job you have trouble. Get over personal problems quickly.

Getting Pictures

Pictures dominate television. Communicate with the photographer what you've been told about the story. Help the photographer with information and stay out of the way. Unless you can pick up the camera and shoot better pictures, you're better off letting a professional do the job. The photographer is just as much a professional as you are, often with more experience and a better understanding of what's needed

Sidebar 3

Videotape Log

Many television journalists do a dreadful job of organizing visuals. Producers scribble notes about possible shots. Reporters think something is on a tape, but they can't find the precise soundbite.

A videotape log is a great device. Take the time to screen the material with the editor. Identify the story name, the date, the field cassette number and the time code of each shot with notes about the shot or the substance of the sound bite. Make copies of these log sheets for the producer, reporter and editor.

VIDEO TAPE LOG SHEET

PAGE # __1__

STORY TITLE: _Crime_   LOGGER: _Harper_

DATE: _1/22/98_   FIELD CASSETTE #: _One_

DESCRIPTION OF FOOTAGE: PROTECTION CASSETTE #: _One_

BETA #: _One_

TIME CODE	NOTES
1:00:00-1:00:37	General View of crime scene
1:00:38-1:00:42	~~Police~~ Various shots of police
1:00:43-1:01:30	Interview with eyewitness
1:01:31-1:02:15	SOT of Police Capt. John Jones
1:02:16-1:03:45	Standups #2 is best at 1:02:30

A video logging sheet should provide descriptions of the shots, times and information on interviews. A good log saves time in the editing room.

for the visual package. The reporter and producer should focus on the basic information of the story, including lining up eyewitnesses to augment the visuals.

In most cases, the reporter will want to do a standup, which is recording commentary on camera. A standup creates an on-air presence and to give credibility to the story. There are two basic types of standups: a bridge that provides a transition between one aspect of the story and another and a standup close that provides a final thought to the story or that recasts information that may not have visuals to support the information. In the case of the fire story, a standup could provide a transition from the initial information about the fire to the eyewitnesses and victims. You might close with a standup after having learned that fire fighters had difficulty bringing the blaze under control because a plan to increase water pressure in the area had been defeated in a recent city council vote.

Editing the Story

Now that you've reported the story, you need to write and edit it for broadcast. More and more, reporters have to write and edit on location. It's important to look at the

Sidebar 4

Television Scripts

Everyone has his or her own preference about preparing a script. But there are some standards. A television script should have two columns, which can be set up easily through any word-processing program.

On the left side, the reporter should list specific editing instructions such as the type of shot and the location of the shot on a videotape. The right side should include the narration, sound bites and natural sound. VO, or voiceovers, are often in all capital letters, but capitals and lowercase letters can be used. SOTs, literally sound on tape or sound bites, should be the reverse of the narration track. Write out the entire sound bite—not just the beginning and end.

5/15/97
Dance
Adam Levine

dance troupe performing (Tape three, 43:04) exaggerated walk (Tape three, 42:20)	**VO** AT A SCHOOL IN THE LOWER EAST SIDE OF NEW YORK CITY EXISTS A LANGUAGE PROGRAM. PART ENGLISH LESSON. PART DANCE CLASS. IT'S A WAY TO TEACH SOME OF NEW YORK'S NEWEST IMMIGRANTS HOW TO SPEAK ENGLISH.
Group of women in circle (Tape one, 15:13)	**SOT** Hands. Hands. Elbows. Elbows. Shoulders. Shoulders. Arms.
Group from behind teacher (Tape one, 18:52)	**SOT** Look right, left, center. Look right, left, center.
Students faces (Tape three, 41:01)	**VO** FOR 90 ENGLISH-AS-A-SECOND-LANGUAGE STUDENTS AT LOWER EAST SIDE PREPARATORY SCHOOL,
Eyes (Tape one, 1:10) or (Tape three, 19:36)	THE MEMBERS OF THE MICHAEL MAO DANCE COMPANY HAVE YANKED THEM FROM THE SEDATE
Mouth (Tape three, 40:24) or (Tape one, 29:43)	CLASSROOM TO LEARN ENGLISH IN AN ENTIRELY FOREIGN CULTURE— MODERN DANCE.
Men in a circle	**SOT** Hands. Fingers. Wrist.

Preparing scripts is handled differently at various broadcast outlets. In most cases, copy should be double-or triple-spaced to allow for correction. The script should include the date, the writer's name and the story name, or slug. Television scripts usually have two columns with the editing directions on the left-hand side.

visual material and sound bites you have before writing. That way, you can write more precisely to the material you have. It's often better to use an audiotape recorder in addition to the camera, so that you can isolate and choose the sound bites you intend to use from an interview.

Sidebar 5

Doing Longer Television Stories

Maryanne Reed

Assistant Professor, West Virginia University

WETM-TV, Elmira, N.Y., WOKR, Rochester, N.Y., and WTAE-TV, Pittsburgh, Pa.

Television stories are not only short news bursts. Stories between three and five minutes often run on network news broadcasts. Television magazine programs generally offer 15- to 30-minute news stories. Documentaries often run 30 minutes to an hour. Techniques differ from person to person and broadcast to broadcast. Here is how I approached a documentary on Jewish traditions in West Virginia.

Long-form television stories, including documentaries, should focus on specfic topics and people such as the Jews in West Virginia rather than approaching a story from a broad perspective, which can lead to superficiality.

The Idea

My idea for producing the documentary came from my own family history. I'm Jewish, and my great-grandparents immigrated to Davis, W.Va., from Lithuania around the turn of the century. My greatgrandfather, Simon Fox, was a peddler who settled in Davis because it was a thriving logging town, where he could open his own retail clothing store. I grew up hearing about his family's life when they were the only Jews in Davis. I was fascinated by the contrasting themes of compromise and commitment that ran throughout their story. For example, my great-grandparents and their children never gave up their Jewish identity. Nevertheless, there was no synagogue in Davis, so the family regularly attended church services in order to experience religious community.

I began with a general premise that I was going to produce a video documentary about the Jewish experience in Appalachia. I intended to produce a piece that looked at several Jewish communities in Appalachia. I planned to include an explanation of the historical process of Jewish migration to Appalachia—how and why Jews migrated from northern cities to small-town Appalachia. But, primarily, I was interested in documenting the Jewish experience in Appalachia—what it has meant to live as members of a distinct minority in a region known to be hostile to outsiders. I was particularly interested in exploring the conflict that many Appalachian Jews face between their desire to

Talk to your photographer about the best shots that will match the information you want to say. Remember, you have only 200 to 250 words to say what's important. A picture can be worth a thousand words, but you have to make certain the information from your voice puts the pictures in context.

Doing standups and recording tracks aren't easy. You may get nervous. Take a minute and think about a quiet place or something you love—a beach, the sky, your child. Clear your mind. Take a few deep breaths. Then go back to work. This is not life and death; it's only television. It's not as important as the event you may have just witnessed, which *was* life or death. So push the adrenaline back and relax as much as possible. It does get easier.

Following are some guidelines for preparing a script. As mentioned previously, scripts should be divided into two columns. At the top of the left-hand column should be the date: Jan. 22, 1997. The second line should be the slug of the story. The third line should be your last name. All copy must be doubled- or triple-spaced. The

Sidebar 5 (continued)

maintain a separate religious and cultural identity and their need to assimilate into the larger community.

The Research

In the course of doing preliminary research, I decided to narrow the focus to the study of a single Jewish community rather than concentrating on several communities. I decided I would be able to explore one community in depth rather than approach the subject superficially. As a consequence, I would be able to produce a more complex and interesting piece. Then I could get to know the people and learn about their hopes, dreams and fears. I could develop a narrative based on their personal stories.

I looked for a small Jewish community whose experience was representative of many other Jewish communities in Appalachia. My preliminary research and my travels led me to the small Jewish community in Beckley, located near the southern coal fields of West Virginia.

At one time, as many as 75 Jewish families lived in Beckley. Jews migrated to coal towns like Beckley in the late 1800s and the early part of the 1900s because of the booming coal economy. Jews first came to the region as peddlers. Later, they opened stores and businesses and became successful small-town merchants.

However, the Jewish population began to decline in the 1950s and 1960s, primarily because mechanization of the mines led to a decline in the once-thriving coal economy. Younger Jews were also encouraged to leave the region by their parents, to become professionals and to live in cities with larger Jewish populations.

At one point in Beckley, the Jewish population dwindled to eight families. And it looked as if the community's one synagogue might have to close because there just weren't enough people in the congregation to support it. But Temple Beth El has recently seen a slight increase. Today, thanks to some economic development in the area, there are now 15 Jewish families in Beckley and several other Jewish families from the surrounding area who attend religious services at the synagogue.

I also chose to focus on the Jewish community of Beckley, in part, because its struggle for survival is very much a present day reality. It's still not clear whether Beckley's Jews will be able to maintain a distinct presence in the town, or whether the congregation will be forced to close its synagogue like so many other small Jewish communities have already done in small-town Appalachia.

The primary focus of my documentary is the story of one small, struggling Jewish congregation in Appalachia and to use that story to address universal themes such as the conflict between cultural identification and assimilation, the search for continuity and community, and and what it feels like to be an outsider.

---

left column will include editing instructions such as tape numbers and time codes of suggested pictures, in and out times of sound bites and take numbers of standups. The right-hand column is the written script. Styles vary from outlet to outlet. I generally use all caps for voice-overs and caps and lowercase for sound bites. Use a style that makes you comfortable. If a name is difficult to pronounce, use a phonetic spelling such as HA-fez AL-asod instead of Hafez Al-Assad. Signoffs for voice-overs or concluding standups should be written in the following style: THIS IS (INSERT YOUR NAME) FOR THE NEWS TONIGHT.

Exercises

1. Put the following into broadcast style:

    a. Mayor Rudolph Giuliani said: "I had a wonderful time. I'll never forget it," as he left Queens.

Suggested Viewings

Broadcast News, prod. and dir. James L. Brooks, 1 hr. 43 min., Twentieth Century Fox, 1987, videocassette. Movies tend more to capture the broadcast journalist for better or for worse than books. This movie stars William Hirt and Holly Hunter in a close-to-the-truth saga of television network news.

Hoop Dreams, prod. Kartemquin Films/KTCA-TV, dir. Steve James II, 2 hrs. 50 min., Kartemquin Films/KTCA-TV, 1994, videocassette. This documentary chronicles two inner-city basketball players and their attempt to become professional stars. The film begins with each of them in junior high school in Chicago. But the documentary also examines their families and their lives.

Edward R. Murrow. "This Is London" and "The Liberation of Buchenwald." Murrow's best reporting from World War II came from on top of buildings and on the streets of London. Buchenwald was a Nazi death camp, which Murrow visited only days after it was liberated by the Allies. These reports, which are available in most libraries either in print or audio recording, are among the finest ever done by one of the finest reporters ever.

---

    b. "I'm pleased to announce that there has been a decrease in subway crime, according to new figures just received today," said Transit Authority spokesman Ken Myers at a news conference this morning.

    c. The chairman made his comments at 10 a.m. this morning.

    d. The fire broke out in a two-story house on Wesley St.

    e. The State Senate will take up the matter on Wednesday. The House has already approved the measure.

    f. The case has gone all the way to the New York State Supreme Court.

    g. The driver of the car failed a breathalyzer test, according to Police Lt. John C. Corcoran.

    h. Robert M. Watson, 34, was treated for several lacerations and is in satisfactory condition, according to Myrna D. Flannery, spokesperson at Mercy Hospital.

    i. The attorney general said, "I will have absolutely no comment until the investigation is completed."

    j. Four men were arrested just about one hour ago after a scuffle in the main city park, police said.

Exercises courtesy of Michael Ludlum, Department of Journalism, New York University

2. Write a news story as a 30-second reader.

Details from a Seattle Police Department Report

April 8, 1994

Victim: Kurt Cobain

Age: 27

Occupation: musician

Victim found by electrician Gary Smith at 8:40 a.m. Smith said he spotted a body in a guest house above the garage. Victim was dressed in a light-colored shirt and blue jeans. A shotgun was found lying across the body. Victim was shot once in the left temple. Smith said he found a single-page note written in red ink.

Police treating the incident as an apparent suicide.

Other background: The level of heroin in Cobain's blood was sufficient to cause intoxication when he pulled the trigger, medical authorities said. A pathologist with the King County Medical Examiner's Office in Seattle said Wednesday that Cobain likely killed himself in the afternoon or evening of April 5. He declined to comment on the toxicology findings.

The time of death is the best estimate based on the condition of the body and evidence at the scene, but Cobain could have killed himself several hours earlier or later, said Nikolas Hartshorne, the pathologist who conducted the autopsy on his body.

"We feel confident that this was a self-inflicted gunshot wound to the head," he said. "There's nothing suspicious about the scene or the circumstances."

Heroin found in Cobain was "a high concentration, by any account," said Dr. Randall Baselt, who heads the Chemical Toxicological Institute in Foster City. But he said the strength of that dose would depend on many factors, including how habituated Cobain was to the drug.

Nirvana's 1991 album "Nevermind" reached No. 1 on the Billboard album charts and sold 10 million copies worldwide. The band forged into the mainstream, and its ground breaking success led the way for fellow Seattle super groups Pearl Jam, Soundgarden and Alice in Chains.

Cobain recovered from a drug-induced coma last month in Rome.

His death is the latest in a legacy of rock 'n' roll tragedies whose casualties include Jimi Hendrix, another Seattle-based, left-handed guitar player who died at age 27; Jim Morrison; Sid Vicious and Janis Joplin.

"Now he's gone and joined that stupid club," his mother, Wendy O'Connor, told The Associated Press on Friday in Aberdeen, Wash. "I told him not to join that stupid club."

Ms. O'Connor filed a missing-person report with Seattle police last Saturday after Cobain left a treatment center and bought a shotgun. She said he had been missing for six days.

Cobain's wife, Courtney Love, singer for the band Hole, was in Los Angeles at the time with their 20-month-old daughter Frances Bean.

"We are all devastated by the unbelievable tragedy of Kurt Cobain's death," said Ed Rosenblatt, president of Nirvana's label, Geffen, in a statement. "The world has lost a great artist, and we've lost a great friend."

Cobain was the product of a gritty boyhood in Aberdeen, a rough-and-tumble coastal logging town 100 miles southwest of Seattle. He pursued painting rather than sports and sought a life beyond work in the woods, on the docks or at the lumber mills in town. Cobain and his wife, cast as grunge's reigning couple, had off-and-on heroin habits that were well-chronicled by the media.

Last month, Cobain was in Rome with Ms. Love and their daughter to recover from health problems that had forced the band to cancel two concert dates in Europe. When he mixed the sedative Roipnol with champagne, he went into a coma and was hospitalized for four days.

Two weeks later, Seattle police were called to the singer's home and told by his wife that he had locked himself in a room where several weapons were stored. Ms. Love told officers that Cobain was suicidal. Coaxed from the room, Cobain said he didn't want to hurt himself. Police confiscated four guns, including a semiautomatic rifle and ammunition. They also seized an unidentified bottle of pills.

What's the most important news? List the six most important facts for the story's lead and second and third paragraphs. Here are some other questions you should ask: How was the victim found? Why did it happen? What details should be included about the death? (Remember that apparent suicides or murders should be the business of the police to say, not the reporter.) What background should be included?

3. Write a TV news story from the following information.

   A Bonanza Bus Lines bus struck a newsstand on the corner of Amsterdam Avenue and West 71st Street today.

   It happened about three PM

   The newsstand was completely demolished.

   The proprietor, identified only as a Mr. Singh, crawled from the structure minutes after the incident. He appeared shaken by the incident and was examined at the scene and found to have no serious injuries. He was taken to St. Claire's Hospital by ambulance for observation and further examination.

   The driver of the bus was cut by shattered glass from his windshield. He also was taken to St. Claire's. Both men's condition was reported to be "not serious."

   The front end of the bus was damaged.

   The bus was en route to Springfield, Massachusetts, from New York's Port Authority Bus Terminal. There were 14 passengers on board. None of the passengers were reported to have been injured. No pedestrians were reported injured.

   The accident occurred at the three-way intersection of Broadway, Amsterdam Avenue and West Seventy-First Street. Residents of the area have petitioned the Department of Traffic in the past to do something about convergence of heavy traffic through this intersection in which a number of serious accidents have occurred in recent years.

   Video available:

   Collapsed newsstand—medium shot

   Collapsed newsstand—close-up, panning debris on sidewalk; newspapers, magazines and other objects. 40 seconds.

   Newsstand proprietor talking with police. 16 seconds.

   Front end of bus—smashed windshield, dented front, medium shot. 20 seconds.

   Ambulance, exterior. 12 seconds.

   Crowd watching. 10 seconds.

4. Write a TV story based on the following facts:

    An Amtrak Metroliner derailed two hours ago.

    It was en route from New York Penn Station to Washington, D.C.

    Accident occurred as train was traveling through Edison Township, N.J.

    Amtrak spokesman says 350 passengers were on train, plus a crew of six.

    It was a seven-car train.

    Edison police say some passengers were shaken up, but apparently there were no serious injuries.

    A faulty switch is believed to be the cause, but the situation is still under investigation.

    Because of the accident, all Amtrak trains running between NYC and Wash are two to three hours behind schedule. Amtrak says normal service should be restored by tomorrow morning.

    Available video:

    Long shot of accident scene with milling crowds and workers. 11 seconds.

    Medium shot of locomotive (off the track) and second two cars. 14 seconds.

    Close-up of damaged track. Nine seconds.

    Aerial view of scene from helicopter. 12 seconds.

    SOT of passenger saying: "I was sitting there relaxing and reading and all of a sudden, bang, this loud noise and the train suddenly jolts to a stop. It was scary, but everyone took it pretty well and the train crew was great. It could've been worse. That's for sure." Passenger's name is Ronald Marson, 39, of Manhattan. 14 seconds.

5. The following information is available for a TV story:

    Fire caused heavy damage to a church this morning.

    It broke out at 6:30 in the main portion of the church.

    It took firefighters more than two hours to bring it under control, according to a fire department spokesman.

    The church is All Sinners Episcopal Church, 244 West 14th Street.

    Three firefighters were overcome by smoke and were treated at the scene. There were no other injuries.

    The interior of the church, including the altar, was heavily damaged.

    A fire department spokesman said there are indications the fire was deliberately started. The arson squad is investigating.

    Video available:

    Wide shot of the church exterior. 16 seconds.

    Close-up of a carving over the main door that says "Come unto me all ye that travail and are heavy laden." Nine seconds.

    Long shot of the damaged church altar. 10 seconds.

    Close-up of the damaged altar. 10 seconds.

12 The Law

William Marshall
Professor, Case Western University School of Law, DePaul
University School of Law, Minnesota Office of the Attorney
General and Office of the White House Counsel

Chapter Outline

"Lawyering" the Media

The media's role in First Amendment theory

News gathering

Confidential sources

Privacy and defamation

Sidebar Tips for non-lawyers

An airplane crashes in a farm field on the outskirts of a major city. A local TV station camera crew arrives at the scene within minutes after the crash. The cameraman runs up to the wreckage, where he gets extraordinary footage, including a close-up of a male and female standing over the wreckage, holding each other tightly. From emergency medical service personnel at the scene, he learns that the couple was apparently in the field at the time the plane crashed. The two people refuse to be interviewed.

Meanwhile, back at the station a reporter obtains information that the pilot of the plane was Nate Kaminsky, 45, a former Gulf War pilot. The reporter contacts a friend who had also served as a pilot in the Gulf and is told by this friend that he knew Kaminsky personally. The friend is at first reluctant to speak. But after the reporter promises him absolute confidentiality, he tells her that Kaminsky was known to use illegal drugs such as hallucinogens and methamphetamines while flying reconnaissance missions. She also learns from an acquaintance of Kaminsky that, in college in the early 1970s, Kaminsky was notorious for his drug use and was once reputed to have danced naked on the college green under the influence of LSD.

The reporter also learns from government sources that Kaminsky has had a commercial pilot's license for 10 years and has no black marks on his flying record. He does, however, have a criminal record for drug use stemming from his years in college.

Finally, the reporter searches the Internet for helpful information and, much to her surprise, locates a Web site entitled "Gulf War Pilots," which includes a full portrait of Kaminsky. She prints out the picture and gives it to her producer to use on the evening news. The producer is, of course, delighted with this story. It's dramatic and visually compelling, and the information found on Kaminsky is sure to be an investigative scoop.

The station's lawyers, however, are less enthusiastic. First, they point out that the station may already be liable to the farm's owner for the physical trespass of the cameraman who went onto the field without permission. They are also concerned about liability to the couple videotaped at the crash site. If the footage of the couple is shown, the station could be liable for intrusion on seclusion, invasion of privacy and (depending on the nature of the couple's relationship) false light privacy.

Publication of the information gathered by the reporter at the station also troubles the lawyers. There are potential legal problems arising from the reporter's promise of confidentiality to her source. If she's subpoenaed to testify about her knowledge of Kaminsky, she'll be forced to break her promise under threat of contempt. If the reporter does break her promise (whether by being forced to testify or otherwise), she may be found liable to her source for damages based on breach of promise.

There are also legal concerns about disseminating the background information on Kaminsky. If the story about his drug use in college is true, the station could be liable for invasion of privacy. If, on the other hand, it's false (or the report on his drug use in the Gulf War is false) the station could be sued for defamation. There's even a problem about showing Kaminsky's photograph. It could be a copyright violation, and the station may already be liable on this count simply for downloading the picture.

Accordingly, the lawyers will strongly argue against running much of the story—a practice that journalists less than fondly refer to as "lawyering." The problem, however, is that the lawyers' concerns are legitimate. Publication of this story in its current form will expose the station to serious liability. Moreover, the lawyers' concerns are supported by an even stronger factor. The financial threat to the station only partly depends on whether the station will be found to have committed the infractions. An equal if not greater threat to the station is the cost of litigating the matter in the first place.

Of course, all is not completely lost. After the story is "lawyered," there will still be something to put on the air. The station can safely report that there has been a plane crash on the outskirts of town, that Nate Kaminsky was the pilot, and that he has had a commercial pilot's license for 10 years, and has no black marks on his record.

"Lawyering" the Media

If it's true that a conservative is only a liberal who has been mugged, then perhaps it is equally true that those who advocate legal constraints on the media are those who have been subject to some abuse. When I graduated from law school, I thought of myself as a staunch media defender. I continue to oppose most media regulation, but I have also learned that the best argument for muzzling the media is the media. I remember as a young attorney, I was involved in a high-profile abortion case involving a challenge to a law that placed technical restrictions on public funding for abortion services. After a preliminary court decision, a television station asked me for an interview to explain the meaning and impact of the judicial action. I spent almost an hour off camera with the reporter, explaining to her the court's decision and what it meant for the availability of abortion services to poor women. During the pre-interview, the reporter asked a number of good questions and seemed legitimately concerned about presenting an informative story to her audience. When she finally turned on the camera, however, she began an entirely new line of questioning that had nothing to do with the effect of the court's decision. Rather, she wanted to know the case's political meaning in the ongoing battle between the pro-life and pro-choice forces—issues about which she knew I was in no position to comment. Why she asked only these questions still remains a mystery unless her only purpose was to get me to say something embarrassing, or to create the always amusing visual of an inexperienced interviewee scrambling to come up with noncommittal responses. Whatever her purpose, however, I was reasonably sure it wasn't to inform the public. Her story did have another effect. It has caused me to hesitate to grant interviews in sensitive cases and to treat press inquiries as suspect rather than as legitimate attempts to glean information.

This chapter will place the practice of "lawyering" in context by presenting an overview of some of the legal concerns that face journalists. First, this chapter will discuss the value that the law, and particularly the First Amendment to the U.S. Constitution, ostensibly gives journalism. Second, it will address some of the legal issues raised by news gathering, including the use of confidential sources. Third, you will learn about defamation and invasion of privacy, which govern journalists' liability to individuals.

However, this chapter doesn't and is not intended to provide legal guidance on any specific circumstance. To begin with, the law governing journalistic practice depends on specific facts and varies from state to state. Any journalist who has legal questions should immediately consult an attorney. Also, this chapter is not all inclusive. First Amendment law alone can fill volumes. The legal issues journalists confront are varied, and a full inventory of issues can't be provided here.

The Media's Role in First Amendment Theory

Unlike virtually any other profession, journalism is thought to have a constitutionally protected role in the American political system. First, journalism is important because of its role in creating and fostering an informed electorate. A viable democracy depends on voters having sufficient information from which to make intelligent choices. And, at least according to constitutional theory, the media are the vehicles that provide the information on which intelligent choices can be based. As the U. S. Supreme Court has stated:

> Enlightened choice by an informed citizenry is the basic ideal upon which our open society is premised. . . . Our society depends heavily on the press for that enlightenment.

Second, according to First Amendment theory, the media must also be protected because of the importance of their role as a check on government. Free media, it's theorized, are critical to exposing government corruption and guarding against government abuses in the exercise of power.

For these reasons, the media have enjoyed considerable success in the courts in curbing governmental attempts to interfere with the journalistic enterprise. The courts have effectively abolished the crime of seditious libel—a tool that other societies have routinely used to suppress those who criticize the government. Similarly, the courts have virtually prohibited the government from imposing prior restraints against materials it finds objectionable. In the Pentagon Papers case, which is formally known as *New York Times v* United States (403 US 713, 1971) the Court allowed two newspapers, the *Times* and the *Washington Post,* to publish classified government documents about the Vietnam War in 1971. The government had argued that the publication of these papers could compromise national security objectives, including the lives of persons involved in the Vietnam conflict. The Supreme Court ruled unanimously for the newspapers' right to publish.

The Court has protected the press from the imposition of discriminatory taxes levied by the media's political opponents. And the Supreme Court has been steadfast in protecting the editorial role of the press. Editorial opinion, whether expressed in text or by caricature, has been accorded nearly complete legal protection. You may have seen the movie "The People Versus Larry Flynt." Flynt is the editor of *Hustler* magazine, *Hustler,* which ran a deliberately untrue depiction of evangelist Jerry Falwell. But the Court (*Hustler* magazine *v* Falwell, 485 US 46 1988) defended Flynt's right to use caricature as political commentary.

In other areas, however, the protections accorded journalism are far less absolute. It is to these areas we now turn.

News Gathering

Although the media enjoy broad constitutional protection under the First Amendment, a constant theme runs through the Supreme Court's cases, which give journalists cause for concern. The Court has frequently stated that, although the First Amendment stringently protects the press, the press is entitled to no greater protection than the average citizen. What triggers constitutional protection, in short, is not judicial concern for the press as an institution but concern for the particular constitutional rights that the press is exercising.

ABC's television news magazine, "Prime Time Live", used undercover tactics in investigating the supermarket chain Food Lion. A jury found the network guilty of fraudulent activities.

In an important decision (First National Bank *v* Bellotti, 435 US 765, 802 1978), then-Chief Justice Warren Burger wrote: "I can see no difference between the right of those who seek to disseminate ideas by way of a newspaper and those who give lectures or speeches and seek to enlarge the audience by publication and wide dissemination. . . . In short, the First Amendment does not 'belong' to any definable category of persons or entities."

Nowhere is the significance of this distinction more apparent than with respect to gathering the news. There is a simple cardinal rule. A member of the media has no greater right to be in any location than does any member of the general public. In our example of the air crash, the photographer is no more entitled to enter a site and be immune from trespassing laws than is anybody else. And, if the police or fire department orders a crowd of onlookers to disperse, the photographer has no special right to ignore those instructions.

This general rule of no special access has a particularly damaging implication in its effect in undercover investigations. It's generally not a violation of the law to pretend to be someone you're not. It's generally acceptable, for example, for a journalist or anyone else to enter an Amway meeting, pretending to be an ordinary consumer. However, an undercover journalist has no special protection from laws prohibiting the use of electronic equipment or from laws that prevent false representation on job applications or consumer credit forms. In one case, for example, a trial court insisted in treating undercover reporters hired by ABC as if they were actual employees of the organization they had infiltrated—in this case, the Food Lion supermarket chain (Food Lion, Inc., *v* Capital Cities/ABC, Inc., et al. 887 F. Supp. 811 1995). As a result, a jury found ABC liable for causing another company's employees (actually, ABC's own agents) to violate their duty of loyalty to their employer (Food Lion) by investigating the company's illicit activities.

The journalist fares no better when seeking access to public buildings, sites or records. State Sunshine Acts, open meeting laws and the federal Freedom of Information Act are applicable to everyone, not only the media.

There's no right, for example, to have access to a prison, closed portions of a municipal airport or the personnel files in the mayor's office. And these rules don't change even if there are accusations of prison overcrowding, breaches in airport security or charges of cronyism against the mayor.

The only exception to the access rule concerns public trials. The public, and the press acting as the public's surrogate, has a right to attend most judicial proceedings.

Confidential Sources

Another common misperception is the notion that a reporter has a constitutional right to protect sources. In the landmark case of Branzburg *v* Hayes (408 US 665 1972), the U.S. Supreme Court held that the First Amendment does not provide journalists with the "privilege" to refuse to disclose their sources. A reporter can face a sentence of criminal contempt if he or she refuses to testify. The Supreme Court wasn't persuaded with the arguments that failure to allow "reporter's privilege" would cause sources to dry up, would chill press coverage of certain matters out of fear of government subpoena and would allow the government to commandeer the press as a tool. Rather, the Court was motivated primarily by two policy arguments. First, the Court was concerned that the grant of such a privilege would unduly interfere with criminal law enforcement. Second, the Court raised the same argument made in the access cases. If the average citizen can be compelled to testify, so can the reporter.

A number of states do have in place so-called shield laws, which offer a reporter privilege in certain circumstances. Shield laws, however, allow far less than the absolute protection that reporters often assume exists. Many shield laws, for example, allow the state to force a reporter's testimony if information is unavailable from any other source. Shield laws also may not protect a reporter from testifying in civil cases against the media when the propriety of a reporter's conduct needs to be determined to establish liability. And even the most stringently drafted shield laws may give way to a criminal defendant's constitutional right to subpoena "exculpatory material," evidence that may support the defendant's innocence.

Finally, a reporter's promise of confidentiality to a source may pose legal problems if the reporter decides not to keep his or her word. In Cohen *v* Cowles Media (501 US 663 1991), a person sued the Minneapolis *Star Tribune* for breach of confidentiality for identifying him as a source after he'd been promised his name wouldn't be revealed. The newspaper defended its decision to identify the source because the individual was a political opponent of the politician the story focused on. Therefore, the source was an important element of the news story. The Supreme Court, however, held that the reporters' breach of promise entitled the plaintiff to damages.

Privacy and Defamation

The most common intersection of the law and the media occurs in the area of civil damages—actions against news organizations by plaintiffs alleging they've been harmed by a news story. The two major types are privacy and defamation.

Privacy

Privacy is divided into four areas. The first, intrusion on seclusion, is, as its name suggests, akin to trespassing. In the plane crash story, the cameraman's close-ups of the couple near the crash site could raise potential liability.

The second area of privacy is misappropriation, which protects people from commercial exploitation of their name or likeness, normally in the context of advertising rather than news reporting. For example, a lipstick manufacturer may not use the image of a movie star to advertise or sell its product without permission.

The third area of privacy, false light privacy, arises when the defendant publishes false information that harms the plaintiff's privacy. This is recognized in only a few states.

The fourth area, disclosure of private facts, occurs when the defendants publish private information about an individual that would be highly offensive to the reasonable person and that is not newsworthy. As you might suspect, there is significant doubt about the legal parameters of what this covers. Is a news report that a surfer eats insects sufficiently offensive to trigger liability? Equally problematic is the question of when a story is, or isn't, newsworthy. The courts are skeptical toward the media's defense that, because they report on a matter, it's newsworthy.

But how can the media be punished for publishing something that is, by definition, true? The U.S. Supreme Court has yet to rule directly on this issue, although it has held that the media can't be found liable for breaching privacy rights when they disseminate information from a government record or an official account. In two important cases, the media relied on official sources and published the names of rape victims without their consent. The court ruled that the newspaper had the right to do that, irrespective of ethical considerations. (*Florida Star* &. B.J. F 491 US 524 1989 and *Cox Broadcasting v* Cohn 420 US 469 1975).

Defamation

The First Amendment has had a pronounced role in defining defamation, which deals with any injury to someone's reputation. In this area, the Supreme Court has constructed elaborate First Amendment defenses to protect the media from damage suits.

The media were not always so well protected. But, in the case of *New York Times v* Sullivan (376 US 254 1964), the rules of defamation were dramatically changed. On March 29, 1960, the *New York Times* ran a full-page advertisement entitled "Heed Their Rising Voices." The ad was designed to generate support for the civil rights movement. The ad claimed that "thousands of Southern Negro students [were] engaged in widespread non-violent demonstrations in positive affirmation of the right to live in human dignity as guaranteed by the U.S. Constitution and the Bill of Rights" and that the efforts of these students were being met by "an unprecedented wave of terror by those who would deny and negate that document which the whole world looks upon as setting the pattern for modern freedom."

In 1960 the standards governing defamation suits were matters of state law, and generally the states agreed on four basic elements necessary to sustain a libel suit. In order to win, the individual seeking damages would have to show that a statement was harmful to his or her reputation, was distributed, specifically concerned the individual bringing the lawsuit and caused actual damages. If successful in demonstrating these elements, the plaintiff might still have to overcome a number of defenses available to the news organization—including that the statement was true.

Sidebar

However, the individual claiming he or she was libeled did not have to prove that the news organization had acted irresponsibly, and this is still the law, that the intent to harm the individual's reputation is not important.

It was against this legal background that City Commissioner L. V. Sullivan of Montgomery, Ala., sued the *New York Times* for its publication of the "Heed Their Rising Voices" ad. The ad's third paragraph, stated: "In Montgomery, Ala., sued after students sang 'My Country, Tis of Thee' on the State Capitol steps, their leaders were expelled from school, and truckloads of police armed with shotguns and tear gas ringed the Alabama State College Campus. When the entire student body protested to state authorities by refusing to re-register, their dining hall was padlocked in an attempt to starve them into submission." Paragraph six, in turn, read as follows: "Again and again the Southern violators have answered (Dr. Martin Luther) King's peaceful protests with intimidation and violence. They have bombed his home almost killing his wife and child. They have assaulted his person. They have arrested him seven times—for 'speeding,' 'loitering' and 'similar offenses.' And now they have charged him with 'perjury'—a felony under which they could imprison him for 10 years."

The problem was that some of the information in these paragraphs was false. For example, as the U.S. Supreme Court later noted in its opinion, "the campus dining hall was not padlocked on any occasion, and the only students who may have been barred from eating there were the few who had neither signed a pre-registration application nor requested temporary meal tickets. . . . [The] police did not at any time 'ring' the campus, and they were not called to the campus in connection with the demonstration on the State Capitol steps. . . . Dr. King had not been arrested seven times but only four; and although he claimed to have been assaulted some years

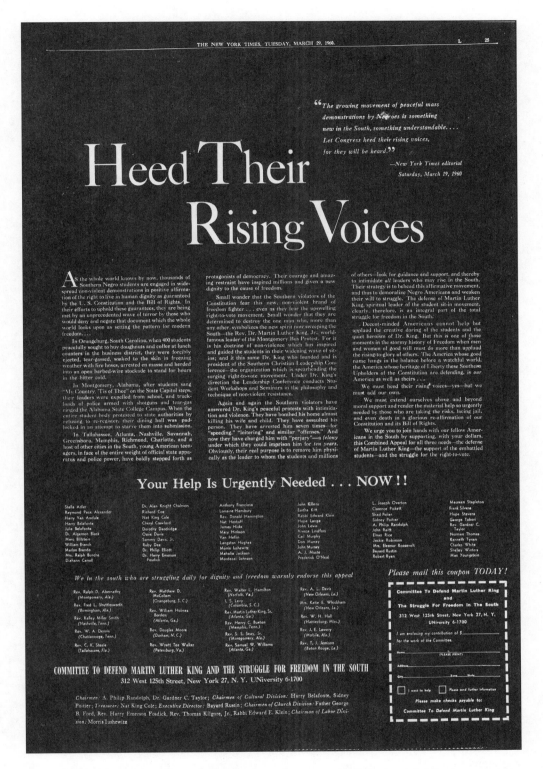

The *New York Times* accepted and ran a full-page advertisement in 1960 for the civil rights movement. A government official in Alabama sued the newspaper, saying he was defamed in the ad. The U.S. Supreme Court disagreed and established greater protection for news organizations when reporting about public officials.

earlier in connection with his arrest for loitering outside a courtroom, one of the officers who made the arrest denied there was such an assault."

Commissioner Sullivan's claim was that the inaccuracies contained in these paragraphs defamed him. The merits of Sullivan's libel claim, however, were not apparent even under the then-existing law. One problem was that the advertisement's statements didn't appear to refer to Sullivan. He wasn't identified by name, and there was nothing apparent in the text tying him to the activities. Sullivan's libel action, thus, didn't appear to satisfy the legal requirement that the purported libel must concern the plaintiff.

A second weakness in Sullivan's case was that, even if the ad were understood to apply to him, it wasn't clear that his reputation would be tarnished and he would suffer injury. Indeed, it was more likely, given the time period, that his reputation would be improved by the suggestion that he was fighting against the student uprisings.

The Alabama jury, however, was not deterred by these legal niceties. It found that the third paragraph was concerned with Sullivan, based on his contention that the word *police* would be understood as referring to him as the Montgomery city commissioner charged with supervising the police department. The jury also accepted Sullivan's even more convoluted argument that he would be understood as being one of the "Southern violators" in the sixth paragraph because, by referring to the police as among these "Southern violators," the allegations would be applied to him. The jury also apparently accepted Sullivan's claim that his reputation was injured by the story's inaccuracies. The jury awarded Sullivan $500,000 in damages, even though only 394 copies of the *New York Times* had sold in Alabama and only 35 had sold in Montgomery.

The case was appealed to the U.S. Supreme Court. The Court, obviously aware that the damage award more accurately reflected Alabama's distaste for northern newspapers than it did concern for Commissioner Sullivan's reputation, did not find the Alabama decision amusing. The problem, however, was that there were no simple grounds for reversal, because libel law was a matter of state, not federal, law. Thus, if the Court were to reverse the Alabama decision, it would have to take the unprecedented step of injecting a federal constitutional component into what previously had been entirely within the state law domain. That's what the U.S. Supreme Court did.

In *New York Times v Sullivan*, the Court held that the First Amendment requires that a public official cannot win a defamation action against the press unless he or she can show that the press acted with "actual malice"—defined by the Court as knowledge of falsity or reckless disregard for the truth. But even at this point the *Times* was not yet off the hook. Having changed the law, the Court was obligated to apply its new actual malice standard to the facts of the case before it. The *New York Times,* the Court held, did not act with actual malice, even though some information in the ad was wrong and even though the *New York Times* published the ad "without first checking the news stories in its own files," which would have confirmed that some of the information was false. According to the Court, the people in the *Times* organization responsible for publishing the ad didn't act with actual malice because they permissibly "relied on the 'good reputation of many of those whose names were listed as sponsors of the advertisement.'"

As the facts of the Sullivan case indicate, some protection for the press from state libel law was clearly in order. The original verdict in Sullivan can be only explained as the product of a blatant attempt to silence anti-government criticism and not as an attempt to redress the purported reputational harm suffered by Commissioner Sullivan. The Supreme Court's decision, therefore, is rightly celebrated as a powerful protection against government censorship.

Moreover, the financial threat against the press posed by pre-Sullivan libel law also can't be understated. According to columnist Anthony Lewis, for example, the financial stability of the *New York Times* would have been extremely precarious had the Supreme Court not reversed the Alabama decision. And, although libel suits were not as prevalent in the 1960s as now, there is no question that upholding the verdict in Sullivan would have had a snowball effect in making libel suits more attractive as huge damage awards became more and more common. Pre-Sullivan libel law, in short, might have easily threatened the financial viability of the press as an institution—particularly when damage awards were in the hands of juries that were becoming increasingly more hostile to press interests.

However, the Court did not end its treatment of defamation law with its holding in *New York Times*. For example, although the actual malice standard was originally limited to cases brought by public officials, it was later expanded to cases involving public figures—loosely defined as those who have the power, influence and capacity to respond to negative stories comparable to public officials. And in later cases the Court adopted a host of procedural protections for defendants. Indeed, the Court went so far as to hold that actual malice could not be proved even by a showing that a defendant engaged in no investigation before uttering the allegedly defamatory statement.

The actual malice, however, has not been an unmitigated boon for the media. For example, the standard requires judicial inquiry into the subjective state of the reporter—did he or she know the story was false or was he or she reckless with respect to the veracity of the story? This would subject the reporter to searching discovery and investigation. The rules have also had an effect on journalistic practice that some regard as unfortunate. For example, applying the actual malice standard to cases involving public figures tends to direct the media to easy stories about celebrities rather than investigative stories into serious private malfeasance. Similarly, the rule that the defendant need not investigate to escape liability under the actual malice standard clearly seems to encourage sloppy journalism.

And it is certainly notable that the actual malice has brought to bear in full force the law of unintended consequences. First, it tends to raise the reputational stakes for media defendants. No longer is the question whether the media made a mistake and, therefore, are obligated to reimburse someone for his or her injury. Rather, actual malice frames the question as whether the media acted with intentional disregard of the truth—a finding that most responsible media clearly want to avoid. For this reason, media defendants do not like to settle. This leads to yet another problem. While the changes in defamation law ushered in by *New York Times* have created a number of buffers to media liability, the existence of those buffers has made defamation law more complex and its litigation accordingly much more expensive. The result is that, on the one hand, defamation litigation is now much more expensive while on the other the costs of settlement are incredibly high in terms of reputation and professionalism. Is there any wonder that lawyers want to avoid stories that might trigger litigation?

Exercises

1. Research the *Times v* Sullivan case. Did the U.S. Supreme Court make the right decision?

2. Research the use of names in rape cases. Should a news organization publish the names of rape victims?

3. Research the Nebraska shield law. Should reporters have the same protection as doctors, lawyers and the clergy?

Suggested Readings

Lewis, Anthony. *Make No Law: The Sullivan Case and the First Amendment.* New York: Vintage Books, 1992. The author, a *New York Times* reporter, analyzes the case that could have bankrupt the newspaper but instead made legal history.

Smolla, Rodney A. *Suing the Press.* New York: Oxford University Press, 1987. The author assesses the growing tendency of individuals and businesses to bring lawsuits against the media.

13 Ethics

Ford Risley, Ph.D.
Assistant Professor, College of Communications, Pennsylvania
    State University
Florida (Jacksonville) *Times-Union* and the Atlanta *Journal-
    Constitution*

Chapter Outline

Codes of ethics

Ethical problems

    Telling the truth

    Deception

    Faking stories

    Plagiarism

    Conflicts of interest

    Gifts

    Lure of money

    Political involvement

    Invasion of privacy

Solving ethical problems

Sidebar 1 Ethical principles

Sidebar 2 Food Lion vs. "Prime Time Live"

Sidebar 3 Less obvious forms of plagiarism

Receiving a small, wrapped package remains one of the most memorable moments of my newspaper days. At the time, I was working on the business desk of a large daily newspaper. One week I wrote a profile of a man well known in the city's business circles. It was a generally positive story of someone who had built a large and successful real estate company from scratch. After the story appeared, the man called to thank me for writing the story. He also said to stop by his office the next time I was in the neighborhood.

Wanting to keep him as a source, I visited his office a few days later to say hello. After thanking me again for the story, he handed me a small, wrapped gift and said, "This is for your wife." I was speechless. No one had ever offered me, much less a family member, a gift in connection with any newspaper story I had written. I also knew that taking the gift would be a clear conflict of interest.

I told the businessman that, although I appreciated his thoughtfulness, I couldn't accept the gift. "It's not for you; it's for your wife," he insisted. I declined again, but when he persisted I decided to leave with the gift and talk to my editor. Back at the office, I explained what had happened. He wanted to know what the gift was. We opened the small box and inside was a pair of diamond earrings. "Get back over there and give those things back," my editor said without hesitation. I returned the earrings that day.

I'd like to think the businessman didn't have anything dishonest in mind by offering me the gift. By all accounts, he was a generous person and was simply showing his thanks, something generally acceptable in the business world. But accepting gifts from anyone connected with your work isn't acceptable for ethical journalists. It's a clear conflict of interest.

As a journalist, you'll undoubtedly be confronted with ethical questions throughout your career. Most aren't as simple as the decision of whether to accept a gift. But there are guidelines to follow.

Codes of Ethics

In the 19th and early 20th centuries, many newspaper reporters and editors saw nothing wrong with accepting gifts. The gifts took various forms, but the most common were free passes for concerts, sporting events and, most commonly, the railroad. A few editors of the era, most notably Lucius Nieman of the *Milwaukee Journal,* criticized the "pass system," as it was known. Speaking to a group of publishers in 1887, Nieman was blunt in discussing why the railroads provided passes: "Because it pays to give them to you."

Despite such warnings, it took a major national scandal to force journalists to take a hard look at their ethical practices. Concern for journalism ethics began in the 1920s during the Teapot Dome scandal. Teapot Dome, near Casper, Wyo., was a federally owned oil reserve to provide the Navy with emergency fuel. The fields, however, were given to private developers without competitive bidding. To ensure that their employees and members understand the ethical practices they're expected to follow, many mass media organizations have crafted codes of ethics. The American Society of Newspaper Editors approved a code in 1923. Three years later, the editor and publisher of the *Denver Post* was censured by the ASNE for his part in the Teapot Dome scandal. Another government scandal, the Watergate burglary in 1973, prompted a second round of code writing. The Society of Professional Journalists adopted an ethics code in 1973, followed two years later by the Associated Press Managing Editors.

A *Wall Street Journal* reporter used his newspaper column to seek personal financial gain—a clear violation of journalism ethics and the law.

Today, codes of ethics take two forms. The first category is made up of codes written by nationally recognized professional organizations such as the Society of Professional Journalists, the American Society of Newspaper Editors, the Radio-Television News Directors Association, the National Association of Press Photographers and the Public Relations Society of America. The second category contains codes developed by individual media organizations, including most major newspapers and broadcasting networks.

The codes of ethics share several themes: accuracy, fairness, objectivity, truthfulness and respect. Their general tone can be seen in this excerpt from the code of the Society of Professional Journalists:

```
The public's right to know events of public importance
and interest is the overriding mission of the mass media.
The purpose of distributing news and enlightened opinion
is to serve the general welfare. Journalists who use
their professional status as representatives of the
public for selfish or other unworthy motives violate a
high trust.
```

Unlike some professional codes of ethics, including those for law and medicine, the codes of most national mass media organizations are not enforceable. The exception is the code of the Public Relations Society of America, which obligates members to identify other members believed to be "guilty of unethical, illegal or unfair practices." (See Chapter 14). The code also requires that members appear before a judicial panel investigating breaches of conduct. Members of the Society of Professional Journalists have debated the inclusion of a clause requiring the organization to condemn breaches of the code. Members eventually decided against including it because it would infringe on the autonomy of individual journalists.

Sidebar 1

Ethical Principles

Philosophers have developed various principles that can be considered when confronted with ethical dilemmas. Following are five philosophic principles that can be helpful for mass media practitioners.

1. Golden Mean. Ancient Greek philosopher Aristotle argued that, when there are two extreme positions in a situation, one should seek the middle ground, or Golden Mean. Aristotle preached moderation between the extremes of excess and deficiency.

2. Categorical Imperative. Immanuel Kant, an 18th-century German philosopher, devised the idea that what's right for one is right for all. In other words, you should act only as you wish others would act.

3. Utilitarianism. John Stuart Mill's claimed that, in determining what's right or wrong, we must ask what will give the greatest good to the greatest number of people. Utilitarianism, as it's known, argues that ethical behavior is that which produces the greatest balance of good over evil.

4. Veil of Ignorance. Twentieth-century philosopher John Rawls has suggested that, in making ethical decisions, you should step back from actual circumstances and step behind a "veil of ignorance," in which roles and social differences don't exist. Ethical decisions are best made when you're equal with all members of society.

5. Golden Rule. The Judeo-Christian ethic calls on you to "do unto others as you would have them do unto you." At the heart of the Golden Rule, as it's often called, is the idea of fairness, treating people in the same way you would expect to be treated.

The lack of enforcement is one of the most repeated criticism of codes of ethics. Without enforcement, critics say, the codes are little more than statements of responsibility. Others argue that, because of the complexity of most ethical cases involving the mass media, the codes provide only minimal guidance. Most ethical dilemmas, they claim, must be made on a case-by-case basis.

Ethical Problems

There are myriad ethical issues that journalists and media organizations can face. Let's look at some of the most common ones.

Telling the Truth

Truthfulness is at the heart of journalism. Readers, listeners and viewers rely on news organizations to tell the truth to help them make important decisions. When journalists lie, they betray the trust of their sources and their audience. They also lose credibility, and without credibility no news organization can be successful.

Deception

Deception covers a wide range of practices, but at its heart is not being truthful with someone in order to get a news story. Journalists practice deceit when they misrepresent themselves, go undercover or use a hidden camera or tape recorder. Such practices are a time-honored journalistic traditions going back to such early 20th century "muckrakers" as Nellie Bly and as seen on modern television news magazine shows such as "60 Minutes." But does that make deception right?

Sidebar 2

Food Lion vs. "Prime Time Live"
Many people concerned with the ethics surrounding undercover journalism cheered when a jury in Greensboro, N.C., found ABC liable for using deceptive tactics in a story about the Food Lion supermarket chain. The ABC news magazine show "Prime Time Live" had broadcast a report in 1992 accusing Food Lion of selling spoiled food. The show's producers had faked resumes to get jobs at the supermarket's stores. Then they used hidden cameras to catch employees repackaging old meat and falsifying expiration dates. Food Lion sued ABC, claiming the report had cost the company billions of dollars in lost sales. But it didn't sue for libel on grounds of unfair or inaccurate reporting. Instead, Food Lion argued that producers of the show had fraudulently misrepresented themselves and that the surreptitious use of cameras amounted to trespassing. The 12-member jury found in Food Lion's favor, saying that "Prime Time Live" had gone too far in pursuit of the story.

Reaction among the media to the verdict was mixed. Some said that the jury's decision would have a "chilling effect" on aggressive investigative journalism. But other observers said there was a lesson for the press in the verdict. Writing in the *Washington Post,* Jonathan Yardley noted succinctly, "There's a right way to cover the news and a wrong way." In the case of the Food Lion story, ABC had clearly violated proper ethical standards.

The absolutist would say no. But most journalists wFould argue the answer is not that simple. Exposing dishonesty, corruption and malfeasance is one of the duties of responsible journalists, and to do so sometimes requires deception because it's the only way to learn what's happening. Most responsible journalists would argue that, for deception to be used, the abuse must be in immediate need of correction and the news media must be the only means to correct the abuse.

Faking Stories

Journalists are not telling the truth when they fake stories, inventing things that are simply not true. The most publicized example of this occurred in 1981 when Janet Cooke, a young reporter for the *Washington Post,* wrote the heart-wrenching story of an 8-year-old heroin addict named Jimmy. Cooke won the Pulitzer Prize for "Jimmy's World," but it turned out later that Cooke had fabricated the story and had invented the character of young Jimmy. The *Washington Post* gave back Cooke's award, and the newspaper suffered serious damage to its reputation and credibility as a result of the fabrication. "Jimmy's World," of course, is an extreme example of faking stories, but journalists also are faking things when they embellish or make up quotes for stories. Photographers are guilty of the practice when they tamper with the scene of news events before snapping a picture. And radio and television reporters are guilty when they mislead listeners and viewers into thinking the reporter is at the scene of an event when he or she had simply added his or her voice over a tape of the event.

Plagiarism

Plagiarism is the practice of presenting another person's work as your own. It's never acceptable. Even so, there have been numerous incidents of reporters, columnists and editors using the work of others and not giving them credit. The *Fort Worth Star-Telegram* had a series of plagiarism incidents, including a columnist who was fired after writing a column similar to a story that appeared in the *Washington Post.*

Sidebar 3

Less Obvious Forms of Plagiarism

Roy Peter Clark, Poynter Institute

- Taking materials verbatim from the newspaper library. Even when the material is from your own newspaper, it's still someone else's work. Put it in your own words or attribute it.
- Using materials verbatim from the wire services. Sometimes writers take Associated Press material, add a few paragraphs to give some local flavor and publish it as their own work. Even though it's a common practice, it's not right.
- Using materials from other publications. Some blame electronic databases for a whole new explosion of plagiarism. Sometimes writers steal the research of others without attribution. And sometimes they use others' work without realizing it.
- Using news releases verbatim. The publicists are delighted, but you should be ashamed—especially if you put your name on an article. Rewrite it except for the direct quotations, and use quotes sparingly. If you use an entire release, cite its source.
- Using the work of fellow reporters. If more than one reporter works on a story, use a byline on top and put the other names at the end of the story.
- Using old stories over again. Columnists, beware! Your readers have a right to know when you're recycling your material. Some of them might catch you at it, and there goes your credibility.

To their credit, most news organizations take swift action when plagiarism is discovered, making a public apology and disciplining or firing the guilty party. In the case of the *Star-Telegram,* the paper not only took action against the guilty writers but revised its policy on plagiarism to make it more clear to employees.

As a journalist, you have a responsibility to provide readers, listeners and viewers with original and fresh reporting whenever possible. When you can't do that and have to rely on the work of others, you owe it to the audience to let them know the source of the information.

Conflicts of Interest

Journalists have a responsibility to be free of any private interests that might conflict with their ability to report a story fairly and objectively. Conflict can come in the form of gifts, financial reward or involvement in politics.

Gifts

As already noted, accepting gifts, or "freebies," was a widespread practice among reporters for decades. But responsible journalists soon recognized that the practice was fraught with problems because it set up a distinct conflict of interest. Those who provided the gift in many cases expected the reporter to either give or withhold publicity. Even if nothing is expected in return, the public might reasonably perceive that a reporter who accepts a gift can no longer be objective.

For those reasons, most media codes of ethics pay particular attention to the practice of accepting gifts. The Radio-Television News Directors Association code establishes that members "will decline gifts or favors which would influence or appear to influence their judgments." And the Society of Professional Journalists code notes that "gifts, favors, free travel, special treatment or privileges can compromise the integrity of journalists and their employees. Nothing of value should be accepted."

Lure of Money

Another problem that can set up the potential for, or at least the appearance of, a conflict of interest is accepting money for work not directly related to a journalist's job. Some of these conflicts arising from the lure of money are obvious; others are less so. There are several recent examples.

R. Foster Winans, a *Wall Street Journal* reporter, wrote the newspaper's "Heard on the Street" column, which contained financial information about companies that could affect the price of their stock. Before the news items appeared in the paper, Winans gave financial information to a stockbroker friend so that he could buy or sell the stock in the companies and garner large profits. In return for the information, the stockbroker paid Winans thousands of dollars. Winans' tactics eventually were discovered, and he was convicted of violating securities laws. He had been unethical in using information he had learned in the course of reporting for the financial benefit of himself and a friend.

Other potential conflicts of interest are not as obvious. For example, should reporters and commentators be permitted to accept speaking fees from businesses or organizations they report on as has become widespread practice in recent years? And should reporters and editors who cover business news be allowed to own stock in local companies they report on?

Political Involvement

Conflicts of interest also can arise from a journalist's involvement in politics, as well as participation in some civic and advocacy groups. Columnist George Will was widely criticized for helping prepare Ronald Reagan for his 1980 presidential debate with Jimmy Carter. Few would argue that a journalist shouldn't hold political office for obvious reasons of conflict of interest, but should the same hold true for the family member of a journalist? The husband of the publisher of the Natomas (Cal.) *Journal* was a candidate for the Sacramento City Council. When the *Journal* supported his candidacy, many readers complained, saying that the newspaper was not being objective in its coverage.

Likewise, there is disagreement over whether journalists should participate in advocacy groups such as Greenpeace or the National Organization for Women (NOW). Former *Washington Post* ombudsman Richard Hardwood has said, "You have every right in the world to run for office or participate in a political or lobbying activity. You don't have the 'right' to work for the *Washington Post*." On the other hand, ethics professor Louis Hodges has said, "If you're not involved in the community and you're totally neutralized, you end up not knowing enough about the community, not being able to get enough leads and so on in order to do your job."

Invasion of Privacy

An individual's right to privacy frequently clashes with the public's right to know and with what journalists believe is their responsibility to report. The following situations pose some of the most difficult ethical questions for media organizations.

Crime and Accidents

One of the most controversial areas in the right to privacy debate involves the naming of sex crime victims and the alleged perpetrators.

Because rape and sexual abuse are such physically and emotionally damaging crimes, most news organizations historically have withheld the names of victims unless they grant approval. On the other hand, some journalists argue that sex crime accusers, as well as the accused, should be publicly named so as not to maintain a double standard. And the U.S. Supreme Court has ruled that news organizations can't be punished for publishing information either lawfully obtained or taken from the public record.

Do news organizations have the ethical responsibility to publish the names of suspects in nonsexual criminal cases? This dilemma gained new prominence with the case of Richard Jewell, the man initially accused of setting off the bomb that killed one person and injured dozens at the 1996 Olympic Games in Atlanta. Using tips from unnamed law enforcement sources, the *Atlanta Journal* broke the story of Jewell being the FBI's main suspect. NBC and the Cable News Network soon followed with their own stories about Jewell. A media frenzy ensued. Dozens of reporters and photographers sat outside Jewell's home for weeks and recorded his every move. Jewell and his attorneys complained that the media were invading his privacy. But he remained the subject of intense media scrutiny until the FBI announced he was no longer a suspect in the bombing.

Photographers and videographers also have to be concerned with invasion of privacy when shooting pictures of crime scenes. "If it bleeds, it leads" has been a common saying in television news for years. Yet many journalists believe that especially graphic photos of crime scenes serve no journalistic purpose. CNN issued an on-air apology shortly after it showed graphic video of the dead body of entertainer Bill Cosby's son. The young man was murdered after his car broke down on the Los Angeles freeway. A CNN anchor said showing the video had been a mistake and that it was inappropriate. Moreover, the public decried the photographers chasing the car in which Princess Diana later died.

Illness

Most people also consider illness to be a private matter and historically news organizations have respected that privacy. For example, most news organizations withheld for years that President Franklin D. Roosevelt suffered from polio, even though he held the nation's highest elected office. Today, the health of the country's top political leaders is considered newsworthy because of the important positions they hold. The public has the right to know, many journalists argue, if a politician's leadership abilities could be affected by an illness.

Journalists are more divided when the illness affects less-influential individuals, particularly those with such a personal disease as AIDS. In 1992, a sports reporter for *USA Today* received a tip that former tennis star Arthur Ashe had AIDS. When questioned directly about the illness, Ashe avoided giving an answer. But, when the newspaper pursued the story, Ashe held a news conference and announced he had contracted the virus through a blood transfusion administered during surgery. Ashe also criticized *USA Today* for pursuing the story and called it an invasion of his privacy. Most editors defended *USA Today* because, they said, Ashe was a public figure. But other media observers criticized the newspaper, arguing that the harm it had inflicted was greater than any public benefit that might have been gained.

Former tennis star Arthur Ashe criticized *USA Today* for pursuing a story that he had AIDS, which he received from blood infusion during a heart operation. Ashe, who later died as a result of the virus, called the newspaper's actions an invasion of privacy.

Solving Ethical Problems

As a guide to help mass media practitioners make ethical decisions, media ethics professors Clifford Christians, Kim Rotzoll and Mark Fackler have adapted a model of moral reasoning devised by Dr. Ralph Potter of the Harvard Divinity School. The model, known as the "Potter Box," has four steps:

1. Define the situation. It is absolutely essential that you clearly understand the situation confronting you. In other words, you must be a good reporter and have all the facts.

2. Identify values. The next step is to determine your personal values, along with those of your media organization and the community it serves. Often these values conflict with one another.

3. Apply ethical principles. Examine the ethical principles outlined in this chapter and see which best apply to your situation. There may be more than one.

4. Choose your loyalties. Finally, you have to decide where your loyalty lies. Is it to your media organization, readers, listeners, viewers or your sources?

It's important to view the Potter Box as an organic process and not merely isolated questions. There are no clear answers in many ethical cases.

Exercises

Now that you have an introduction to some of the ethical issues involving the mass media, consider the following case studies. Use the Potter Box method of evaluating ethical situations in answering the questions.

Case Study 1

You're the police reporter for your hometown newspaper. One of your jobs is to gather each day's crime reports and compile them in a regular feature called the "Police Blotter," which has your byline on it. While going through the reports one morning, you see an arrest report for a case of driving while under the influence of alcohol. You recognize the woman's name on the arrest report. She's an old high school classmate who also sings in the church choir with you. Shocked to see her name, you pause over the report for a few minutes, but eventually you copy down the information on the arrest report and go back to the newspaper office. As soon as you sit down at your desk, the phone rings and you hear a sobbing voice. It's the woman who was arrested for drunk driving. She says she knows you see all the police reports and wants to explain what happened last night. She says that she and her husband had gotten into a fight and that she had gone out to have a few drinks and blow off steam. She has never been arrested, she tells you, never even received a traffic ticket. If the arrest report is published, she says, she'll be publicly humiliated and unable to face her friends, especially her friends at church. She begs you not to print the arrest report. What do you do?

Case Study 2

As the news director for your television station, you've received several tips that a local manufacturing plant, the largest employer in the area, is negligent in its safety standards. The sources tell you that fire exits frequently are blocked, safety equipment is substandard and supervisors aren't listening to employees' complaints. Company officials insist they are complying with all safety regulations, but you believe the complaints could be valid. Do you assign an off-air member of your staff (someone who's not recognizable to the public) to get a job with the company and report on what she sees inside the plant? Should you try to find a way to get a hidden camera into the company and videotape what the sources claim is taking place? If the station staff member is required to lie in order to get the job with the company, should you tell her to do so?

Case Study 3

You're a photographer for a daily newspaper, and you're working the Saturday shift. While driving home from lunch, you see an ambulance, police cars and a large group of people along a quiet section of a beachfront park. Curious about what has happened, you park the car, get out and approach the crowd of people. The crowd is circled around the body of a young boy who has drowned. Paramedics were unable to revive him, and, as you walk up, they're preparing to cover him with a sheet for transportation to the morgue. As the paramedics work, his parents are crying hysterically. A police officer is trying to restrain the boy's mother, who wants to continue holding him. Do you take photos of the paramedics covering up the boy and the reaction of the grief-stricken parents? What if you decided to take photos and you artfully captured the poignant scene? Should your newspaper run the photographs? You later take a photo of the covered body and the parents, who have turned their back to the scene and are being led away by a consoling police officer. Would this be a more appropriate photo to publish in the newspaper?

Suggested Readings

Christians, Clifford G., Mark Fackler, and Kim B. Rotzoll. *Media Ethics: Cases & Moral Reasoning.* New York: Longman, 1995. This book provides a method for making ethical decisions and a variety of ethical cases for all forms of the mass media.

Knowlton, Steven R., and Patrick R. Parsons. *The Journalist's Moral Compass.* Westport, Conn.: Praeger, 1995. An introduction to some of the most important journalistic principles along with an overview of the problems that journalists confront in living up to the principles.

Lambeth, Edmund B. *Committed Journalism: An Ethic for the Profession.* Second Edition. Bloomington, Ind.: Indiana University Press. 1992. This book offers a framework for the practice of ethical journalism.

14 Public Relations Practice, Writing and Planning

Ginger Rudeseal Carter, Ph.D.
Assistant Professor, Georgia College & State University
The Opelika-Auburn (Ala.) *News*, The Marietta (Ga.) *Daily Journal*
and *Neighbor Newspapers* and *The Jasper County* (S.C.) *News*.
Jasper County School District and Georgia State University.

Chapter Outline

What is public relations?

The journalist and the practitioner: More alike than you'd think

RACE: The formula for performance in public relations

    Research

    Action

    Communication

    Evaluation

    The formula in a crisis

The basics of public relations writing

Media relations in a nutshell

The ethical practice of public relations

Sidebar A common thread

For years in Atlanta, the local Society of Professional Journalists chapter held a "Hacks vs. Flacks" softball game. The local press (the "Hacks") took on local public relations practitioners (the "Flacks") in a good-natured nine innings. Over the years, though, the benches on the "Flacks" side increasingly filled with former "Hacks." Is it a sin? Treason? Heresy? The spread of free agency?

The shift of reporters into public relations represents the reality of today's media industry. The truth of the matter is many of the public relations industry's finest are former print and broadcast journalists. A look at three months' worth of classified ads in the newsletter for the Georgia Chapter of the Public Relations Society of America shows that one main requirement for PR positions is former media experience. The logic of this requirement is simple: Who better to pitch stories to the media than the former recipients of those pitches? And who better to write news releases or produce video news releases than professionals who did the same for a media outlet?

There are other truths involved in the frequent cross-over from print and broadcast journalism to public relations. Public relations salaries are frequently higher than those in print and broadcast journalism, especially in the midlevel range. The hours are often more routine than in a newspaper or broadcast outlet. And, in the long run, the work of public relations can be very similar to a day in the local news bureau. Many public relations offices are run like newsrooms with beats assigned to specialists. For instance, broadcasters are often assigned to work with other broadcasters.

So who makes the switch? For example, of 12 of my college friends—journalism majors who worked on the Georgia State University *Signal* in the mid-1970s—only Jim Auchmutey, an award-winning feature reporter for the Atlanta *Journal-Constitution,* is still working on a daily newspaper. Within this circle of 12, eight are in public relations full- or part-time; one is a journalism professor and two are lawyers. These are not startling statistics, but they represent a trend.

There are other examples, beginning with my own career. After years of covering high school sports and the local cop shop, I took on my first public relations job as the public information officer of the Jasper County School District. I later worked as a public relations specialist for Georgia State University and directed a statewide anti-prejudice program called "A World of Difference." Brent Gilroy, a former reporter for the Greenville (S.C.) *Piedmont,* the Marietta *Daily Journal* and *Building Design Journal,* took a different route. Now vice president of business development for Powell-Tate, a Washington, D.C., public relations firm, Gilroy served as press secretary to former Georgia Rep. Buddy Darden. He said his news skills were a valuable asset when he began working with the media.

The PR profession is an honorable one, requiring many of the same talents as the print and broadcast media. This chapter will define and discuss public relations practice in addition to some basic methods of public relations writing.

What Is Public Relations?

"Why did you select public relations as your major?" the question on the scholarship application read. "Because I just love people, and I love PR!" came the response from the young applicant. Nowhere did she mention a love of writing, a love of information dissemination or a love of free and responsible media. Personality and people skills are not the only attributes of a successful public relations practitioner today.

For years, the Goodyear blimp has been an effective way to promote goodwill for the tire company by providing panoramic shots of sporting events.

Public relations is so much more than looking nice and meeting people. The industry is fighting to put aside this old stereotypical image of the PR person. But how does one define public relations today? There are many definitions, but the best one merges history, scholarship, *Webster's Dictionary* and common sense. As PR great Paul Garrett, former vice president of General Motors, put it, "We need not so much a fresh definition of public relations as a fresh point of view with regard to it." So let's look at public relations through its attributes rather than as a rigid definition.

Public relations is a management function. This means that there's an institutional commitment to the process. Your organization's management knows what you're doing and why you're doing it. Most of all, it supports you in it. That permits a greater realm of opportunity and operation, as well as a support system. Frankly, this is no different from the management backing of a civic journalism project. The action is for the greater good. This element has become the most important one in the definition of public relations, and it's a fairly new attribute.

Public relations is planned and deliberate, not spur-of-the-moment, seat-of-the-pants hucksterism. *Planned* means that before the first release is written the practitioner has constructed a road map for reporters. There's a goal and a stated objective. *Deliberate* suggests some cultivation of a source and strategy.

Public relations is performed in the public interest. In their book *Toxic Sludge Is Good For You,* John Stauber and Sheldon Rampton suggest that the practitioner frequently ignores what's best for the public while focusing on the client's needs. In fact, there are examples of all media performing in this manner. This concept deserves thought: What about a product/person/event serves the public? What's the angle? If you could write the key impact paragraph of the story, what would it say? Odds are that the information has a link to the public.

Public relations involves interactive, two-way communication. In the early days, public relations was more publicity than anything else. The old model of communication looked something like this:

Did the receiver get the message and, more important, did the receiver act on it? Who knows? This model didn't permit any other variables.

Today, however, public relations relies on two-way communication with the reporter. With the advent of the Internet, e-mail, fax and overnight delivery, the process has been speeded up. Public relations is not practiced in a vacuum—not successfully, at least.

- Noise—such as external functions, interference, technological malfunctions—encircles the message.

- People listen to and evaluate the message.

- Feedback is reciprocal and constant.

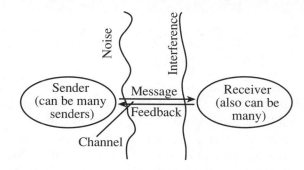

Communication
Environment

Sidebar 1

A Common Thread

In spite of the legendary adversarial relationship between journalists and public relations practitioners, the relationship is symbiotic. Reporters count on PR practitioners for information and tips on the news; PR practitioners count on reporters to place their stories. Both sides have motives, of course. And, in the strictest sense, all are involved in propaganda. There are other commonalities:

- Both journalism and PR are mass communication fields concerned with the dissemination of information to the public.

- Both journalism and PR put a high priority on the news value of an event or activity.

- Both journalism and PR are made up of committed communicators.

- Both journalism and PR are involved in the gatekeeping process—that is, both fields make a decision about what should run and what shouldn't.

- Both journalism and PR depend on making the public act, think, do, change or move. Both are engaged in agenda setting or making the public think about something for the purpose of action.

- Finally, both journalism and PR are concerned with legal and ethical behavior in the performance of a daily job. Both fields have professional organizations with codes of ethics to guide members' behavior.

Public relations targets its audience. Reporters examine two questions before writing anything: Who is my audience, and why do they care? The questions also apply to public relations; press releases are specifically crafted for an audience just like news. Who is the audience for your release, and why should it be used? This is the essence of targeted public relations.

All these elements add up to a definition of a broad, growing field. As the field and its jobs change, so will the definition. Just as the role of the journalist has changed over the years, so has the role of the PR practitioner.

The Journalist and the Practitioner: More Alike Than You'd Think

If we can define public relations, can we also define the attributes of the PR professional? All the admonitions for journalists in earlier chapters of this textbook also apply to the budding public relations practitioner. Being well-versed in the news and issues of the day—as well as the reporters who are reporting that news—is a key requirement of the PR job. You must know who is covering what, and you must know who needs your information.

During my career as a public relations specialist at Georgia State University, it was my job to let the public know about research at the university. I sent out news releases daily on the activities within my colleges. I also watched the happenings of the day so I could place the university's "experts" in the news. When terrorists struck, I used the mail, phone and fax machine to let reporters know that Georgia State had a professor who specialized in terrorism. When the U.S. Census reported that people were moving from the city to the suburbs at a rapid clip, I passed along the name of a geography professor. An earthquake in South America put our local geologist on the news.

Being informed about news and society is essential to the public relations job. How can you be a good and effective communicator without knowing what's going on?

RACE: The Formula for Performance in Public Relations

Now that you know what public relations is and how you fit into the picture, how do you do it? Is there a basic way to approach a PR campaign?

Whether you're planning for a special event or trying to get coverage for someone else's event, there's a simple formula available that will help you plan. Most public relations textbooks or primers suggest adherence to a formula represented by the acronym RACE. *R* is for research, *A* is for action (as in, what action will meet your goal?), *C* is for communication, and *E* is for evaluation. The RACE model is especially good for planning for or creating a special event. Some agencies even have worksheets to break down this process and to use along the way. Consider it every time you have a PR problem to solve. No matter what the problem, these four stages will help solve it. RACE can be broken down into a plethora of subquestions and outcomes.

Research

What's your problem? What's the history of the problem? How has it been handled before? What are the goals and wishes of the sponsors? How much money is available to work on the problem? Who can you call on for assistance in your project? What's your timeline for the project? Who's your audience? Why do they care?

At the end of the research for the project, a question or an overall goal should be stated. This is most useful when evaluating the success or failure of the project. Above all, the team has a foundation and a plan of action to move forward on. Don't scrimp on this step!

Action

What materials do you need to prepare for this event or to disseminate this news? Should you hold a news conference? Do you need a press kit? Do you need any photographs for the media? Who will staff the event? Who are your experts? Who's on your mailing list? Are the addresses and names correct and updated?

At the end of the action planning, the materials for the project will be prepared, proofed, printed and disseminated. This step could take several days, or it could take several months. More individuals are drawn into the process at this stage.

Communication

Have you invited everyone in your audience, either formally or informally? Have you met the deadlines for the media to permit the publication or broadcast of this material? Who should you call to personally pitch the story? What sort of feedback is available for you to work with?

At this stage of the project, the media materials are disseminated, and you work with the media. Up to the day of the event, this becomes a checks and balances system. At this stage, don't lose sight of your goal. Don't become discouraged. Above all, keep the information available and updated. In today's market, new technology, such as e-mail and the World Wide Web and its sites are useful at this stage. For example, when planning for a recent conference, I was able to communicate via e-mail with the op-ed editor of the Atlanta *Journal-Constitution* through the critical editing of an article. No more telephone tag! I also used the conference's information-filled Web page to inform reporters of the conference's program. Instead of sending a bulky information packet, I sent an abbreviated version and directed reporters to the Web. The reporters from the Atlanta *Journal-Constitution*, Associated Press and C-SPAN all used this information to update their works in progress.

Evaluation

Were there kinks in your plans? Did you get the attention you had hoped for? Did you make any new media friends who will be receptive to your information in the future (a journalist would call these "sources," and many PR people call them that, too)? Did you stay within budget? Did you fail? If so, why? I once planned a large and lavish press conference with a nationally known track star. At the hour of the conference, there was a four-alarm fire in one of Atlanta's oldest historic neighborhoods. No one showed up for the press conference. What could I have done to avoid this?

Evaluation also suggests that you collect your news clippings and mentions and send them to the person you're representing. This is a courtesy, but it also provides closure on the job. This also allows you to reinforce the importance of the public relations role.

The Formula in a Crisis

This formula also works for crisis public relations, although the process is expedited. When a crisis happens, PR professionals must think on their feet. The rule of thumb is never to lie to a reporter, or it will come back to haunt you. It has been reported that Jody Powell, press secretary to former President Jimmy Carter, asked not to be told about the plans to rescue American hostages in Iran in 1980. Powell said he would rather tell reporters the truth—that he didn't know anything—than lie when he did know details he couldn't disclose.

The Basics of Public Relations Writing

One week, my professor at Georgia State sent me to the mayor's office to work with Press Secretary John Head. I balked at working in the PR office for a week—I protested that I didn't even know how to write a news release. "Write it like a news story," my professor said. "It's really nothing more than that." Twenty years—and thousands of releases—later, I still write news releases like basic news stories. Good PR writing uses all the attributes of good news writing. Why not? If you want to communicate with a reporter, you have to speak his or her language. This is more than courtesy, but that's a simple name for it.

The basic format for a news release is simple. First, place the release on letterhead paper. About one-third of the page down type

`For Immediate Release`

`The date`

`Contact: Your name`

Many firms have a variation on this format, but this slug line should provide basic information. When did the event happen? Does the reporter have to wait to use the release? Who can help the reporter if he or she has a question?

Next type a headline. Use standard English and use capital letters and lowercase type style. Make it bold or underlined if you'd like to, but this isn't necessary.

`Former President and Mrs. Carter to speak at town hall meeting March 6`

At a glance, a reporter knows if this is something he or she needs.

Then write your lead. Generally speaking, a standard inverted pyramid news lead is best in this situation. What do you need people to know?

`A Georgia College & State University professor won the Pulitzer Prize for feature reporting Thursday.`

Practitioner Mary Jean Land uses a format of lead called "Stop Digging Here," which also would work for the basic release lead:

S (subject): Former President and Mrs. Carter

T (topic): Their presidential years

O (organization): Sponsored by Georgia State and six other colleges

P (place): At the Carter Presidential Library

D (date): March 6

H (hour): At 1 p.m.

You've quickly organized your facts and can include what's most essential in the lead. As you know from earlier chapters in this book, once the basic facts are gathered, it's easy to piece together a lead that reads

`Former President Jimmy Carter and his wife, Rosalyn, will talk about the presidential years in a town hall-style press conference at 1 p.m., March 6, at the Carter Presidential Library.`

Use whatever style of reporting you'd like for the rest of the story, as long as it looks like a story. If you have a personality who has done something, interview him or her and write a short feature. Include quotes when possible. Reporters may say they don't need quotes, but, if you offer good ones, reporters will use them. (See Chapter 6 for more information on using quotations.)

How long should a news release be? I've written some releases as short as one page and as long as four pages. Like any news item, you should write it for what it's worth. Don't force a story to be longer than it is. You wouldn't do that as a journalist, so why do it as a public relations practitioner? Use "Add 1" or "Page 2" at the top of the second page.

Your last paragraph should list additional contacts. A statement that says, "to interview Professor Wilson, call (912) 555-1212, or call Mary Doe for more information" lets the reporter know that more information is available. When your release is about an upcoming event, the last paragraph is a good place to include information such as price, directions and other details: "The conference will be held in Suite 2 of the Smith Building, One Park Place, located on the corner of Peachtree Street and Park Place in downtown Atlanta. Admission is $15 and includes lunch." When you've finished a release, put –30–, ### or a similar mark at the end. This lets the reporter know you're through.

Use AP style. Spell check and then proofread your release, because you don't have a copy editor to clean up behind you. If you can, have someone else proof the release. Make sure your grammar makes sense and you haven't misplaced your modifiers or mixed your metaphors. Check the calendar and make sure March 6 is really a Thursday. These may sound like picky suggestions, but some reporters like to make fun of news releases with errors in them. I know one reporter who will throw away a news release with a typo in it. I also worked in a newsroom where reporters posted news releases with errors in them, looking for the biggest mistake of the week. You won't be there to see your work laughed at, but remember: If your release is on someone's bulletin board, it won't make it in the paper or on the air. Note the example of a working news release. Keep it clean, keep it simple.

Must you always use a news release format for informing the media? No, but most practitioners use a version of it. A backgrounder is a sheet that gives detailed information and is part of the press kit; the tip sheet might be a personal letter, memo or note to the reporter. The planning for the event will dictate what's needed. Most offices still produce reams of news releases a year, making it the workhorse of the public relations field.

Media Relations in a Nutshell

During the process of a campaign or placement, the PR practitioner is ultimately forced to contact a media representative. This interaction is what is generically known as media relations. Personal contacts go a lot further than cold ink on paper. But some people are better at media relations than others; it depends on their confidence level on the telephone. When you've made a personal contact and know the person, this call is far simpler; when it's a "cold call," the first contact, then it's more difficult.

The first rule of business is that, before you consider the pitch, do your homework. Remember: Who is your audience, and why do they need this story? Make sure you're calling the right person and give ample time for action. I once worked for a weekly paper with a Monday noon deadline. The PR person from an Atlanta hotel called the Monday before Thanksgiving at 5 p.m. to pitch me Polynesian Thanksgiving recipes. First of all, she missed my deadline. Second, the paper didn't print recipes. Third, the people of Smyrna, Ga., weren't exactly Mai Tai Turkey kind of people. She wasted her time trying to reach me. Had she done her homework, she never would have called me.

NEWS

Georgia State University

Department of Public Information
University Plaza
Atlanta, Georgia 30303-3083
404/651-3570
FAX 404/651-3667

For Immediate Release
Contact: Ginger Carter   (404) 651-3579
           Gary Moss or George deGolian   (404) 651-3311

GULLAH TALES NOMINATED FOR ACADEMY AWARD

Gullah Tales, a film by Atlantans Gary Moss and George deGolian, has been nominated for an Academy Award for Best Live Action Short Film.

"We're delighted by this honor. We made an excellent film, and we feel it deserves the recognition," said Moss, producer/director of the Georgia State University Office of Educational Media.

Written and directed by Moss and produced by Moss and deGolian, *Gullah Tales* weaves a colorful tale of an underdog, faced with an impossible situation, who comes out the winner. It is narrated in Gullah by Janie Hunter, a well-known Gullah storyteller from John's Island, S.C. The entire film features authentic Gullah language, settings and costume. Dr. Clara W. Howell served as executive producer of the film.

Direct Cinema Limited, the distributor of Gullah Tales, entered the 22-minute film in the competition.

"The other films in the category were all Hollywood produced with Hollywood actors and bigger budgets," Moss said. "*Gullah Tales*, which only cost $30,000 to make, was not produced as an entertainment film but as an educational film."

The nomination, deGolian added, is unique for filmmakers from this part of the country.

"There haven't been many nominations from the South, which makes this even more of an honor," he said. "For an educational film to be nominated for an Academy Award is unprecedented."

The two men who play lead roles in the film, Jerry G. White and Stace McDaniel, live in Atlanta. White, who played John in the film, said he was very excited about the nomination.

"It speaks to the quality of this film that it was nominated," he said. "I am pleased to have been part of the cast of the film."

Gullah Tales, which was supported by grants from the Georgia Endowment for the Humanities and the South Carolina Committee for the Humanities, was filmed on location at Middleton Place in Charleston and Hofwyl/Broadfield Plantation in Brunswick, Ga. It is the third film in Moss' series on American folk life. The first film, "Man of Lightning," is the story of the American Indian, and the second, "Old Dry Frye," is based on an Appalachian folktale. "Old Dry Frye" won a Georgia Emmy Award for best entertainment special in 1986.

30

Good public relations writing uses all the same attributes of good writing. The basic format for the news release provides news, important details and contact names and addresses.

The second rule is to know the reporter's deadline. Would you call Dan Rather in New York at 6:20 p.m.? No, because you know he's about to go on the air. Plan to make your call when you know it's not deadline. In newspapers, the deadline time depends on whether it's a morning or an evening paper. As a dry run, call the receptionist and ask when the deadlines are. In television and radio, check broadcast time and plan around it.

When you connect with a reporter on the phone, the second words out of your mouth (after you identify yourself) should be "Have I caught you on a deadline?" If the reporter says no, you have the green light to pitch your story. Have the details in front of you. Make it succinct. Don't babble or ramble. Now that we have e-mail and fax, it's easy to say, "I'll zip the details over to you if you'll give me your fax number." Be aware, though, that some reporters don't want to give out those addresses and numbers. At one time, the *New York Times* newsroom changed its fax number every month so PR people wouldn't inundate the machine with releases.

Most important, don't ever call a reporter and ask, "Did you get my release?" This is a waste of time and, frankly, an insult. If it's that important, pitch it personally. If it's not, mail it and take your chances. In media relations, sometimes the reporter comes to you for an expert or more information on an event. The guidelines are similar. Remember the deadlines and get back to the person as soon as possible. If you don't have someone or can't help, be honest and say so. (Nothing makes a reporter angrier than a forced expert.) Truth, once again, is the most important thing.

The Ethical Practice of Public Relations

Ethical public relations is not an oxymoron, any more than ethical journalism is. Public relations practitioners, in general, consider good character, trust and honesty important elements of their work.

Both the Public Relations Society of America (PRSA) and the International Association of Business Communicators (IABC), two prominent organizations made up of PR consultants, have strict codes of ethics. The code asks members to pledge "to conduct ourselves professionally, with truth, accuracy, fairness and responsibility to the public: to improve individual competence and advance the knowledge and proficiency of the profession through continuing research and education." The Code of Ethics warns practitioners against lying to a client, making guarantees of placements, taking kickbacks and invading a client's privacy. Violation of PRSA's code of ethics could mean expulsion from the organization. However, the PRSA code applies only to PRSA members.

The material covered in Chapter 13 of this textbook applies to the public relations professional as well as the journalist. Ethics exist as a road map for behavior, and PR professionals strive to keep their behavior above board.

Exercises

1. Check out the public relations textbooks in your department or school's reading room, or examine books in your library. Look at the books' definitions of public relations. How has the definition changed over the years?

2. On the World Wide Web, do a keyword search of public relations agencies. What do you find?

3. Interview a public relations practitioner about job requirements. In a short essay, discuss how journalistic training is an asset to the public relations professional.

4. Review advertisements for public relations positions in your local newspaper or in a newsletter from the Public Relations Society of America or the International Association of Business Communicators. How many require media experience? What other requirements are listed for these positions? (Note: Sometimes positions for exotic dancers or club hostesses are listed under public relations. Determine the legitimate public relations jobs by the content of the advertisements.)

5. Your school wants to begin an annual media day for local high school seniors. Using the RACE model, work through the four steps. You have a $500 budget for all elements of the day, including invitations, programs and publicity. You will also be reaching out to students whose schools are within 45 minutes of your campus. Break into groups of three or four and plan the event.

6. Read an account of the Tylenol poisoning scare or the Exxon *Valdez* tragedy and evaluate the company's public relations effort for its application of the RACE model. Did the company do the best possible thing in responding to a crisis?

7. Your local professional chapter of the Society of Professional Journalists is bringing ABC news anchor Barbara Walters to town to speak. As an added benefit, Walters will spend two hours with journalism students at your school. As the student president of the SPJ chapter on campus, you've been selected to write a news release about the visit. For your college media and the local newspapers, write a news release that announces the visit. You can set the date three weeks from now, and you should figure that the school paper has a Thursday noon deadline for Friday publication.

8. You're the director of public relations for the Central Steel Warehouse, a large steel fabricating factory on the outskirts of town. At 9 a.m. today, you receive a call from the manager of your assembly department. He tells you a 20-foot-high stack of pipes has collapsed and that at least three workers are caught under the pile. The manager has called 911, and police and rescue squads are on the way, but the rumor mill is already at work. In fact, the minute you hang up the phone, the local radio reporter is on the line saying he's heard there's been an accident. What do you do?

Suggested Readings

Cutlip, Scott M. *The Unseen Power: Public Relations. A History.* Hillsdale, N.J.: L. Erlbaum Associates, 1994. Cutlip's book is the most contemporary history of public relations.

Cutlip, Scott M., Allen H. Center, and Glenn Broom. *Effective Public Relations.* Englewood Cliffs, N.J.: Prentice-Hall, 1964. This book is the definitive textbook on public relations.

Stauber, John, and Sheldon Rampton. *Toxic Sludge Is Good for You.* Monroe, Maine: Common Courage Press, 1995. This book takes an interesting look at the darker, less ethical side of public relations.

15 Advertising

Ron Schie
Assistant Professor, West Virginia University
McDonald, Babb & Clarkson and Tektronix International Inc.

Chapter Outline

The future

Freedom of speech

The changing environment

Creativity

Design

Strategy

Writing

Sidebar Information is important

Do you want to know how much people disagree about advertising? Take a look at these three views:

- "The force of the advertising word and image dwarfs the power of other literature in the 20th century," said author Daniel J. Boorstin.

- "Historians and archaeologists will one day discover that the ads of our time are the richest and the most faithful reflections that any society ever made of its entire range of activities," the late media maven Marshall McLuhan said.

- "Advertising is selling Twinkies to adults," argued analyst Donald R. Vance.

This chapter will explore where advertising is today and where it's going in the future. The chapter will discuss technology's impact on the advertising industry, then come back to some suggestions for creating successful advertising, many of which are communication basics learned during my many years in advertising.

Advertising is a career path for bright, creative, enthusiastic people who are willing to work long days. Although some of the brightest people I've ever met work in the advertising business, I'm not going to try to convince you that it's brain surgery. Yet over the years I spent in advertising I developed a healthy respect for the people and the process. When done poorly, advertising makes me cringe with embarrassment. But advertising done well makes me laugh, cry, stand up and applaud and, yes, sometimes go out to the store and buy.

I never wanted to be an advertiser. I thought I'd write plays, songs, poetry or books. Instead, I spent 20 years thinking in 30- and 60-second blocks of time and writing headlines and body copy to sell everything from beans and onions to computer chips and oscilloscopes. There were magical days when ideas clicked and clients cheered. There were torturous days and nights when things just wouldn't fall into place or, worse, when the best ideas were rejected. It was often exciting and fun—other times, frustrating and exhausting. It's a business that devours ideas and demands hard work and commitment from the people it chooses.

Brain surgery it's not; selling it is. At a seminar, I heard Don Schultz, professor of integrated marketing communications at Northwestern University, use an example of a "knock-knock" game to explain advertising. As an advertiser you must place yourself outside the door of your prospective customer and, when he or she answers the knock, know what to say to keep the door open and make a sale. The point he was making, of course, is that as an advertiser you must have something meaningful to say—something that will communicate a benefit to that customer—or the door will close in your face. You must have a strategy. Advertising is simply delivering an effective sales message to prospective buyers of a product or service. Unfortunately, it's not always so easy, as is apparent by some of the awful advertising that's out there.

Advertising's role throughout history has been to match buyer with seller. Today, in our economic system, we have an abundance of products and services for the use and enjoyment of consumers. Most of our present economic system goes well beyond simply supplying life's necessities, as other motivating factors fuel the existing "shop 'til you drop" mentality. For better or worse, advertising plays a major role in this activity. Potential buyers still look to advertising to provide information about products and services.

Perhaps advertising's greatest importance to our economic system is how it subsidizes other media. Commercial radio and television stations depend almost entirely on advertising revenue for income, and advertising constitutes two-thirds of the income for newspaper and magazine publishing.

The Future

Today, we're experiencing an information transition as we move from the linear world of reading and writing to the graphic universe of the next century. Technology is giving companies new and more effective ways to reach customers and prospects. Database marketing, home shopping channels, infomercials, electronic coupons and the World Wide Web are all emerging as the cost effective ways to deliver messages. These new channels of information offer variety, convenience, flexibility and customization.

Advertising will be an important part of the future as this new information delivery system develops and expands. Just as advertising subsidizes the traditional media, it will also be the primary source of income for the new media. Advertising will continue to be an economic fact of life in a mass distribution economy, as in the past, it will be more effective and less costly than other alternatives.

Freedom of Speech

As outlined in this book, speech is protected under the First Amendment. But, in case after case, commercial speech has been less protected than other forms of speech. This is in part caused by the legal system's failure to adequately define commercial speech. And yet, this reluctance reflects the view of the public, who are wary of advertising and the media. Media are blamed for the loss of community, the corruption of youth, the promotion of sex and violence and any number of other societal problems. Because of the profit motive and the media's dependence on commercial advertising, the public's uncertainty and suspicions are great.

New media and new marketing communications techniques that are now possible are viewed by the public with this same distrust. It's natural to fear the unknown, and new technologies will undoubtedly lead to demands for regulation. Advertising must proceed into this new media world with caution. Already suspicious of advertising, consumers may develop even stronger negative attitudes toward marketers, and this could result in government intervention.

The Changing Environment

The media scene has been changing for some time, and along with these changes the advertising industry has been in a state of transition. The days when an agency could place most of a client's budget with the three major networks are long gone. In 1994, Edwin Artzt, chairman of Procter & Gamble, called for ad agencies to "get involved with the new media or lose their business." In 1995, network television dropped from reaching 90 percent of the U.S. population to about 60 percent in less than 20 years. The advertising industry took notice.

The computer has changed the very nature of the media. "Narrowcasting" is becoming the buzzword. That's where a highly customized industry caters to specific audiences, or "niches," in a marketing and advertising strategy. Selective content for a specific audience can be provided with reasonable cost and efficiency. New media have been created to reach select groups of consumers, and the old media have been reworked to meet the more specific demands of today's consumer. Production of mass quantities of identical messages don't work as well as they used to.

Some of the most dramatic changes are taking place in the interactivity consumers have with media. New media, but also traditional media, are increasingly offering opportunities for audience members to communicate and receive a quick response. Television news programs, home shopping programs and advertisers are providing phone numbers, e-mail addresses and fax lines to establish a flow of information. It is no longer the monologue as in the past, but a dialogue.

Access to a wider variety of entertainment and information is easier than ever. But for selective, interesting media and vehicles, access can be involved and time-consuming. The "new media" can require considerable effort to gain exposure. Think of the number of steps involved in accessing e-mail, and this is one of the more user friendly of the totally interactive "new media."

Other factors influence advertising, including the move toward a global economy and the changing demographics of the American population. Businesses and industries continue to expand markets outside the United States. There is really no choice. Competition for the U.S. consumer, as well as for international customers, is wide open with technology enabling relatively small companies to compete with giant corporations. Even the U.S. domestic market increasingly becomes more global and multicultural.

New consumer groups are emerging such as the Hispanic population, which grew 17 percent in only five years to nearly 28 million people in 1996. Hispanics now are about 10 percent of the U.S. population.

Globalization and multicultural diversity in our society places particular demands on advertisers. Markets fragment and divide into niche segments, requiring individual messages for specific groups of consumers.

What do these developments mean for creativity and success in advertising? First, messages need to be specific and individually targeted at a savvy and sophisticated consumer. Second, the computer, not long ago reluctantly accepted by the advertising industry, will be the tool for the advertising industry. The computer is an important advertising tool used by artists, designers, writers and art directors to develop and produce materials for both print and electronic media. Copywriters now compose, edit and proofread with speed and ease. Art directors no longer need typesetters and photo houses because a personal computer can generate type and graphics. Finished "comprehensives," or "comps," are produced quickly for client review and approval meetings. A comp is as complete a representation as possible of a print advertisement without finished artwork. This means the ad's design is complete; the typeface has been chosen and has been either hand-lettered or more likely computer-generated to approximate the final product. The ad is as close to final as possible because the comp is used to sell the idea to the person making the final decisions.

Slides and color comps are easily generated and used for presentations. With a television commercial, the storyboard is the visual layout of the commercial. As the concept is revised and finalized, the script becomes more detailed and the storyboard art more finished. A finished storyboard is equivalent to a comprehensive in print.

To make the storyboard even more realistic, the frames may be shot on slides for presentation to the client. If the frames are recorded on videotape along with a rough soundtrack, the storyboard is called an "animatic." Animatics are frequently used for client presentations and market research sessions.

The computer is only a tool, however. Art directors must exercise caution and not allow computerized processes or software to define the creativity. Unfortunately, the attitude exists that anyone possessing appropriate hardware and software instantly becomes a talented designer or art director. In reality, what he or she possesses is the ability to design mediocre but technically well-produced work.

Creativity

We all think we know creativity when we see it or hear it. But determining what qualifies as "truly" creative or agreeing on a definition of *creativity* is not as easy. We know it's what clients pay big money to obtain. It's what's necessary to break through the cluttered media environment.

Advertising has always been the business of ideas, and that has never been more true than it is today. Still, it remains difficult to agree on just what a creative idea is. The addition of new technologies and media may complicate the argument even more.

Design

Advertising design has changed drastically in recent years and continues to evolve. Rules for specific layouts and word counts for print advertising today seem meaningless. Traditional formulas, which stated that scenes in commercials should be limited in number and remain on the screen for three to six seconds, seem almost laughable when compared with the rapid-fire delivery of MTV and others like it. Images and type are often layered and placed anywhere around the page.

Whereas graphics have evolved and have become more complex, the language of advertising tends toward simplicity. No longer must headlines be a certain type size or length. If no headline works, so be it. If a longer headline fits the strategy, as many words as necessary can be used. And the cynicism of audiences reared on advertising is evident in overly exaggerated, hyperbole-filled messages that wink at you from the page or screen, or perhaps the other extreme, with honest, straightforward messages as if in reaction to previous exaggerated claims and half truths. In either case, the changes are evident.

This is not to say that there's no place for traditional design. The designer's task is to combine the old and new in strategically innovative ways. Audiences will continue to adapt to these new forms of marketing communication.

Technology will speed up and deepen this process. Now, rather than clipping a coupon from a newspaper or magazine, the customer can simply double click with a computer mouse on the advertisement. Instead of driving to the shopping mall to buy, the customer can order on line. But advertising will also become easier to avoid, and separating content from advertising will be a relatively simple process.

"Ads will no longer be limited by time and space. Customers will choose to interact with advertising that truly assists them in making decisions," says Avram Miller, vice president of business development for Intel Corp. "Not only will ads be more pertinent, customers will be able to order products while interacting with these ads, thereby increasing the value of the experience."

IMC is an acronym an advertiser needs to know. It stands for integrated marketing communications. Creators of advertising must use all the tools at their disposal to develop a strategy. It must start with the consumer's needs and wants, not necessarily what the manufacturer wants to feature. The strategy must have a clear, concise, easily understandable and competitive sales message—one message—to deliver to each consumer. This message may be carried through advertising, public relations, a promotional event, store displays, packaging and direct marketing. Each part of the strategy must reinforce and support the others as a single communications system.

Following is an example of integrated marketing communications. With Olympics marketing more cluttered than ever, Coca-Cola made an early decision to

Pepsi and Coca-Cola have developed advertising strategies to promote their brand names throughout the world.

break from the mold of linking a sponsoring brand to athletes. The company decided instead to link Coca-Cola Classic to fans. "We decided not to do Olympics advertising during the Olympics," Coke's marketing chief Sergio Zyman said. Coke began airing ads entitled "For the Fans" four months before the games started in 1996. Shortly thereafter, the Olympic Torch Relay began winding its way across

Sidebar

America, courtesy of Coca-Cola. The marketer made maximum use of the relay, generating national interest with celebrity torchbearers and local interest with a grassroots nomination program that enabled thousands of ordinary Americans to carry the flame. In all, more than 5,500 torchbearers participated in the relay. "With the torch, we said to our consumers, 'We want you to have the chance to be at the Olympics, even if you're not going to Atlanta,' " Zyman said. Meanwhile, in stores, Coca-Cola ran a fairly standard under-the-cap consumer sweepstakes, "Red Hot Olympic Summer." And, in Atlanta during the games, the company sponsored Coca-Cola Olympic City, an entertainment, shopping and dining complex. The sum of all the parts was an Olympic sponsorship that stood apart from most of the others by underscoring, again and again, one of Coke's core brand values. "The Coca-Cola brand stands for bringing people together," said Steve Graham, vice president of marketing communications at AT&T Corp. and a former Coca-Cola manager.

Strategy

You're standing outside the consumer's door, ready to knock and make the sale. What are you going to say to get the door open and your message heard? You need a strategy.

Ideally, you should develop your strategy before you start to create. After all, the strategy is the map to guide the creative team through successful execution. But strategy development is an ongoing, dynamic process, and you may come up with ideas that change your direction. Don't be afraid to refine or even totally rewrite your strategy. Just make certain that the strategy you end up with is tight, not vague and open to interpretation.

Your strategy should include the following:

- The product or service—what it is, what it does, how it's used and what it will do for your target

- The target. This is not a meaningless demographic, but a description of who this person is. Write to an individual.

- The competition. If the targeted individuals don't buy your product, what do they buy instead?

- The problem your advertising will solve. Here it's good to summarize research findings that identify the problem. If people don't know your product is in the marketplace, then "awareness" is the problem. It could be a "negative perception" problem, price or something else entirely.

- The advertising objective. What will your advertising do? It should solve the problem you identified.

- Product features and benefits. This is where you get into what it's going to do for your target. For example, the product has a feature such as vitamin E oil, which translates into the benefit of smoother, softer and healthier skin.

- The tone and character. This is simply a statement that describes the feeling your advertising will convey: wild and fun, sensitive and caring, traditional and trustworthy.

The importance of this process is that you learn to think through your ideas. You don't have to work in a sequence. Just make certain you hit all the points as you think through the process. It's the way to come up with good advertising.

Writing

Nike has developed an image as a high-power sport company by advertising with high-profile sports stars like golfer Tiger Woods.

Now it's time to write. I believe in getting words on paper quickly. There's plenty of time to edit and rewrite later. Sometimes it helps just to write out what you want to say. Don't worry if it's clever or memorable. Just get it on paper.

You want your advertising to differentiate your client from the competition, but don't be different just to be different. Your difference has to be relevant to the benefit of the product you're selling.

Make sure your ad is true. Make sure the claim in your ad can't be contested. Above all, you want to be believed. There are certain core values that will never change. People want to feel better, look better, be richer and be respected. Fads and trends come and go, but these core values stay the same.

Be visual. Keep your copy short. Get people's interest with your headline and visual and then get them to call the telephone number for additional information.

Be simple. Don't worry if someone doesn't like your ad, as long as he or she understands it.

Read award books. Use them for ideas. Appreciate the thinking and let it inspire you.

Read books, magazines and newspapers, as many as you can get your hands on. Go to a library reading room and go through every magazine in the place. You have to keep up with what's happening.

It's all in the details. Never say, "I guess it's good enough." If it bothers you at all, work on it. Fix it. The difference between mediocre advertising and great advertising is often in the details.

Listen. Your mind isn't a faucet that can be turned on and off. If it's not working, if ideas aren't flowing, take a walk. Go to the gym and work out. Don't exhaust yourself, trying to make something work. Leave it and come back, and maybe "Voilà!"

Keep a file of your ideas that get shot down. If they're good, you'll get the chance to use them.

Don't underestimate yourself. If you want to work at a particular agency, give it a shot. Creative people too often underestimate their own talents.

Exercises

Research and analyze these ad campaigns:

Xerox—"Brother Dominic." Needham, Harper & Steers. 1976. Helped establish Xerox as "THE Document Company."

Apple Macintosh—"1984." Chiat/Day. 1984. Called the greatest commercial ever made, it helped launch Apple's Macintosh with a not-so-subtle jab at IBM. The spot, followed by product advertising on TV and a 20-page magazine insert, helped Apple exceed its goal of selling 50,000 Macs in 100 days.

Intel—"Intel Inside." Dahlin, Smith, White. 1991. Stressing speed, power and affordability, the campaign also has had a strong print component over the years. The "Intel Inside" tag line has continued through successive generations of Intel computer chips.

Nike—Simply placed a shoe onto a blank page and added an 800 number that people could call.

The Swoosh. Designed by an art student at Portland State for $35 is the only message Nike needs. Simple, eloquent communication is what great advertising has always been about. But what makes Nike's marketing efforts so successful is the consistency of their integrated marketing communications and advertising efforts over the past 10 years.

Suggested Readings

Gossage, Howard Luck. *The Book of Gossage*. Chicago: The Copy Workshop, 1995. Howard Gossage died in 1969, the year I got into the advertising business. I had never heard of him until a few years ago when I read several quotes he made in *Advertising Age*. Then I picked up this book and was amazed how relevant his views remained.

Rotzoll, Kim B. and James E. Haefner. *Advertising in Contemporary Society: Perspectives Toward Understanding*. Champaign, Ill.: University of Illinois Press, 1996. This book does an excellent job of explaining advertising in a way that cuts through much of the misinformation that often clouds discussions on the subject.

Upshaw, Lynn B. *Building Brand Identity*. New York: John Wiley & Sons, Inc., 1995. Brand identity has never been easy to establish and maintain. With the fragmentation of conventional media and the unprecedented amount of marketplace clutter, establishing a bran is even more difficult today than ever. This book, which contains many examples of understanding consumers and their needs, should be required reading for anyone thinking about a career in advertising.

16 Reading to Write

Robert E. Wernsman Jr.
Instructor and Honors Program Coordinator, Texas Tech
  University
The Huntsville (Texas) *Item, The Big Spring* (Texas) *Herald, The
  Knoxville* (Iowa) *Record, State Center* (Iowa) *Enterprise,
  Melbourne* (Iowa) *Record,* the *Peru* (Neb.) *Challenge* and the
  Wahoo (Neb.) *Newspaper.*

Chapter Outline

Reaching the reader

Identifying the news

Writers read to accommodate their audience

Observation

Sidebar 1 Reading to write

Sidebar 2 Tips

Reading skills, focused on areas of interest for an audience, are crucial to effective communications. That's why all practitioners from journalism to advertising should read.

Journalists read to write well. You are preparing to write for large audiences. To do so effectively you must see your issues clearly. You face a widely divergent population of readers and listeners. Members of every audience vary in their interests, expectations and education levels. How do you reach them with words best serving those characteristics?

Students who read a variety of writing completely and critically will find the answers to these questions most easily. You can't expect to communicate effectively unless you merge the best writing approaches with thorough knowledge of the audience's interests.

Growing numbers of choices are available in our information world. You must be more mindful than your audience of this glut of information. Study your readings closely; focus on words in broadcasts. You must hone such skills to ensure your audience receives and understands your work. Reading skills, focused on areas of interest for your audience, are crucial to effective journalism.

Reaching the Reader

Your readers want truth, variety, accuracy, vibrancy, balance, vigor and brevity. This textbook reflects these issues throughout. To see how we reach such goals, you must dedicate yourself to reading—reading often, comprehensively and with a wary eye. Good writing absolutely depends on it.

The demands on time often collide in the pursuit of effective information delivery. A harried reporter often has limited hours or minutes to gather thousands of words from multiple sources—and then choose the words the piece earns. That's only the first half of effective communication, however. The audience then must be both willing and able to comprehend the message—an audience rushed in dozens of ways. Writing clearly for them is an achievement. Taking your reading seriously only improves your chance of writing success.

Writers read to discover how other writers identify the news. The best writers are the best readers, and that's no coincidence. There's little mystery to the news delivery process, and a classroom unfolds before you every day as you open a newspaper. Reading others' well-chosen words builds vocabularies and provides approaches to stories. You must recognize the difference between what works and what doesn't work in this process to take full advantage when you begin writing.

All this ensures you'll be a clearer, more complete communicator. Your ultimate success at improving your skills depends on the foundation you build by reading— reading frequently, thoroughly and critically. Be sure you have a newspaper within reach while you're reading this chapter. If you have any crayons or marking pens, grab them, too. You'll have a chance to do some coloring.

Writers read to effectively reveal the news. You must practice your ability to answer exactly: What is the news? As a reporter and writer, you must always ask yourself: What did we not know yesterday or an hour ago? This is a critical measure of words' value. Ask yourself: How deep will I dig into a news story to find the news? Not every news story you write is going to open with the news in the first 15 words. The best writers use a variety of approaches. When that time comes, you must use a more creative approach to capture readers' and listeners' attention. However, for your initial writing efforts, identifying and delivering the news directly is of paramount importance. Reading newspapers reveals this process to you.

Writers read to learn to tell readers "Who cares?" Answer that question about any story you read, hear or write. Any of them failing to make this clear discourages readers. So, who will care? Once you begin the writing process, you should have a clear answer to this question. It will be even clearer once you complete the reporting process. If it isn't, there's little reason to write the story.

The journalist frequently serves as the eyes and ears of the audience. Knowing for whom you're watching and listening clarifies your writing significantly.

The quality of your coverage as a news writer informs your readers and listeners. It enables them to take action, to vote, to support, to protest, to rest assured. Whatever the response, you must inform them fully so they can decide wisely. It's no simple task to be a news writer, but you can reduce its complexity. Read daily those who deliver news professionally. Which writers appeal to you? What about their writing interests you? Consider how they address the "Who cares?" issue and how they serve their audience. Is their work informative? Is it clear?

These issues grow in value when you read frequently, helping you to distinguish good habits and avoid weak choices. Rapidly, part of this craft's mystery fades. Writers read, so grab your newspaper.

Identifying the News

The first ability of the novice news writer must be identifying the crucial: news. Whether it's in your reading or your reporting, the news should be clearly evident. You must know the news before you can decide how to present it. Learning to peg the news by reading your newspaper makes it all the easier when you sit at the keyboard and work to do the same in your newswriting. It makes no difference whether it's a brief or on the front page.

Sidebar 1

Reading to Write

1. All writers, including journalists, read.

2. Writers, including journalists, read to learn to write.

3. Journalists read to identify news.

4. Journalists read to reveal news.

5. Journalists read to determine who cares.

6. Journalists read to learn the value of words.

7. Journalists read to accommodate their audience.

8. Journalists read to learn to find information.

9. Journalists read to bring color to their writing.

10. Journalists read before writing.

Now's the time to grab your newspaper and choose a news story. Find a short one, because length is no measure for newswriting success. A sound, well-told story of six to eight paragraphs requires as much or more attention to detail as a lengthy article. In one sitting, read the story thoroughly and critically without distraction. Answer these questions:

Did the writer find the news?

Is it obvious in your first reading?

Did you have to return to a previous paragraph to clarify an issue?

If the report you're reading isn't clear, you're likely reading a confused writer's work—confused about the purpose or the subject matter. The writer should choose a lead focusing on the most important news element or use a creative feature lead and reveal the news substance within an appropriate sequence. In either case, the "Who cares?" issue should be clear and easy to identify. Broadcast writers appeal to the listener's sensibility. While readers can refer back when writing is unclear, you're on a one-way street without reverse in radio and television. With either media form, there is no reason it should lack clarity. The best writing for print sounds best when read aloud as well.

Now, without referring to it a second time, can you summarize the focus of the story from your newspaper in a single sentence? The best writers do exactly that before they write their articles. Appropriately called a focus sentence, it appears above the story for the writer and editor to view. It assists the writer in achieving and maintaining focus; it tells the editor the core of the report. Editors can use such sentences to their advantage when writing headlines. Just as headlines summarize the story in a few words, the focus sentence summarizes the piece in a single sentence.

Try this: Without returning to the original story in your newspaper, write a single sentence that effectively captures the focus of the story. Imagine you have your roommate's attention for only one sentence and must convey the story's essence. It isn't always simple, and for that reason novice news writers often resist the practice. The payoff for identifying the news first and explaining it simply arrives later, when you challenge your story and it clearly answers the "Who cares?" question.

Now, consider the third question: Did you have to return to a previous paragraph for clarification? The sooner you recognize this as painful in your reading, the sooner you'll avoid inflicting such pain on your readers. Listeners, of course, have no choice because they can't go back. Keep your writing as clear for listeners as for readers, and you'll move more easily between media styles.

Question why you had to return for clarification. Was it to understand who was speaking? An unclear "he said" will confuse your readers and waste their time. Or was it a mysterious "it" confusing the flow of your reading? Such hurdles only frustrate experienced readers expecting the story to flow logically. Your daily newspaper reading will reinforce the need for such clarity.

As you become a more practiced reader, analyze stories for simple presentation of complex information. Writing for the media is closer to technical writing than the average reader knows. You must comprehend facts, figures, percentages, addresses, relationships and trends—and then write about them in a manner attracting and serving your readers. Can you simplify the complex information? You have no choice. Explaining complex issues is an important aspect of your job.

Writers Read to Accommodate Their Audience

Whether they're reading or listening, members of the mass audience always bring limitations to the task of receiving words. The audience's time, space and attention frequently are not in your favor when delivering information. It's not simple competing with such typical daily challenges as wet diapers, an unbalanced checkbook and a steaming pot of spaghetti. Besides, you compete with dozens of television channels, movie and cartoon videos, video games, e-mail and Internet choices for audience time and interest.

What considerations can you give your readers and listeners to keep your writing before them? Get to the point. Don't bury your news deep in the first paragraph. You've read elsewhere in this book how to approach classic storytelling, and advocates of lengthy, fully developed writing occupy a rightful place in the mass media. However, before you can effectively tell a story of any length, you must first understand the story. Your ability to write with brevity, clarity and purpose at this stage lays the foundation for those deeper, more-developed articles.

Writers read to learn to find information. News writers can only be as successful as the material they gather. Before writing, you must fill a basket with the answers you've gathered from your interviews and document searches. Sift through your material; organize, write, refine and polish. But, if you bring an empty basket to your keyboard, you face few options besides returning to creative writing or poetry. There's nothing wrong with those choices, except you're in the wrong classroom and textbook if they're your preference. Whereas some writing professions may freely create their own product, you must have solid facts, examples, references and quotations in this field.

Factual information from witnesses and documented details, along with experts' commentary and perspectives, comprise the meat of your news report. Your information basket must be full and you must select good fruit from bad—strong quotations, action verbs, a variety of views—when delivering your goods.

Where do you find your goodies? You're looking for worthy information from worthy sources. That's the foundation of your story and you can't disguise its absence. Where do we find such sources? Witnesses and participants are primary, as are expert and documented information; these are three essential elemants. Consider them as integral to an information circle needed by every newsgatherer-writer. Among your best sources as experts are professors on campuses, who are informed individuals accustomed to explaining complex information to uninformed people. Consider an information circle available to every newsgatherer-writer. If your efforts accommodate all sections of this circle, you assure yourself of an impressive basket of goodies.

Sidebar 2

Clarity is an important demand people bring to news reading or listening. Sentences build on sentences into logical paragraphs; paragraphs build on paragraphs into a logical news report. Here's the test: The presentation fails when readers must return to an earlier paragraph to clarify what they've just read. Organized articles eliminate backtracking.

Observation

Observation is crucial to gather information successfully in each of the three primary categories; it enhances the depth of story detail. Observation requires you use as many of your senses as possible—see it always, smell it when you can, touch it if possible and listen intently. Taste? Be sure your material is worthy of your audience's consumption: truth, fairness, completeness, and balance. Don't feed them anything else.

Do examples of observation appear in your stories? This is information an alert news gatherer often notices without benefit of someone's words. You observe people's actions on the news scene—any reactions by the source during an interview—or by questioning the presence of an unusual framed plaque gracing the source's office wall. Observing enhances.

What examples of observation appear in your stories? Some descriptions can emerge only from a reporter at the scene, vividly describing the color of a person's clothing, the scope of a disaster, the broad smile of a proud parent or the unspoken hesitancy of a wary interview subject.

Likewise, being knowledgeable about your subject provides your report with depth. Only through reading and research can you give your readers the background that keeps a story in context. What is the historical aspect of this situation? What happened a year ago? Are trends developing? What earlier reported developments from two days or two months ago, affect the latest development?

No matter how experienced the news gatherer, one aspect never changes: Questions are essential. Good reporters question always, and then effective writers deliver the answers to those questions. They do so in a unique dual fashion, however. Accomplished writers provide answers without revealing the questions; answers explain unstated questions without the reporter's presence intruding. Likewise, the best reporters ensure the story leaves no questions unanswered in the reader's or listener's mind. It's a significant responsibility.

Clearly, writers read. Writers read to compile the vocabulary needed to communicate efficiently. Writers read to learn to convey new information effectively. Writers read to answer, "Who cares?" Writers read to appreciate the value of their words and their audience's limitations. Effective writers read to provide a balanced, colorful report. Most importantly, writers read before they write. Read.

Exercises

1. Identify a story that appears to be delivering its news in summary lead fashion—typically containing the who, what, when, where, why and how in the first two paragraphs. Read only those two paragraphs. Put the newspaper down or turn off the radio or television. Can you recount the essence of the story? Write a single sentence from the information you drew from the story. Condense and summarize to avoid repetition and to ensure clarity.

Where do you find your goodies? You're looking for worthy information from worthy sources. That's the foundation of your story and you cannot disguise its absence. Where do we find such sources? Consider an information circle available to every news gatherer-writer. If your efforts accommodate all section of this circle, you assure yourself of an impressive basket of goodies.

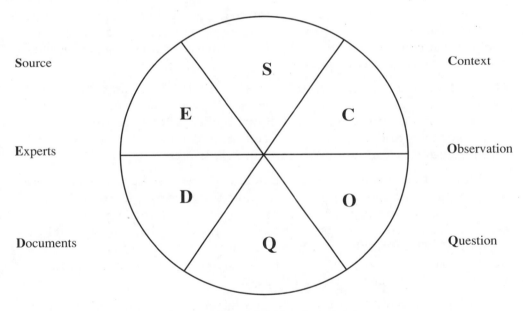

Source   Context

Experts   Observation

Documents   Question

(Readers: Picture Trivial Pursuit pie pieces)

These six elements are crucial in fulfilling your responsibility of answering the typical five *W*'s and the *H*. The five *W*'s are who, what, where, when and why. The *H* is how. These are the basic building blocks of any story.

The list comprises your fields for harvest. Your basket fills with information drawn here. Arranged on the right are your personal responsibilities. Fulfill those tasks while gathering and you serve your audience faithfully.

2. You can use this story to apply the color concept.

WASHINGTON—Rising numbers of U.S. college students are studying overseas, and many aren't going to the traditional universities in Europe, a survey found.

They're venturing farther afield, to Africa, Australia and the Middle East.

The number of American students studying abroad rose 10.6 percent to 84,403 in 1994-95, continuing a 10-year upward trend, a report released Sunday by the New York-based Institute of International Education said.

Foreign student enrollment in U.S. schools, meanwhile, rose less than 1 percent the past two years.

"As recently as a decade ago, studying abroad was considered a luxury," said Richard M. Krasno, the institute's president. "I think it's now considered a more instrumental part of undergraduate education."

He speculated that American students are warming to the idea of studying abroad because they are being exposed to other cultures on their own campuses. Many also recognize the importance of a second language and international experience in competing for good jobs, he said.

"When I first went to school, they said:, 'Here, study French. If you ever go to France, you'll be able to order off a menu.' Now, it's seen as a career asset," said Wayne Decker, director of the office of international studies at the University of Arizona.

Amy Hofsheier, 21, a student at the University of Arizona, is off to Israel next month to study five months at Ben Gurion University in Beersheva. She's majoring in archaeology and Judaic studies and hopes to see the country and improve her language skills.

"I think for myself. It's really a necessity," said Ms. Hofsheier, who hopes to do archaeology work in Israel one day. "The majority of the kids are still going to Spain and France, but I think interest is opening up to other places." The institute has conducted an annual statistical survey of the foreign student population in the United States since 1949.

Bring your coloring tools. Mark blue for the source, yellow for the documents and red for the experts. These are your primary elements. Then, add some purple to what reflects context and background, orange over the observations made by the reporter and green for those questions you realize are answered without stating them. The final three elements complement your report.

By the way, there's no penalty for coloring outside the lines. This material frequently overlaps. Now, let's consider what the idea of colors offers the newswriting process. Are there comparable amounts of blue, red and yellow? If so, there's balance. Is there an abundance of one color over another? Do only two colors appear without benefit of the third? Could unexplored sources, if contacted, add to this story or make it clearer? Would documents add to the depth and clarity? Your coloring can reveal any deficiencies in your story. A writer can resolve these deficiencies by gathering more information from additional experts, more documents or further elaboration from the primary source. By giving the audience such additional information, the story carries greater useful detail.

Suggested Readings

Gould, Stephen Jay. *Wonderful Life*. New York: W. W. Norton & Company, 1989. This book reveals both quality writing and an excellent story of the past, which holds powerful and important revelations about society's future.

Ritzer, George. *The McDonaldization of Society*. Thousand Oaks, Calif.: Pine Forge Press, 1996. The shape of our future? This may be it. Describing a society that is becoming compartmentalized, uniform and repetitious, this well-written book challenges long-held assumptions and notions.

Resumes, Cover Letters, Work Samples and Tips for Getting a Job

17

Michael L. Mercer

Assistant Professor, Department of Journalism, Auburn University
Intern, general assignment reporter, farm reporter, education
reporter, copy editor, assistant city editor and columnist for
the Jackson (Tenn.) *Sun.*

Chapter Outline

Preparing to write a resume

Writing a resume

After the introduction

Work experience and other skills

References

Writing a cover letter

Sending work samples

Hunting for a job

Sidebar 1 An employer's rant

Sidebar 2 Resume reels

Sidebar 3 First jobs

Journalism professors pride themselves on preparing students for the workplace: teaching them how to spot news, sniff it out, write lilting leads, seek excellence in editing, shoot awesome pictures and prepare great graphics. But professors often give short shrift to showing students how to market these abilities for internships and entry-level jobs through the preparation and presentation of effective resumes, cover letters and samples of their work.

Numerous books, handouts, computer programs and self-proclaimed experts are loaded with how-to information concerning the preparation of resumes, cover letters and work samples. But the most valuable resource for journalism students needing help in this regard should be their professors. Professors should do more than offer to critique a student's resume, cover letters or work samples during office hours. Rather than confine this advice to individual students in the office, professors should seize students' concerns about job hunting and prepare a unit, a series of lectures and audio-visual presentations, showing how basic newswriting, editing and graphic skills come into play on a resume.

Preparing to Write a Resume

The resume is simply a marketing tool. But, in developing a resume, journalism students should be applying the 5 Ws and H principles of basic newswriting. The subject of the story is *you*. An effective resume should tell *who you are, what you are, where you are, when you're available, why you're available and how you got to this point*. If your resume fails to answer any of these questions or related ones, it's not an effective resume.

Your resume should reflect your ability to write a news story. Remember, a resume is a sample of your writing, your ability to communicate with words in a profession that calls for a wordsmith and grammatical guru. Can you get to the point—that is, the news of the story about your search for a job? Can you get this information high up in the story, preferably in the opening volley? Can you be accurate, brief (one page is recommended) and clear? Can you be fair to yourself and the potential employer, letting the employers have the information they need in tightly written fashion to make sure you're the right person for the job? Or will the employer find errors that will make them lose faith in your writing, editing and proofreading? Will the employer even question your very commitment to accuracy in this profession?

Brevity also is a virtue. If you're well-prepared to enter your profession, it will show. Don't feel the need to overwhelm the prospective employer with a ream of extracurricular activities and achievements. He or she will be impressed if you can display your ability to tell a lot in a little space, preferably a page. And don't feel as if you have to crowd every inch of the page. White space can be attractive, if you know how to use it.

Write a resume a potential employer can read within 30 seconds or less. Employers are busy people. They don't want to spend a lot of time figuring out if your resume suggests you might be a good find. Make your qualifications readily and easily apparent. There wouldn't be a job available if an employer didn't need you, so he or she wants to find someone quickly—someone who will put an end to the job search. Time is money. Employers appreciate a quick, one-page synopsis of your candidacy for the job.

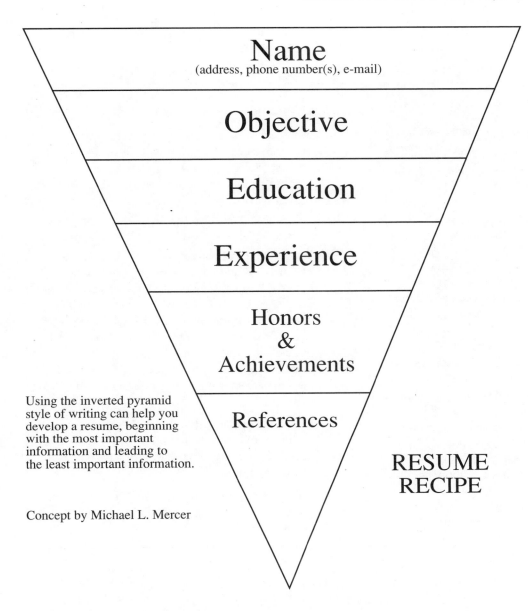

Using the inverted pyramid style of writing can help you develop a resume, beginning with the most important information and leading to the least important information.

Concept by Michael L. Mercer

RESUME RECIPE

Don't fill a page with lists of jobs you've done just to fill it up. Fill the page with quality, not quantity. Don't worry too much if your resume looks skimpy. You're still in college. No one expects you to have done it all. If you're applying for an internship or entry-level job, no one expects you to know it all. Most employers are looking for competent, trainable people, those they can mold and shape. They're looking for potential, not overnight successes and superstars.

Before writing your resume, know who will be reading it. Do your homework. Send your completed resume, cover letter and work samples to someone you can reach through a telephone call to follow up. Also, know something about the job you're seeking. The more you know about the potential employer and the position, the better you'll be able to focus on designing your resume for that position.

Ideally, a resume should give an employer a verbal picture of you and your potential in the job you're seeking. If you're seeking an internship and the target

Sidebar 1

An Employer's Rant

Flora J. Garcia, Production Manager, Time Online

I posted a call for resumes for a couple of good jobs. By the next morning, I had a couple dozen resumes and letters—MOST of which I could read. Several of the offenders had way too much experience to be making these errors.

A significant number were sent to the e-mail in my signature, not the one I requested in the body of the message (so that I can try to send thank-you letters to everyone and keep track of things). I asked that people INCLUDE their resume in the e-mail, and still a good number were sent as attachments, some of those even to the wrong e-mail.

I've seen at least one typo in the first sentence, my name has been radically changed and I have a good dozen where there are line wraps that make the letter really hard to read.

Folks, if you're applying for a journalism job, these things REALLY matter. Does it mean you absolutely won't get the job? Probably not, but you have to make up for it. Following directions is important. If you're only this careful with your initial representation, how careful are you going to be with your work and my company's reputation?

Here are some really obvious hints:

1. Test your resume. Send it to a couple of friends on different mail programs. Make sure any odd characters are OK, that there aren't any wraps that get strange and that it basically looks easy to read. It can't be pretty in ASCII, so that should take some of the pressure off, but it CAN be readable.

2. Follow the directions. If they say e-mail a letter explaining X and Y, please make sure you talk about X and Y. If they say e-mail, that's what you do at the computer, not with the phone. The number of responses people get to these things is too big that calling is a good thing. I don't mind if people call to make sure I've gotten stuff (especially if they don't expect me to call back), but I'm sure there are people who do mind even that.

3. Check the spelling of every single word, especially the name of the person you're writing to. I can pretty much say getting that wrong is going to put you in the out pile.

4. Know that some of us are going to check to see what sort of posting activity you've been involved in.

employer has no internships and no plans to start them, you're wasting your time and the employer's. If there's a job opening and you know just what you need to know in seeking the job, the odds are already in your favor. Employers are usually anxious to fill job openings as long as the money's budgeted to fill them. Bosses don't want to dilly-dally on finding new employees because the money may dry up. If they wait too long, the position may be frozen or eliminated. If you send a good application to a prospective employer, chances are he or she will be excited to get the package in hopes you're the one needed for the job.

Writing a Resume

If you're having trouble developing a resume, try the newswriting approach. After all, the news is you're looking for a job and you want the world to know it.

As previously mentioned, like any story or news release, the resume should try to answer the 5 *W*s and *H*—who, what, where, when, why and how. The resume has a similar structure. It can be prepared in the familiar inverted pyramid, or top-heavy, style of writing, with the most important information (or the news) at the top and the least important information following in the body or bottom of the "story." Be sure your resume provides background and sources. You're the primary source for attribution because this is your resume. Secondary sources are the people and places with whom and where you've prepared yourself for this moment in your career.

Ultimately, the entire resume will answer the WHO question. But, for starters, the most prominent feature on the resume should be your name, no one else's and no other category such as your objective, education, employment history or lack of it, computer skills, honors and achievements, professional affiliations, extracurricular activities or references. Your name should stand out on the resume, whether you center it at the top of the page, put it at the side or try something different and off-beat. Whatever you do, remember that your name should capture the reader's attention first. Make your name the biggest feature. Use the largest appropriate typeface. Your name is the headline for the news story you want them to read.

Companies often receive many resumes for job openings. A variety of computer programs or resume services allow you to experiment with various type sizes for your name. Run the alternatives by friends, colleagues, associates and professors for their feedback before you're satisfied. Listen to their counsel. But, regardless of what they say, you're the boss. It's your resume, not theirs.

Whether you use a nickname or a more formal given name, choose the name you want to be known as. If you want to be known as Charles rather than Chuck, that's fine.

Telling someone who you are on the resume also requires listing an address and telephone number. If you're a college student not living at home, most likely you will have two addresses and two phone numbers: a campus address while you're at school and a home address. Specify which is which.

Using Associated Press style for addresses, numbers and other items on your resume is advisable. It shows you know AP style, which is the most likely standard of style in a workplace. It shows no one has to teach you about style. That means you're ready to hit the ground running. Also, it helps you show consistency in the use of the language. Avoid using postal abbreviations, just as you would in a news story. Write phone numbers in AP style, with the area code in parentheses, and a space between the area code and the rest of the number. If there's an extension, write "Ext." and the number of the extension, which is AP style. If you have an e-mail address, use it as well. Use of e-mail suggests you're high-tech, up-to-date and have a license to drive on the information superhighway. Online job listings are becoming more popular, and many of these outlets require the use of e-mail or the electronic transmission of resumes. Some employers impressed by your credentials may contact you via e-mail before calling or writing you.

After the Introduction

Once you've introduced yourself by name, address, telephone number and e-mail, the next logical step for your resume would be to ensure you have an objective. The objective is a matter-of-fact statement of what you seek. Of course, your simple objective is to get a job. But, for resume purposes, a simple, preferably one-line sentence should suffice. Why state an objective? An objective shows you've done some preparation for the position you seek. Don't assume just because you sent a resume and cover letter that no objective is necessary. You wouldn't be sending a resume or cover letter if you weren't seeking a job, right? An objective on the resume shows you're focused.

Don't use a wishy-washy objective. For example, don't use the objective "seeking a challenging job that will utilize my talents to the utmost and lead me to management." A lot of jobs might qualify under that description. Be much more specific. Name the job, even down to the place you want to work—for example, "Entry-level reporter at *The News* or summer internship at *The Sun.*"

If you know the date you can come to work, share it. It might give you an edge over others who are similarly qualified but can't state their availability.

If you're focused, then prospective employers should be focused on what you want, too. Your objective should lead them to read on and determine if you're prepared to meet your goal. Without an objective, you both risk losing sight of what you're trying to sell.

The next area you should address on the resume is how much post-secondary education you've achieved. Don't list the year you graduated from high school. Graduating from high school is a noteworthy achievement but not worth putting on the resume if you're in college. You had to finish high school in order to go to college, or you earned a high school equivalency diploma. List the post-secondary institutions you've attended and the diplomas you've received. If you're still working on your diploma, say so by listing the anticipated year of graduation, along with the degree you'll receive and the field it's in. List the institutions in reverse order, starting with the one you're in now before listing those in the past. Give general dates of attendance in months or years.

If you're proud of your grade point average, list it in the education slot. If you're not, don't list it unless the employer requires the information on the application. Most employers are smart enough to know a high GPA isn't everything. They'll be much more concerned with your other qualifications, your preparation and especially your performance, which they'll determine by samples of your work.

Employers will want to know what practical experiences you've had and could bring to a job. If you've had enough journalistic experiences, consider listing them in reverse order under a separate JOURNALISTIC EXPERIENCE or PRACTICAL EXPERIENCE category. If that's not possible, list other work experiences you've had under a general WORK EXPERIENCE or OTHER WORK EXPERIENCE category. Prospective employers generally like to hire busy people who already have some work experiences. Give the general dates of your work experiences.

Work Experience and Other Skills

Don't take any work experiences for granted. If you've worked a lot of places in a short time, you don't have to list all of them. But, if you've worked in a fast-food restaurant, don't overlook the very positive vibes prospective employers might get from such a listing. They know you have a work history somewhere and that you can juggle more than one thing at a time. Customer service skills are sorely needed in most jobs, so any previous job serving customers can demonstrate your good public relations skills. Employers also value teamwork, the ability to work and get along with others. And attendance at a job is always an issue, so a potential employer can get some idea whether you would even show up for work or how often you did.

Do you have any special skills, or have you earned any honors or achievements? List them if they're appropriate to the job you're seeking. They will help you stand out from the crowd.

If you know how to work with several computer programs, say so. But don't state your "knowledge of how to work with the program." Just list the program. "Knowledge" suggests only that you've heard of the program or are familiar with it. Until you've been tried-and-tested, no employer really can be sure just how much expertise you have. But listing programs you've worked with tells the employer you're at least computer literate or trainable.

Let's say you were on the staff of your high school newspaper. Listing that job on a resume says a lot more than just the fact you went to high school and graduated. This lets the employer know how far back you started thinking about a journalistic career, when you started acquiring the skills necessary for the job and the sacrifices you made to be on the staff. If you were an editor, say so. This indicates your leadership ability and potential to work in a team and produce a publication. Being an editor called for you to make judgments and tough decisions. If you were a leader in any organization, don't just say you were a member. Listing the leadership says both: You were a member and you were a leader. It says you either sought leadership or others saw leadership potential in you. It's an early sign, too, that you can handle the politics that come with any job.

Volunteerism also is highly prized by employers. If you were a candy striper, let a prospective employer know. If you received an award for giving blood, that's a plus. Someone who volunteers time and talents for a community or civic organization is a welcome job candidate. Were you president of the church choir? Great! Nobody made you do it, right? That's another sign of leadership—sacrifice and service— since most people don't sing in choirs, and rehearsals are required.

References

Never say "References Available on Request." Prospective employers may never ask you for them. They shouldn't have to. While you're hoping someone will call you to ask for your references, he or she may be already on the phone, calling another well-qualified applicant's references because they were already listed.

Remember, employers are busy people who expect you to be busy, too. Why should they have to call you and ask for references when you could have so easily listed the name, title, address, telephone number and even e-mail of the people you want them to call? You may never have the opportunity again to make a first impression with your application package, so list at least two references on your resume. Why wouldn't you want to have people already listed who will speak positively about you when you're seeking a job? By not listing references, you not only run the risk that another applicant will get an edge, but you might not be available when an employer calls you to get them. Believe it or not, you've already indirectly given an employer some references by listing places you've worked or gone to school. What's to keep a smart boss from calling those places to inquire if anyone's ever heard of you? By listing references, you're directing the potential caller to the right person and the right place.

Who should be your references? If you're in school or about to get out, ideally one of your references will be a professor who's had you in class and knows your classroom work habits, your attendance and in some instances your character. But

Volunteerism is highly prized by employers, so include these activities in a resume. Having an employee volunteering time and talents for civic organizations is a welcome sign.

not all your references should be academic. At least one should be an off-campus or community person who's familiar with your work habits or volunteerism.

Make room for references. Sometimes people suggest they don't list references because they take up too much room on a resume. But, if you can list one, you can list up to three in the same general space. Don't stack references on top of each other and force the resume to go over a page. Instead, place one reference's name, title, address and telephone number on the left side of the resume in a bottom column. List another reference in the middle column and a third in the right column.

Writing a Cover Letter

Writing a cover letter is a necessity. Remember, it also is a sample of your writing like the resume and work samples. Paragraph indentation is recommended rather than using the flush-left approach. Indented paragraphs are easier to read.

You should send a cover letter along with your resume and work samples in your application package. Even if you hand-deliver the package for an interview, include a brief cover letter.

Developing an effective cover letter doesn't have to be a nightmare. In the first sentence or paragraph, simply tell the person why you're sending the package. If you want a job, say so in the first sentence. Just as you would in a news story, get to the point. Tell the person how you heard about the job, what you know about the job and how you qualify for the job.

COVER LETTERS

In a cover letter, you should briefly state your interest in a position and describe your qualifications. Most cover letters include three paragraphs. You may encounter situations where your letter will be longer. Remember that the cover letter should be as concise as possible and easy to read. As in the case of resumes, recruiters rarely spend much time reading lengthy cover letters.

- Try to address it to an individual (call the company and ask to whom it should be directed). If you cannot get a name, write, "Dear Sir or Madam:" as the salutation.

- Tailor your letter to the organization or position that interests you. This means writing a letter for each resume you mail. This will take longer, but is worth the effort. General letters have a poor success rate in obtaining interviews. You may be able to use some of the same language in letters, but always target the person to whom you are mailing the letter. Employers will recognize a form letter and will likely interpret that as laziness or lack of real interest in their company.

SAMPLE COVER LETTER

Street Address
City, State, Zip Code

Date

Person's name
Person's title
Address of Company
City, State, Zip

Dear Person's Name:

Tell the person to whom you are writing why you are writing. If you are applying for a position, tell them where you heard about the position. If you found out about the job in the classified ads, note that. For instance, "I would like to apply for the sales position listed in the State on May 1, 1997". It could be that someone told you about the position. If this is the case, you would state that "John Smith recommended that I write you concerning employment opportunities with your company".

Here you want to tell the employer how you are qualified for the position. This paragraph should strongly outline your strengths that make you the best person for the position. Elaborate on the information in your resume, but do not repeat it. Remember to be concise and list five specific examples of your skills. This is also a good place to make reference to your resume. For example, "As you can see from my resume, I have two years of experience in marketing".

Ask for an interview in this paragraph. Be assertive. Tell them you will call in two weeks or on a certain day to follow up. If you say you will call, be sure you do. Thank the person for considering you for the position.

Sincerely,

A cover letter should complement a resume and vice versa. Neither takes the place of the other. You can sound businesslike in the letter, but don't expect to mask your lack of qualifications or embellish your positive traits by using high-sounding phrases. Write in a conversational tone and be personable. A letter should speak to people. Be brief, concise and precise. And be assertive. Don't start off with a statement such as, "I am writing to you about the possibility of seeking to apply for so-and-so job." Instead, try something like, "I want to be your next (whatever the job is)."

Three paragraphs ought to be enough with the closing paragraph, once again, on the assertive side. Don't write, "I'll be looking forward to hearing from you." Instead, tell the employer you'll be calling just as soon as you think he or she has gotten the letter. Your initial call is just to determine if the company's received your application package, but show the company you mean business by following up. Ask if someone's had a chance to look over your application package. If not, say you'll be calling back again in a few days. If someone's read it, ask (1) his or her impression of your work and (2) what your chances are for getting an interview. As long as the vibes are good, be persistent in your phone calling. But don't become a pest. When it becomes apparent a particular place is not interested in you or if you get the run-around, move on and call somebody else.

Sending Work Samples

Your resume and cover letter look good. Now, you need to prepare your work samples or portfolio. Don't expect to be hired without good samples. In fact, your published work will be the bottom line for a prospective employer to decide whether you're worth hiring or not. It won't take many samples to make this decision. Make sure these are samples of your best work. If you're a writer, send about five of your greatest hits. Make sure the stories, like your cover letter and resume, are error free.

Send about two samples of hard news and two features. Make the fifth sample a column or review to show the employer how you think and express yourself. If the clippings have photographs with them, include the photographs. Like most people, employers are apt to read stories with pictures first, because these stories are more attractive and draw the reader's attention. Don't send gray-looking clips that lack visuals unless the stories are truly good reads with excellent leads.

Send your work on 8-by-11-inch paper if possible. Prepare your clips professionally. Mount them with glue or tape and then reproduce the page so the pasting can't be seen. If you're a copyediting candidate, you want to display great headlines you've written and pages you've designed. Send copies of photographs, not the originals. If slides are called for, make sure you don't send your only pictures. Graphic artists and public relations and advertising specialists also should prepare representative samples of their best work. If you want to preserve color, go ahead and have the more costly color reproduction done. If you have a small, hard-to-read clipping you want to submit, there's nothing wrong with enlarging it for easier reading. Don't be sloppy at this point. Your presentation reflects your professionalism.

Sidebar 2

Resume Reels

A television resume reel, which includes work examples for a job, should be no more than six to seven minutes long and on VHS. If you're interested in working on camera, the first minute should show a variety of standups, including a live shot. It's likely that a news director will look at the first minute. That's where you show who you are. In short, it's a bit of a meat market. A montage of standups with dissolves is perfectly acceptable. The next three minutes should be two 90-second stories on breaking news. The next part of the tape can be any longer features or anchoring you've done. The final segment can be biographical material of no more than 30 seconds.

If you want to be on air, that's what you emphasize. If you want to be a producer, that's what you emphasize. If you want to be a photographer, emphasize that. You should not say you can do it all unless that's the only job available. Figure out what you want to do and stick to it.

Sometimes it's useful to go to a small market. But, if you're going to be frustrated by working in small-town America, that will show. So don't go there if you can't be seriously interested in what goes on there. You would be doing yourself and the town a disservice.

Your printed resume should be one page and should emphasize your professional experience. High school track honors and glee club are not what employers are interested in, although community service does interest local stations.

Some agents take beginning reporters and producers if the agents see promise. Having an agent costs 5 to 6 percent of your beginning gross salary. But it might be worth it to have a good insider player with a cogent analysis of your work and potential.

Hunting for a Job

It's a job finding a job. So, if you're looking for one, be it entry-level or an internship, let everyone know who you think can help you. Knowing somebody has never hurt in a job search and never will. If you know people already in the business, they know somebody already in the business, too. If they don't have an entry-level job or internship at their workplace, they know someone else who will. Attend job fairs. Pick up business cards. Get to know recruiters and the companies they represent. If you attend a job fair and see an opening for an interview, take a seat even if it's a company you're not sure you want to work with. Since you're not sure you want to work there, spend the time getting the information you need to be sure you're not passing up a great opportunity to get your foot in the door for that needed experience everybody else wants you to have before they'll hire you.

Don't forget to let your favorite professors know you're in the hunt for a job. Many of them have friends and contacts still in the business. Tap into the professors' network. And several associations, including the American Society of Newspaper Editors and Society of Professional Journalists, publish annual internship guides.

Don't expect to land any internship or entry-level job without first preparing yourself for the task, developing the skills and using marketing savvy to show someone you're ready. If you're well-prepared, it will show in your resume, your cover letter and your clips.

Sidebar 3

First Jobs

Following are how the authors of this textbook got their first jobs:

Pat Berg, University of Wisconsin, River Falls

I wandered into my first reporting job, literally. I'd heard that the St. Paul *Pioneer Press* was looking for a correspondent for western Wisconsin. I gathered every clip I could find and took them to the paper. I didn't know visitors were supposed to sign in at the front desk, so I went up to the newsroom on my own and found my new boss. After reading my clips, she agreed to give me one assignment. That came a few days later. Was I surprised when she told me to cover a meeting that began at 7:30 p.m. and call in my story by 9! I remember I wrote two leads during the meeting, one for each possible outcome. I also sent notes to participants, asking them to verify the spelling of their names. And I propped open the door to an office across the hall from the meeting so I could get to a phone as soon as I got the story. After the first assignment, anything was do-able.

Glen Bleske, California State University, Chico

I first met Sandra Baker, a Gannett publisher for a trio of weekly newspapers along Florida's Space Coast, at a job fair when I was a college junior. She encouraged me to call her when I graduated, and I did. I was lucky. My letter, resume and clips arrived just a few days after one of her editors had quit.

The first day on the job, I had to edit stories, write headlines and lay out pages. It seemed an impossible task to meet deadline. The next week we began pagination. I had one day to learn the system. I learned a lot those first weeks, including the fact that I loved journalism.

Anita Caldwell, Oklahoma State University

The shape of music notes. That's how I got my first job. I had been immersed in music—I was playing it, teaching it, writing it and hanging out with friends who produced it. One day, I was visiting a friend who spent hours as a music copyist, deciphering musicians' handwritten scrawls and writing them out on music paper for what eventually would become camera-ready copies of sheet music.

It had to be a labor of love. The dizzying array of little black dots, dashes and other symbols would surely start jumping around the page after hours and hours of tediously drawing perfect circles, stems and lines.

What a great story, I thought. How many people could know who is behind the sheet music they see in their favorite music stores? Computers had not yet become a significant part of our lives as they are today and the ones that were in existence didn't have the hardware/software needed to do the job well.

I convinced an alternative weekly to use the idea. After a few more stories with the weekly, I landed a job at a small-circulation daily.

My first few stories were awful. But I kept writing. And somehow I got much better. And then I got pretty damned good. And I never looked back.

Ginger Rudeseal Carter, Georgia College & State University

My first job in journalism was as a part-time sports reporter for the *Opelika-Auburn News*. I was a master's student as the time, and I wanted to keep writing while I pursued the degree.

I went into the office and inquired about openings. The sports editor, Jimmy Johnson, said he needed folks to regularly cover high school sports and assorted community stories. I was paid by the story.

My first assignment was at Tallapoosa High School, a Friday night game. I followed the directions Jimmy gave me to the stadium—and found myself outside Tuskegee, Ala. I found a map and found my way back to the stadium.

For the next two years, I wrote two or three stories a week for the paper. I interviewed Pepper Rodgers, the former Georgia Tech coach, and covered the opening of the newly renovated Jordan-Hare Stadium at Auburn. I covered two state playoff teams. There weren't many women covering high school sports in the late 1970s, so I had my share of problems with coaches and players. The pay wasn't much, but the job taught me about perseverance. That job continues to be my favorite newspaper position of my career.

Christopher Harper, Ithaca College

I started out as a photographer at my hometown newspaper, the *Idaho Statesman*. The paper wanted someone to work as a shooter for part of the summer and write the second half of the summer. I had taken two photography courses in addition to print courses.

Sidebar 3 (continued)

I had skills the newspaper needed and parlayed that into a job. I then worked for the newspaper whenever I came home for Christmas and spring vacations.

I decided I needed to leave Idaho when I was offered a full-time job at $105 a week. That's just a bit more than $5,000 a year. It wasn't THAT long ago. Now I've worked for a wire service, two newspapers, a news magazine, a radio network, a television network and a number of online publications.

Adapt to the market is my mantra. The best job I ever had was covering the Chicago Cubs and the Chicago White Sox as a backup sports writer for the Associated Press. Think about it: free food and three hours a day watching baseball. Well, I guess some people wouldn't think that's heaven. I did!

James H. Kenney Jr., Western Kentucky University

The story about getting my first job in photojournalism is actually more of a job-hunting tip. While I was still in college, I applied for a job at the Hanford Sentinel in California. There were two of us being considered for the opening.

The weekend before my interview, I went to Hanford and shot a town festival. I developed the negatives and made contact sheets (small positive images made from the original negatives) and brought them with me to the interview. My intent was to give the photo editor an idea of how I would shoot a typical assignment for him.

The photo editor liked my work, but I found out later he was more impressed that I had taken the time and effort to shoot the assignment before I got the job. The effort showed him that I not only wanted a job, but I wanted *that* job. I was told that it was the deciding factor in getting hired over the other candidate.

Michael Mercer, Auburn University

I was introduced to the newspaper industry in January 1970 when I began working part time as a janitor for *The Jackson* (Tenn.) *Sun.* I was a high school senior at the time, and my father was a full-time janitor for *The Sun.*

I worked three years as a janitor, mostly 15 hours a week split between Fridays and Sundays while attending a local college, where I was majoring in mathematics and certifying to teach math to grades 7–12.

In 1973, *The Sun's* new owner, Cowles Corp., discovered I had never filled out an application to

work at the newspaper, so I was asked to do the paperwork. On the application, there was a space to fill in any of my activities. At the time, I was assistant editor for the college newspaper, so I mentioned that.

When my supervisor found out I was writing for the college newspaper, he told me the new publisher was seeking some local writers and wondered if it was OK to pass that information on. The next thing I knew, the supervisor reported the new publisher wanted to meet me. The publisher (now a journalism educator himself) asked to see samples of my work.

When I brought him samples (mostly columns), he apparently was impressed and asked me if I wanted to intern there in the summer of 1973. Since I already had a summer job working at a local college, I told him I could only devote about seven weeks to the full-time internship. He said that was fine. At the end of the internship, the newsroom kept me on was a part-time reporter my senior year in college. It was a good thing, too, since my janitorial job was phased out, anyway. When I graduated in 1974, I covered my own graduation. The newspaper ran a front-page, color photo showing me in cap-and-gown writing notes.

I worked full time for *The Sun* from 1974 to 1994.

Mark Paxton, Southwest Missouri State

My first job out of college was as a reporter at the *Charleston Daily Mail,* the afternoon newspaper in the capital of West Virginia. I can summarize in one word how I got that job: experience.

Each semester I was in school, I worked on the student newspaper, doing everything from reporting to being editor. I had to write stories on deadline. I had to design pages. I had to decide which stories we would run and which we wouldn't. That kind of experience simply can't be duplicated in a classroom.

I also worked outside the college. I had two summer internships—one at the afternoon newspaper in my hometown and one in the public relations department at an oil company. In addition, I spent my Friday nights one autumn helping my hometown morning newspaper cover high school football. When it came time for me to graduate, I had plenty of clips to show prospective employers

Sidebar 3 (continued)

what kind of work I could do, and I could also demonstrate my willingness to work hard. The result? I had my first job guaranteed two months before I walked down the aisle to get my diploma.

Maryanne Reed, West Virginia University

When I graduated from Northwestern University in 1987, I hit the job market, with a master's degree in broadcast journalism and high hopes. But it ended up taking me six months and 18,000 miles to find that first on-air job in television news.

I started my job search from my parents' home in Lancaster, Pa., first sending out resume tapes to television stations with advertised openings. After two months and lots of rejection letters, I decided to be more aggressive in my job search. So I planned a series of "road trips" in which I peddled my wares, much like the traveling salesmen of the 1950s.

I drove around the country in my parents' 1979 powder-blue Buick Riviera, meeting with news directors in small and medium television markets. With my box of resume tapes in tow, I traveled as far north as Portland, Maine, as far south as Dothan, Ala., and as far west as Cedar Rapids, Iowa. I put myself up in cheap motels and lived on all-you-can-eat breakfast buffets and peanut butter and jelly sandwiches.

From this experience, I sharpened my reporting skills. Each time I came to a city, I had to find my way around quickly, and I had to learn as much as possible about the community and the television market, so I could come to the interviews prepared.

I also learned to be persistent, another helpful personality trait for a reporter, because I was rejected for jobs quite often, and I was frequently insulted. One news director in upstate New York said I had a voice for newspapers. And I was occasionally stood up. I often sat in the waiting room of television stations for hours, only to be told the news director was too busy to see me that day.

When I was done, I had met with more than 50 news directors and had four job offers. I ended up taking a job as general assignment reporter at WETM-

TV in Elmira, N.Y., the NBC affiliate. The pay was around $12,000 a year, and I worked long, grueling hours, but I learned a lot. In this position, I did everything from shooting video to setting up my own lights and running my own TelePrompTer.

Ford Risley, Penn State

My first job was a two-year stint as a reporter with the *Daytona Beach News-Journal.* I don't remember how I heard about the job, but I was hired to work in one of the newspaper's bureaus. There I covered two small communities: the self-proclaimed "Fern Capital of the World" along with another town that was a haven for spiritualists.

Eventually, I moved to the main newsroom, where I covered government affairs of several beachfront cities. It was a terrific experience because the communities were facing all the problems associated with growth: traffic, housing, taxes and environmental concerns. But the best part of the job was the extraordinary group of young journalists I got to know. We became good friends, spending many hours socializing and talking about the news business. I'm proud to say that virtually everyone has stayed in communications-related professions. Several have gone on to work at outstanding newspapers such as the *Los Angeles Times,* the *Minneapolis Star-Tribune,* the *Orange County Register* and the *Pittsburgh Post-Gazette.*

Carol Schlagheck, Eastern Michigan University

In early 1976, I was a senior at Bedford High School in Temperance, Mich., and editor of the high school newspaper, *The Goalpost.* I got a call from an advertising saleswoman at the local weekly. She was plotting to found a competing paper. Was I interested in helping? By February of my senior year, I was editor of *The Bedford Journal.* I wrote all the stories, took all the pictures, pasted up pages and sometimes delivered papers for $2.50 an hour. Best job I've ever had.

Sidebar 3 (continued)

Ron Schie, West Virginia University

Returning from a two-year stint in the Peace Corps, I wanted to get a job in television production. I wanted to write for TV and thought the production experience would help me to understand the medium and meet people working in the business.

A friend of a friend helped me to get an interview at WNBC-TV in New York City. And I was hired, not in the production area, but as a traffic coordinator. Traffic coordinators were actually in the spot sales department. They're responsible for scheduling when commercials will run and often serve as liaison between the ad agencies and the production staff. This gave me the opportunity to come into contact with advertising people who often knew of job openings. Not wanting to be a traffic coordinator, I took the first job that gave me the chance to write. Though ad copy it was, and not the scripts that I dreamed of writing, it was only temporary. But years later, I'm still in advertising and loving it. Soon I will write that play I learned how to do in college.

David Tait, Carleton University

I missed the interviewers from the *London Free Press* when they came to my journalism school in my final year, even though it was the job I wanted most. I'd been called away as part of a disaster research team. Jim O'Neail, the city editor, let me stop at the paper on my way back, but I was so tired and nervous that I booted the interview, badly. Hearing that my connecting flight wasn't until late, O'Neail bought me dinner and got me talking about my field work with the research team. I told story after story about all I'd done and all I'd learned. He hired me, after all.

Robert Unger, University of Missouri–Kansas City

Getting that first job, for me and my generation, was far different than it is for yours. I graduated from the University of Missouri–Columbia in 1967, and that put me on the market in 1969 after a couple of years in the U.S. Army. That was pre-Watergate, before the journalism boom and before our profession began to pay like one.

Still, it wasn't all wonderful. Yes, I had offers—four, in fact. I chose the *Chicago Tribune,* even though I was offered $10 a week more by the *Muskegon Chronicle.* So I started for $160 a week in January 1970, taking a dramatic pay cut, in real terms, from my officer's pay in the Army.

Despite all that, I think the rules are still about the same: Walk the line between confident and cocky, and concentrate more on what that prospective employer needs than on what you want. Above all, remember that the everyday practice of journalism is the great equalizer. College heroics, memberships and popularity matter little after the first day. And talent ALWAYS rises to the top.

Robert Wernsman Jr., Texas Tech University

"Your Grandma Rose called from Wahoo." How innocent a message that seemed. My sweet Grandma calling a soon-to-be mid-1970s journalism degree-holder. Granted, job prospects seemed few at the moment, but this was an optimistic time despite no solid leads from letters of inquiry yet.

Then, Grandma called. Retired after a fruitful life of teaching youngsters in Prague, Neb., she was living her last years in the county seat town. The return call revealed a most pleasant surprise: "The *Wahoo Newspaper* [yep, that's the actual name] is looking for a sports editor."

Aaahh! The chance to return home, cover the sports of nine high schools and a college. So you can go home, in a sense, and instill an enthusiasm for local news and sports coverage. But as you network for that first job, never forget: return calls to Grandma. You just never know.

Don't waste time preparing a package for a company where you don't want to work. You still might get the job, but your distaste may affect your attitude and your job performance. Do your homework on companies where you want to work. Find out what kind of person they're looking for and learn who the key players are in the hiring process.

You might want to consider ensuring you have an answering machine or an answering service provided by your telephone company when you're looking for response to your application packages. If you have an answering machine or answering service, consider changing greetings and adopt a shorter I'm-not-here-please-leave-a-message greeting instead. Not many employers have the patience to wait for a long, cutesy message to end. The greeting with all kinds of musical backgrounds you reserved for friends and family isn't appropriate for folks who mean business and may want to do business with you when they call.

Follow up immediately and professionally on any packages you send to a prospective employee. If you get an interview, dress professionally and be prepared to ask as well as answer questions. If you get a job offer, give the prospective employer an answer as soon as possible. If you need help making a decision, ask for some time and the deadline for the decision. Ask friends, professors and professionals for their advice. When you make your decision, let the prospective employer know as soon as possible so he or she will know whether to stop looking or not.

Exercises

1. Take your resume and apply the principles outlined in this chapter. What would you do to improve your resume?

2. Write a cover letter for an internship or a job. What should you emphasize to get the position?

Suggested Readings

"Internship Directory," Society of Professional Journalists Reports, 1996. SPJ, 16 S. Jackson St., Greencastle, Ind. 46135-1514, (317) 653-3333 or http://www.spj.org This directory provides listings of available internships throughout the country. Local SPJ chapters often have information about possible openings in their sections of the country.

"Newspapers, Diversity & You," Dow Jones Newspaper Fund. 1995. This is an excellent booklet that features facts and figures concerning journalism careers. It has a sample resume and cover letter as well as tips for developing them, job-hunting tips, information about various internships and scholarships and testimonials from journalists about what turns them on about journalism.

18 The Emerging World of Online Journalism

Christopher Harper
Professor, Ithaca College
Idaho Statesman, Associated Press, Newsweek, ABC News and
"ABC 20/20"

Chapter Outline

Online at the *Chicago Tribune*
   Darnell Little
   Stephen Henderson
Virtual Melanin
Writing online

Cornelia Grumman of the *Chicago Tribune* is a new breed of journalist—the digital journalist who uses techniques from print, broadcast and online reporting.

Cornelia Grumman presses the sixth-floor button on the elevator at the Henry Horner public housing project. The City of Chicago has planted flowers outside the building, where gangs and drug pushers really run the West Side neighborhood. The elevator doesn't work well and reeks of urine. After two tries at the button, Grumman finally rides to the fifth floor and walks up one flight of garbage-laden stairs. Two young boys climb on a safety fence that's supposed to keep them from falling into the garden below, but the fence seems more like a cage to keep them in.

Grumman, a reporter for the *Chicago Tribune,* wants to know what people on welfare think about massive changes in the federal program. She visits 24-year-old Melineice Reed and her three children, who live in a well-kept, but tiny, three-room apartment. Reed has lived in the projects all her life. The next day she has an interview for a job as a cleaning woman, and she's a bit nervous. "Do you have anything to wear that's nice?" Grumman asks. "Nice enough," Reed says.

Nearby, a group of worshipers gathers at a Baptist church for Sunday services. Grumman finds several people willing to talk about the federal plan that would limit benefits to the poor. One woman, Demitraius Dykes, has spent all of her 26 years on welfare. A recovering drug addict, she has five children. Dykes says she's trying to turn her life around, attending a course in office skills. "I don't want my kids to grow up and think they should sit around and wait each month for their check," she says. Grumman scribbles notes, runs a tape recorder and takes a picture later. Although she doesn't like using video cameras, Grumman wishes she had one along for this interview, because Dykes is a good talker.

Grumman is one of a new breed of journalists—the digital journalist. Although more than 200 American newspapers offer an online edition, most are simply an electronic version of the printed newspaper—a "shovel-down" version, as it's known on the Internet. The *Tribune,* however, is one of the few newspapers in the country that has devoted reporters to work exclusively for the Internet edition. The reporters write stories, take pictures, operate video cameras and even create digital pages. With 20 other staff members, the seven reporters produce one of the most innovative online editions available today.

Communicating through digital media may mean more preparation than for other media. A computer story or presentation may start with a storyboard, which contains an online version of a page's content, graphics and computer links to other material.

At the turn of this century, the U.S. Census Bureau used a counting machine and punch cards developed by the man who eventually created IBM. Do you know what the Census Bureau found? The top job in America was as a farmer. Printers stood at No. 24 on the list of the top jobs. By 1965, printers were off the list. Even though digital computers—the type we use today—had been around for nearly 50 years, computer users didn't make the top 30 jobs. By 1995, math and computer scientists and computer programmers both landed spots on the top 30 jobs list. Together, they represented the sixth-largest category of jobs, with 2.2 million workers. The top five jobs were retail salespeople, teachers, secretaries, truck drivers and farmers. Just beneath computer types were janitors and cooks.

As we enter the next millennium, computer work rather than farming is likely to be the job of choice, unless, of course, you'd rather be a janitor or a cook. That's cook, not chef!

Hundreds of American publications are on line. If you don't know about online journalism, you'll be left behind with the hot metal typesetters and the hard-drinking, chain-smoking reporters in fedoras.

Online at the *Chicago Tribune*

Here is a glimpse inside the world of online journalism at the *Chicago Tribune*. The newspaper editors and reporters at the *Tribune* tend toward traditional corporate attire. With few exceptions, the online group tends toward T-shirts, blue jeans and tennis shoes. Grumman, by far the best-dressed, in her business suits, studied public policy at Duke University and the Kennedy School of Government at Harvard. She worked as a freelance reporter in China, including booking rock-n-roll bands there. Another reporter, Darnell Little studied computer programming and developed telephone software for Bell Labs before becoming a journalist. Stephen Henderson wrote editorials for newspapers in Lexington, Ky., and Detroit before joining the *Tribune's* Internet staff.

During the 1996 Democratic convention in Chicago, the Internet edition of the newspaper reached nearly 100,000 users a day—more than most newspapers in the nation—by putting together a mixture of original reporting, audio reports from the *Tribune's* radio station, video clips from two *Tribune* television stations and articles from the printed edition.

Darnell Little

Reporter Little conceived a historical tour of some of the 25 previous political conventions in the city, starting with the one that nominated Abraham Lincoln in 1860. Little, who received master's degrees in both engineering and journalism from Northwestern, went to the Chicago Historical Society to get a visual sense of how to conduct a tour on the World Wide Web.

"The idea was to take people on a tour that was a virtual museum. There were three parallel streams. There was the tour guide—a walk through six conventions. The second was a behind-the-scenes look at what was happening in Chicago at the time. The third part included archives and political cartoons," Little explains. "The reporting is the same as working for a standard newspaper—gathering the information and talking to people. But you put it together and write it differently."

Before writing a story, Little designs a series of storyboards for what each of the main pages will show—a practice used extensively in the film, television and advertising industries. The storyboard contains an outline of a page's content, graphics and computer links to other stories.

After Little reports a story, he then follows his original storyboards, with adaptations, to make certain that the reporting, photography, headlines and navigation make the stories easy for the reader to enjoy.

Little uses the storytelling approach of the *Wall Street Journal* articles on the front page, which he says works well on the Web. The first page uses an anecdotal lead to draw the reader into the story. The second page broadens the story with the nut graph. The other pages flow from these first two pages to allow the reader to follow a variety of links that expand on each report.

The process is called "layering." Because a computer screen contains less space than the front page of a newspaper, the first layer, or page, of a digital story contains a headline, a digital photograph and text that makes the user want to continue to the next layer. The pages are usually less than 500 words with the reader's option, to select a highlighted path set out on a guide. But a user may want to follow another path. He or she could read about the 1860 convention and want to learn more about what was happening in Chicago during that period. After searching through the archives of that time, the user can proceed to the next convention or even skip ahead to another convention. The layers provide a logical way to proceed, but the layers can also enable the user to read the digital page in any order.

"I write the story in chapters," Little says. "What works the best is when you have a design on the Web that is the equivalent of the layout of a magazine and your eye and attention are focused on one part, which is easily digestible, and it flows and leads you into other parts."

Stephen Henderson

When he wears his Detroit Tigers baseball cap, reporter Henderson looks like a young Spike Lee. Henderson studied political science at the University of Michigan and started as an editorial writer at newspapers in Kentucky and Detroit. Within days after his arrival in Chicago, he noticed a story about the 1995 murder rates in the city.

"It wasn't a big deal. It was a story that the paper does every year," he recalls. "I said to myself, 'I bet there's a lot more there.'" Henderson asked the print reporters for all the information about the murders—the time, the neighborhood, the cause of death and a variety of other statistics. He put together a map of the city and allowed every citizen to look for information about his or her neighborhood—again with a click of the mouse rather than a visit to the records office of the police precinct. "We got thousands of people interested," he says. "If we use a big database in telling a story, [we] also have to give the readers a chance to use that database. That's giving people information that's important to them."

Virtual Melanin

It's been a long day for McLean Greaves. Rapper Biggie Smalls had been gunned down only a few days before, and 31-year-old Greaves was working on a Smalls tribute on the World Wide Web. He had been going through videotape and putting up the site nearly nonstop for two days.

Ironically, Greaves then had to turn his attention to the Web site design for Bad Boy Records, Smalls' label, which was supposed to go public soon. He'd have to work around-the-clock to get the Web site done. Simply put, Greaves and his co-workers' sweat equity and long nights are putting their Web site development company, Virtual Melanin, on the Internet map.

The motto from Greaves and his company is: "Brothas and Sistas. Not tall enough for the NBA? Too 'unique' to get signed to a record deal? Don't worry; there's another way to get outta the ghetto: the Internet."

Greaves' clients include director Spike Lee's company, 40 Acres & A Mule Filmworks and the Entertainers Basketball Classic, a famed tournament held each year in Harlem. The premier Web site, however, is Cafe Los Negroes, a cyberspace meeting place for news, entertainment and chat. All of Greaves' sites emphasize "melanin," which are naturally occurring dark skin pigments. "It's everything on the

Virtual Melanin, which takes its name from the pigment that creates dark colors, is a digital company that appeals to African-Americans and Latinos in their 20s and 30s.

Web with melanin," he explains, with an emphasis on attracting Generation Xers, particularly African Americans and Latinos. Whites are also welcome; it's not an exclusive club. The cost of membership is only a click of a computer mouse. The cafe includes an online publication with news and entertainment. There are sections devoted to poetry, new filmmakers, music reviews and even a fashion boutique.

Born in Barbados, Greaves grew up in Vancouver Island, Canada, where there were three blacks in his high school graduation class. He recalls buying hair products through mail order from Chicago because none were available in western Canada. The only time, he says, he could hear black music was by turning his radio a certain way after midnight to hear a Seattle jazz station. So he developed Cafe Los Negroes for those who may not be able to easily access black and Latin cultures.

The World Wide Web opens up huge possibilities, Greaves argues, for news and entertainment at low costs to the customer. Together with Arzie Hardin, a former Wall Street currency trader, and Tyrone Thomas, a top-of-the-line programmer, Greaves has put together a team of about 20 people in design and marketing. The group has stayed in Bedford-Stuyvesant, one of the toughest ghettos in New York City, because it keeps overhead low and allows the group to create a computer literacy among young blacks and Latinos. "We're bringing it right to the streets," he says. "We're basically showing people that they have a voice."

It's not a strident voice. It's confident voice with a good bit of humor. Across the top of Cafe Los Negroes, for example, the site pledges that Ebonics, the street language, isn't spoken there. The company answering machine states, "Remember the next revolution will be computerized."

Greaves stresses the need for entrepreneurial skills rather than protests in the ghetto. "It's different from the old rules of the sixties—protests and solidarity," Greaves explains. "We don't complain about 'the White Man.' That's anachronistic. It worked well when there were the civil rights issues of the sixties. But not now."

The group produces an online newspaper, *Root Stand,* in which Greaves uses his journalistic skills learned at the Canadian Broadcasting Co. He's started to create a team of camera operators to work on a virtual news site. "In the United States, there's a chasm between blacks and whites. If you tap into our world and hear our debates and our issues, you can join in. It doesn't make any difference what race you are. Even if you say you're white, no one on our sites is going to say, 'You can't hang out here.'"

Writing Online

I have worked for newspapers, a wire service, a news magazine, a television network and a television magazine. Today, almost all my work appears online. When I criticized the *Washington Post,* I heard about it, almost immediately via e-mail. When I wrote about pornography on the Internet, I heard about it via e-mail. When I wrote about kids and computers, I heard about it via e-mail.

There's an immediate response to what you write. People out there are reading and listening. And you have to react to their compliments, criticisms and complaints. That's why I got in this business more than 20 years ago: to reach people. That's why Cornelia Grumman, Darnell Little, Steve Henderson and McLean Greaves do it, too.

Exercises

1. Go to the World Wide Web and find the *Chicago Tribune* at http://www.chicago.tribune.com and Virtual Melanin at http://www.vmelanin.com What do you think is good about the presentation, navigation and writing on these two sites?

2. Find a publication you read on the World Wide Web. Apply the principles outlined in this chapter for good writing and navigation. Write down how well you think your favorite publication does in comparison with the *Chicago Tribune* and Virtual Melanin.

Suggested Readings

Gentry, Leah. "Buckbobbill: Journalist." Newspaper Association of America. December 1996. http://www.naa.org The author has been responsible for online media at the *Orange County Register,* the *Chicago Tribune* and the *Los Angeles Times.* This article analyzes writing for digital publications.

Gilder, George. *Life After Television: The Coming Transformation of Media and American Life.* New York: W.W. Norton Co., 1995. The author is one of the best thinkers about the media. This book is a classic about the impact of digital media.

Neuman, W. Russell. *The Future of Mass Audience.* New York: Cambridge University Press, 1995. The author is another of the best minds who ponder the media and their place in society. This book provides a look back and a look into the future of all media.

Style

You won't win a Pulitzer Prize, an Emmy or an Obie for copy that uses proper style, good grammar and correct spelling. But you'll make a lot of friends on the copy desk. Almost every newspaper has its own stylebook, which tells reporters and editors how to use a variety of terms, titles, numbers and even spelling. Many publications use the Associated Press as a guide. But the *New York Times,* for example, varies its style significantly from the AP. Following are some generally accepted guidelines, but it's important to check with a publication's specific stylebook.

Addresses

With specific addresses, abbreviate most designations such as Avenue, Boulevard and Street. For example, you should use 192 Fifth Ave.; 129 Ramsey Blvd.; and 155 Casey St. If the address is not as specific, the designations are usually spelled out. For example, use Fifth Avenue, Ramsey Boulevard and Casey Street.

Dates

Months are spelled out if used without a specific date—for example, February 1949. Note there is no comma between February and 1949.

If a month is used for a specific date, some months are spelled out. These include March, April, May, June and July—for example, July 4, 1995.

The other months are abbreviated:

January is Jan.	October is Oct.
February is Feb.	November is Nov.
August is Aug.	December is Dec.
September is Sept.	

For example, Jan. 1, 2000, is the beginning of the next millennium. Note that a comma follows the specific date and the year.

Numbers

If a number begins a sentence, it's always spelled out—for example:

Eighty people arrived late for the party.

But the sentence would be written differently if the number doesn't begin the sentence:

Nearly 80 people arrived late for the party.

Spell out numbers one through nine unless it's an age or a date:

One person voted against the plan.

His 2-year-old daughter plays well with other children.

She was born Feb. 2, 1996.

You should use a dollar sign and a numeral for money. For example, it is $5 and $5,000. However, it's $5 million and $5 billion. If you use a specific figure such as $5.13, keep in mind that you need a decimal point between the dollars and cents. The same is true for $5.13 million.

Percentages

Percent is one word. Use figures such as 10 percent or 26.7 percent. If the number is less than 1 percent, you should use 0.7 percent.

Government Numbers

Use numerals and capitalize the next word:

1st Ward, 2nd District, 3rd Precinct, 4th U.S. Court of Appeals. Use *the ward, the district* and *the precinct* if the number is not specified:

The ward is a political subdivision in Chicago.

Street Numbers

Spell out street numbers below 10:

Fifth Avenue 10th Street

The same approach is used for amendments to the U.S. Constitution. Use First Amendment and 12th Amendment. For other use of numbers, including fractions, sports scores, dramatic acts and scenes, Roman numerals, page numbers, telephone numbers, weights and others, see the AP stylebook.

Places

Without a city, the state's name should be spelled out.

With a city, eight states are spelled out. These are Alaska, Hawaii, Idaho, Iowa, Maine, Ohio, Texas and Utah. For example, it should be Juneau, Alaska; Honolulu, Hawaii; Boise, Idaho; Des Moines, Iowa; Portland, Maine; Columbus, Ohio; Houston, Texas; and Provo, Utah.

With a city, the other 42 states are abbreviated. You can't remember all of them, so look them up.

Alabama is Ala.

Arizona is Ariz.

Arkansas is Ark.

California is Calif.

Colorado is Colo.

Connecticut is Conn.

Delaware is Del.

Florida is Fla.

Georgia is Ga.

Illinois is Ill.

Indiana is Ind.

Kansas is Kan.

Kentucky is Ky.

Louisiana is La.

Maryland is Md.

Massachusetts is Mass.

Michigan is Mich.

Minnesota is Minn.

Mississippi is Miss.

Missouri is Mo.

Montana is Mont.

Nebraska is Neb.

Nevada is Nev.

New Hampshire is N.H.

New Jersey is N.J.

New Mexico is N.M.

New York is N.Y.

North Carolina is N.C.

North Dakota is N.D.

Oklahoma is Okla.

Oregon is Ore.

Pennsylvania is Pa.

Rhode Island is R.I.

South Carolina is S.C.

South Dakota is S.D.

Tennessee is Tenn.

Vermont is Vt.

Virginia is Va.

Washington is Wash.

West Virginia is W.Va.

Wisconsin is Wis.

Wyoming is Wyo.

For example, it's St. Paul, Minn.; Sioux Falls, S.D.; and Baltimore, Md.

Sexism

Fireman. Use *firefighter.*

Mailman. Use *mail carrier.*

Mankind. Use *humanity.*

Policeman. Use *police officer.*

Be careful about using the word *his* to describe actions that could be done by both men and women. For example, the following is a common error:

A reporter should check his copy.

A reporter can be either male or female. Some teachers prefer this approach:

A reporter should check his or her copy.

A better way to write this sentence is:

Reporters should check their copy.

Time

a.m. and p.m. should be in lowercase with periods. A precise time such at 8:03 p.m. should use a colon that separates the hour and the minutes. A time such as 8 p.m. shouldn't include a colon followed by two zeros. Be careful about being redundant with times. For example, 8 p.m. at night is redundant because p.m. means at night. You can say 8 o'clock tonight. Use noon and midnight. Noon and midnight happen only at the 12s.

Titles

A variety of abbreviations are used for titles, particularly when an individual's complete name is used:

Capt. John James fired the shot. But it is

The captain fired the shot.

Other military and police titles include

The general or Gen. John James (military only)

The colonel or Col. John James (military only)

The lieutenant colonel or Lt. Col. John James (military only)

The lieutenant or Lt. John James

The sergeant or Sgt. John James

The corporal or Cpl. John James (military only)

The private or Pvt. John James (military only)

Political Titles

The governor spoke at the convention.

Gov. John James spoke at the convention.

Other titles include

The lieutenant governor or Lt. Gov. John James

The representative or Rep. John James, D-N.J.

The senator or Sen. John James, D-N.J.

Academic Titles

The university president handed out the diplomas at graduation.

University President John James handed out the diplomas at graduation.

Other titles include

The dean or Dean John James

The professor or Professor John James

Religious Titles

The reverend said Mass.

Rev. John James said Mass.

Other titles include

The bishop or Bishop John James

The archbishop or Archbishop John James

The pope or Pope Paul VI

A variety of titles are generic and should not be capitalized. These titles include carpenter, teacher, steelworker and a host of others.

When the individual's name is used again, the last name should be used. Many editors maintain that women should have courtesy titles such as Miss, Ms. or Mrs. The professors involved in writing this textbook believe this practice is antiquated. Check your publications and follow that style.

Grammar

Make Sure Your Subjects and Verbs Agree

Most of us can remember studying grammar in elementary school or middle school. Some of us can remember diagramming sentences. By the time we reached high school, studying grammar took a back seat to studying literature. In English composition classes in college, we probably spent more time learning how to document sources and how to write thesis statements than we did learning grammar. Some common grammatical errors can be fixed simply and easily. The first of these is subject-verb agreement.

In most sentences, it's easy to figure out the subject and verb. In the sentence "Joe hit the ball," "Joe" is the subject and "hit" is the verb. The trouble comes when the subject isn't so easy to identify.

Consider the sentence, "Beneath the sea lie/lies adventure and danger." What's the subject? It's not "Beneath," although that comes before the verb; rather, it's "adventure and danger." And as we all remember from our grammar lessons earlier in life, a compound subject takes a plural verb. In this case, therefore, the sentence should read

Beneath the sea lie adventure and danger.

Now examine this sentence: "Neither Joe nor the twins is/are going to the fair tonight." The subject is "Joe" and "the twins," so obviously the verb is the plural "are." Correct? Yes. But now turn the sentence around: "Neither the twins nor Joe is/are going to the fair tonight." Now the verb turns into the singular "is." Why? Whenever you have the construction "either . . . or" or "neither . . . nor," and the subject consists of a singular (such as "Joe") and a plural (such as "the twins"), the number of the verb—that is, whether it's singular or plural—is determined by which subject is closer to the verb. It's the only instance in the English language that the position of the subject determines whether the verb is singular or plural. Following are some more subject verb agreement tips.

- In the construction "There is . . ." or "There are . . ." the subject is NOT "There." The subject follows the linking verb "is" or "are." Examples: "There is one man" but "There are a boy and girl."

- The construction "as well as" is not part of the subject. Example: "John, as well as Bill and Ted, is going to the store." "John" is the subject and requires a singular verb.

- These words, when used as a subject, ALWAYS take a singular verb: *each, either, anyone, everyone, much, no one, nothing, someone.*

- When *each, either, every* and *neither* are used as adjectives, the noun they modify always takes a singular verb. Examples: "Every cask of wine was spoiled." "Every" modified "cask," which is the subject. "Cask," therefore, takes a singular verb.

- "Number" can be singular or plural. "The number is" but "A number are." The same rule holds true for the words *majority* and *percentage*.

- *None* is almost always singular. Think of it as "not one." Example: "None of the boys is ready to play."

Nouns and Pronouns Must Agree

Not only must your subjects and verbs agree, but your pronouns and the nouns they refer to also must agree. We all know that verbs come in singular (*is*) and plural (*are*). The same is true for pronouns. There are singular pronouns (*he, she, it, his, her, its*) and plural pronouns (*they, their*).

The trick is making sure you use a singular pronoun when the noun it refers to is singular; you must use a plural pronoun when the noun is plural. The trickiest time to do this is when your noun is a "collective" noun. For example, take the work *team,* as in the sentence "The team won its/their third game of the season." Is *its* or *their* correct? To answer this, determine what the noun is. In this case, it's *team.* How many teams are there in this sentence? Just one? If so, then team is singular, and the word requires the singular pronoun *its:* "The team won its third game of the season."

But what if instead of the word *team,* the sentence used the team's nickname? "The Bears won its/their third game of the season." In this case, how many bears are there? Isn't each member of the team a Bear, and together they make up the Bears? If so,

Bears is plural and requires the plural pronoun: "The Bears won their third game of the season." It gets trickier still. What if the team is the Marshall University Thundering Herd? How many Thundering Herds are there? Just one. Each member is not an individual Thundering Herd, so the team nickname is still singular: "The Thundering Herd won its third game of the season."

One way to check for noun-pronoun agreement is to read back through your work and identify each pronoun, then find the noun that the pronoun refers to (called the antecedent). If you have trouble finding the antecedent, that means your sentence is probably unclear and needs to be rewritten. If you can easily find the antecedent, though, double-check to make sure it and the pronoun are in agreement.

Punctuation

You probably didn't know that there are 13 different types of punctuation. That may be the unlucky reason many of us don't use punctuation properly. These guidelines are only some simple rules. English punctuation is difficult. Keep a grammar book handy. When you aren't 100 percent certain of what to do, you're probably going to use a punctuation mark improperly. Look it up!

Periods

You should use a period to say, "stop, the end." Once a complete thought—recorded in a complete sentence—is finished, a period is usually appropriate:

I finished the test.

Commas

If periods mean to stop, commas simply mean to slow down. Many writers tend to use too many commas. People stick a comma in somewhere where there's nothing better to do.

Commas in a series are slightly different in journalism than in a term paper. For example, here's how commas are used in a series:
I bought cherries, peaches and plums at the supermarket.

Note that there's NO commas between the word *peaches* and the word *and*. Commas in a quotation go before the final quotation marks.

"I don't want to go," he said.

Note where the comma is placed. Many beginning writers want to put the comma outside the quotation marks.

Commas separate ages from a name:

James Mason, 69, died today.

Commas separate a politician's party affiliation from the name.

Sen. Strom Thurmond, R-S.C., has served the most number of years in the U.S. Senate.

Apostrophes

You use an apostrophe to create a possessive—a designation of ownership. But it's a bit tricky. Here's an example:

I spent the afternoon at the Smiths' house.

If the owner's name ends with an *s* or sounds like a *z*, then you put the apostrophe after the *s*:

I went to Chris' house for dinner.

But, of course, there are exceptions. When in doubt, look them up. No one can remember all of them. If you're on a strict deadline and really don't have time to look up the rules, write the sentence differently to eliminate the possessive.

Semicolons

Don't use a semicolon unless you really know how to use one. Most people don't use semicolons properly. When in doubt, use a period. A semicolon separates two thoughts in a single sentence, acting much like a period.

The sky was blue; the temperature was cold.

You could just as easily write these thoughts as:

The sky was blue. The temperature was cold.

Colons

Use a colon to introduce a list or an example as we've used it in this appendix. A colon also occurs in specific times such as 8:03 p.m. Sometimes a colon can be used for emphasis:

He had one goal: first place.

Quotation Marks

You should use quotation marks to demonstrate that something is quoted either in full or in part—for example,

"The sun got in my eyes," the driver said.

The sun "got in my eyes" without any warning, the driver said.
Note that no comma is used in partial quotes used in the middle of a sentence.

Question Marks

A question mark is used at the end of a question. There are few other uses.

Hyphens

A hyphen generally connects words acting as adjectives or to avoid confusion:

"well-connected individual" rather than "wellconnected individual" "know-it-all" rather than "knowitall"

If the first word in such a phrase ends in "ly," however, do not use a hyphen:

"broadly based coalition" rather than "broadly-based coalition"

"usually reliable poll" rather than "usually-reliable poll"

Brackets, Ellipses, Dashes, Exclamation Points and Parentheses

For the most part, use them sparingly.

Words That Cause Trouble

Journalists need to understand words. Hundreds of words cause trouble for writers. A good grammar book written for journalists will help you keep track of troublesome words. Following is a short list of words that give students problems:

1. *Affect, effect. Affect* is usually a verb. Generally, *effect* is a noun. "The effect of the program will be negative." "The program will affect the college." *Effect* can be a verb that means to bring about. "The president sought to effect a change in attitude."

2. *All right. Alright* is never acceptable in professional writing.

3. *Compose, comprise.* A tricky one. See the AP stylebook for more information. Remember that the parts COMPOSE the whole, whereas the whole COMPRISES its parts.

4. *Destroy.* You cannot partially destroy something. Therefore, "completely" or "totally destroyed" is redundant. "Almost completely destroyed" is nonsense.

5. *Hopefully.* This work is an adverb and describes how someone feels. "The student waited hopefully for the check to arrive." Don't use the word to mean "it is hoped." Don't write

"Hopefully, I will pass this class." Write "I hope I will pass this class."

6. *Imply, infer.* A speaker implies, whereas the listener infers.

7. *It's, its. It's* means it is, whereas *its* is possessive.

8. *Its, their.* Remember that collective nouns take a singular possessive. "The faculty will hold its meeting."

9. *Lay, lie.* Another tricky one because the past tense of *lie* is *lay. Lay* (*laying, laid*) is the action word and takes a direct object. "I will lay the book on the table; I laid the book on the table" *Lie* (*lying, lay*) refers to a state of being. "He will lie on the couch." "He lay on the couch until he felt better."

10. *Less, fewer.* Use *less* when referring to a quantity that can't be divided, *fewer* when writing about numbers. "There were fewer bottles of milk in the story." "My glass had less milk than his."

11. *Like, as.* Substitute "similar to" in the sentence. If it makes sense, use *like.* Another way to tell the difference is, "as" or "as if" is usually followed by a phrase that has a verb. "Do as I do." "His house is like a garbage dump."

12. *Over, more than. Over* should be reserved for spatial relationships such as "flying over the city." With numbers, use *more than.* "He earned more than $8 an hour for the work." Unfortunately, many newsrooms use *over* as a substitute for *more than.*

13. *That, which.* Use *that* to introduce material that is needed to understand the word it modifies. In other words, use *which* when the material is an afterthought or could be deleted (put in parentheses). REMEMBER: Use a comma to separate *which* from the word it modifies. "The river, which is polluted, runs by my office."

14. *Flout, flaunt.* You *flout* the law, but you *flaunt* your new sports car.

15. *Nouns.* Let nouns be nouns and verbs do the work. *Impact* is a noun not a verb. Avoid nouns with *ize* tags: *finalize, prioritize and maximize. Use* is better than *utilize.*

16. *Anxious, eager.* You're anxious about passing this course, and you're eager to graduate. *Anxious* implies worry, not eagerness.

17. *Following, after. Following* isn't a preposition. *After* is a shorter word. Use it.

18. *Before, prior to.* Again, *before,* the short word, is preferred. *Prior* to is stilted.

19. *Buy, purchase.* Again, use the common word *buy. Purchase* is pretentious. Avoid it.

Spelling

accommodate

battalion

canceled

embarrass

desperate

fulfill

guerrilla

harass

hemorrhage

inoculate

irresistible

judgment (Note: there is no *e* between the *g* and *m* despite what movie titles use.)

likable

manageable

questionnaire

occurred

restaurateur (Note: there is no *n.*)

seize

separate

skillful

siege

teen-age (adjective)

teen-ager (noun)

toward, not towards (The same rule applies to backward, downward, forward, onward, upward.)

traveled

weird

There are dozens more. When you're not certain, look it up. More important, don't depend on spell check on the computer. As Mark Paxton of Southwestern Missouri State notes:

Ewe must no the rite spellings of many words, or Yule misspell sum words even if the computer says their OK.

After I wrote the preceding sentence, I ran my computer spell-check program. According to it, every word in that sentence is correct. Obviously, some words are spelled incorrectly, which points out the problem in relying on your computer to do your spelling. A computer can't tell the difference between words that sound the same but have different meanings and spellings—for instance, *to, too* and *two* are all

Credits

Photos

Chapter 1
Pg. 2: AP/Wide World Photos; pg. 9: Elaine Thompson/AP photo.

Chapter 2
Pg. 17: AP/Wide World Photos; pg. 18 Mark Elias/AP photo.

Chapter 3
Pg. 25: © Mark Hirsch; pg. 27: © James L. Shaffer.

Chapter 4
Pg. 35: UPI/Corbis-Bettmann; pg. 36: © James L. Shaffer.

Chapter 5
Pg. 44: © Frank Johnson; pg 48: © Steve Fenn/ABC, Inc.

Chapter 6
Pg. 61: UPI/Corbis-Bettmann; pg. 64: © James H. Kenney Jr.

Chapter 7
Pg. 78: Frank Niemeir; pg. 83: AP/Wide World Photos.

Chapter 8
Pg. 93, 95: © James L. Shaffer.

Chapter 9
Pg. 105: © James L. Shaffer; pg. 106: Ron Edmonds/AP photo.

Chapter 10
Pg. 118: UPI/Corbis-Bettmann; pg. 121 (both), 123, 125, 126, 127: © James H. Kenney Jr.

Chapter 11
Pg. 136, 139: © James L. Shaffer; pg. 143: AP/Wide World Photos; pg. 145: © Christopher Little/ABC, Inc.; pg. 148: provided by Maryanne Reed.

Chapter 12
Pg. 159: AP/Wide World Photos; pg. 16: *New York Times* Photo; pg. 169: © Catherine Ursillo/Photo Researchers, Inc.

Chapter 13
Pg. 175: Reuters/Corbis-Bettmann.

Chapter 14
Pg. 181: AP/Wide World Photos.

Chapter 15
Pg. 196: AP/Wide World Photos; pg. 198: © David Tulis/Atlanta Journal/Sygma.

Chapter 16
Pg. 202: AP/Wide World Photos

Chapter 17
Pg. 218: © James L. Shaffer.

Chapter 18
Pg. 228: © Blair Jensen; pg. 229: AP/Wide World Photos; pg. 232: © James L. Shaffer.

Index

A

"ABC Evening News," 145
ABC television network, 136, 145, 159, 171
"ABC 20/20," 136
Academic research, using, 29
Accidents, 63-65
Accuracy, importance of, 98
Action, in RACE formula, 184
Active verbs, 89, 112, 141
Actual malice standard, 164, 165
Addresses, finding, 37
Adobe Photoshop software, 131
Adversarial interviews, 45, 46, 49
Advertising, 191-99
    changing environment of, 193-94
    creativity and, 195
    design, 195-97
    freedom of speech in, 193
    future of, 193
    information gathering in, 197
    strategy development in, 197-98
    work samples for resumes, 220
    writing for, 198-99
Advocacy groups, ethics of joining, 173
Almanacs, as research tool, 27
American Society of Newspaper Editors (ASNE)
    code of ethics (1923), 168, 169
    job hunting and, 221
Ames, Joe, 59
Animatics, 194
Answering machines, using, 226
Art directors, 194
Artzt, Edwin, 192
ASNE. See American Society of Newspaper Editors (ASNE)

Associated Press (AP), 131, 136, 185, 223
    AP style, 90, 187, 215
    plagiarism of material, 172
    as research source, 37
Associated Press Managing Editors code of ethics (1975), 168
Associated Press Stylebook, 90, 91
Atlanta Journal, 174
Atlanta *Journal-Constitution*, 180, 185
Attribution, 9-11, 70
    examples, 92-93
    importance of, 93
Auchmutey, Jim, 180
Audience
    accommodating, 205-6
    in public relations, 182
    reaching, 202-3
    respecting, 143
    targeted in advertising, 192

B

Background, 6
    See also Research
    background interviews, 45
    gathering, 71
    going "off the record" and, 54
    for government reporting, 69-69
    primary sources and, 45
    privacy of information, 156
Backgrounders, 187
Baker, Russell, 51
Beats
    education, 66-67
    fires, accidents and disasters, 63-66
    immigration beat, 58
    obituaries, 62-63
    police and court beat, 59-61

speeches and meetings, 67-69
The Bedford Journal (Temperance, Mich.), 224
Berg, Pat, 43, 222
Better Business Bureau, as idea source, 15
Big story, 75-84
    breaking rules, 83-84
    building, 81
    enormity of, 82
    establishing relationships, 77-78
    explaining complicated subjects, 81-82
    listening and, 77
    manners and, 79-80
    requisites for, 83
    simplicity and, 78-79
Bleske, Glen, 67, 87, 222
Bly, Nellie, 170
Boorstin, Daniel J., 192
Bradley, Bill, 78
Branzburg v Hayes (1972), 160
Breach of confidentiality, 160
Brevity, 212, 219
Bridges, 146
Broadcasting
    codes of ethics, 169, 172
    first jobs, 224, 225
    radio host's view, 143
    television anchor's view, 145
    videotape log for, 146
    Broadcast writing, 6, 135-49
    determining importance, 140-44
    editing stories, 146-49
    identifying news, 139-40
    location and, 144-45
    long-form television stories, 148-49
    obituaries, 62
    photographers as part of team, 145-46
    script preparation, 138-39
    television scripts, 147
Broder, David, 80

Brusic, Ken, 58-59
Budget coverage, 66-67
Building Design Journal, 180
Burger, Warren, 159

C

Cable News Network, 174
Caldwell, Anita, 13, 222
Cameras, 122, 124
Canadian Broadcasting Corporation, 2, 233
Captions, in photojournalism, 130-31
CAR. See Computer-assisted reporting (CAR)
Careers
    in advertising, 192
    finding. See Job-hunting
Carter, Ginger Rudeseal, 69, 179, 222
Cartier-Bresson, Henri, 129
Categorical imperative, 170
Censorship
    avoiding, 84
    protection from, 164-65
Chamber of Commerce, as idea source, 15
Characters, 3, 4
Charleston (W.Va.) Daily Mail, 223-24
Chicago Sun-Times, 83
Chicago Tribune, 76, 83, 225
Chicago Tribune online, 228, 230-31
Christians, Clifford, 175
City directories, as research tool, 27
Civil damages, 160-65
Clarification, 204-5
Clarity, in communication, 203, 206
Clark, Roy Peter, 172
Closed-ended questions, 49
Closure, 3, 5
Codes of ethics, 168-70

in broadcasting, 169, 172
enforcement of, 169-70
manners and, 80
in public relations
practice, 189
Cohen v Cowles Media
(1991), 160
Collective nouns, 109
Color, in photography, 128-29
Comma splice, 110
Commentary, avoiding, 95
Commercial speech, 193
Communication
clarity in, 203, 206
in public relations, 182, 182,
183, 185
in RACE formula, 185
vocabulary and, 207
Community records
as idea source, 16
researching, 28
Complication, 3, 4
Composition, photographic,
124, 126, 126, 128
Comps, 194
Computer(s)
See also Computer-assisted
reporting (CAR)
as advertising tool, 194
digital photography, 131-32
electronic databases, 172,
192, 231
job hunting and, 215, 217
spell-checker programs, 106
use in research, 29
Computer-assisted reporting
(CAR), 33-39
strategy of, 38-39
Confidences, eliciting, 77
Confidentiality of sources,
156, 160
Conflicts of interest, ethics
and, 172
Conjunctions, 110
Content, double-checking, 67
Context, of quotes, 70
Cooke, Janet, 171
Coordinating conjunctions, 110
Copyright violations, 156
Copywriters, 194
Courts
covering, 60-61
researching, 37
terminology, 59, 60
Cover letter
example of, 219
for resume, 218-2
Cox Broadcasting v Cohn
(1975), 161
Creativity, 194, 195

Crime
invasion of privacy and, 174
reporting on, 59-61
Criminal justice system, 61
Crisis public relations, 185
C-SPAN, 68, 185

D

Database marketing, 192
Databases. See Electronic
databases
*Daytona Beach
News-Journal,* 224
Deadlines
awareness of, 66
deadline pressure, 97
media relations and, 189
Deception, ethics and, 170-71
Decisive moment, in
photojournalism, 129-30
Defamation, legal issues of,
161-65
Deliberation, in public
relations, 182
Denver Post, 168
Description
in broadcast stories, 144
in feature stories, 96
Descriptive writing, 89, 206
Design, in advertising, 195-97
Details, importance in
interviews, 50
Dialect, 94
Dictionaries, as research tool, 27
Digital journalism. See Online
journalism
Digital photography, 131-32
Direct quotes, 92, 94
Disasters, 63-65
Disclosure of private facts, 161
Documentaries, 148-49
Double-checking
factual information, 105-6
importance of, 67
for obituaries, 62

E

Economy, advertising and,
192, 194
Editing, first jobs in, 222
Editing stories, 103-13
active verbs, 112
checking spelling, 106-7
double-checking facts, 105-6
eliminating wordiness, 107-8
fixing, 90, 98

noun-pronoun
agreement, 109
parallel construction, 111
revision, 104-5
run-on sentences, 110
sentence fragments, 109
subject-verb agreement, 108
Editorial opinion, protection
of, 158
The Editor's Toolbox (Ryan), 69
Education beat, 66-67
explaining complicated
subjects, 81-82
requirements, 67
Electronic databases
database marketing, 192
in marketing, 172
in online journalism, 231
Emergency workers
as idea source, 14-15
interviewing, 65
Encyclopedia of Associations
(Gayle Research), 27
Endings, 95, 97
Enterprise art, 120-21
Ethics, 167-76
See also Codes of ethics
ethical principles, 170
ethical problems, 170-74
making decisions, 175-76
Euphemisms, avoiding, 29
Evaluation, in RACE
formula, 185
Examples, importance
of using, 96
Experience, listing in resume,
216-17
Experts, as sources, 205
Eyewitnesses
interviewing, 64-65
as story sources, 205
treatment of, 65

F

Face-to-face interviewing, 50
Fackler, Mark, 175
Factual errors, 105-6
Faking stories, ethics and, 171
False light privacy, 161
Falwell, Jerry, 158
Feature stories
in photojournalism, 120-22
quotes in, 96-97
Federal records, researching, 29
Fire house, as idea source, 14-15
Fires, 63-65
First Amendment rights,
157, 158

commercial speech and, 192
"no special access" rule, 159
First National Bank v Bellotti
(1978), 159
Fixing stories, 90, 98
Florida Star case (1989), 161
Flynt, Larry, 158
Focal point, in photography,
126, 126, 128
Focus
of documentaries, 149
of stories, 204
Focus sentence, 204
Follow-up, in job-hunting, 220
Food Lion, Inc. v Capital
Cities/ABC, Inc., et al (1995),
159, 171
Footnotes, 29
Fort Worth Star-Telegram,
171, 172
Fowler, Cheray, 82
Framing, in photography, 128
Freedom of Information
Act, 160
Freedom of speech, in
advertising, 193

G

Garcia, Flora J., 214
Garrett, Paul, 181
General news, photojournalism
and, 119
Georgia State University *Signal,*
180
Gerunds, 111
Gifts, ethics of accepting, 168,
172-73
Gilka, Bob, 131
Gilroy, Brent, 180
Golden Mean, 170
Golden Rule, 170
Government
covering, 68-69
researching, 37
researching documents,
28-29
Graham, Steve, 197
Grammar, 90, 91, 113
See also Spelling; Vocabulary
active verbs, 89
checking and correcting, 72
comma splice, 110
correcting quotes for, 70
in news releases, 187
noun-pronoun
agreement, 109
parallel construction, 111
reference books on, 106

run-on sentences, 110
sentence fragments, 109
subject-verb agreement, 108
Graphics, in advertising, 195
Greaves, McLean, 231-33
Greenville (S.C.) *Piedmont,* 180
Grumman, Cornelia, 228, 230, 233

H

Halberstam, David, 81
Hanford Sentinel, 223
Hardin, Arzie, 232
Hardwood, Richard, 173
Harper, Christopher, 33, 57, 135, 162, 222-23, 227
The Hartford Courant, 14
Harvey, Kay, 46, 52
Head, John, 185-86
Henderson, Stephen, 231, 233
Historical events, photojournalism and, 118, 119, 129
Hodges, Louis, 173
Human element, in photojournalism, 119
Humphrey, Mark, 131
Hustler magazine, 158
Hustler magazine v Falwell (1988), 158

I

IABC (International Association of Business Communicators), 189
Idaho Statesman, 222-23
Ideas
creativity, 195
for documentaries, 148-49
in photojournalism, 131
Idea sources, 13-20
See also Sources
community records, 16
cultivating, 16-17
local, 15-16, 21
local officials, 15-16, 17
schools, 17-19
where to look, 14-15
Identifying news
in broadcast writing, 139-40
in reporting, 203-5
Illness, privacy and, 174, 175
Illustrations, 121-22
Imagination, stories and, 5
IMC (integrated marketing communications), 195-97

Improving stories, 98
Improvisation, 76
Inaccurate reporting, 93
Indirect quotes, 92
Information gathering, 88
in advertising, 197
double-checking facts, 105-6
internet research, 37
for photojournalists, 130
privacy of information and, 156
unexpected information, 53
writing and, 205
Information sheets, 18
Integrated marketing communications (IMC), 195-97
International Association of Business Communicators (IABC), 189
Internet, 34-35
See also Online journalism; World Wide Web
filing stories online, 58
home pages, 58
in public relations, 182, 185
search engines, 35-36, 38
Usenet, 58
Internships, 212, 223
Interviewees
hostile, 52-53
types of, 51-52
Interviews, 43-55
abbreviating narrative in, 53
basic rules for, 50
call-backs, 54
controlling, 51-52
ending, 53, 54-55
environment for, 50
first meetings, 51
interruptions to, 50
key quotes, 53
at meetings, 69
mistakes in, 47-48
note-taking, 50, 54
"off the record," 54
preparing questions for, 46-47
questioning techniques, 48-49
relationship with interviewee, 47
researching for, 46
reviewing notes following, 55
sensitivity in, 65, 66
supplies needed, 47
tape-recording, 49
for television, 52
types of, 45-46

unexpected information, 53
using shorthand, 54
using silence in, 48
Intranet system, 58
Intrusion on seclusion, 161
Invasion of privacy, ethics and, 173-74
Inverted pyramid
in stories, 90
use in resumes, 213, 214-15
Irony, 92
Ison, Chris, 53, 54

J

The Jackson (Tenn.) *Sun,* 223
Jargon, 29, 59
Jennings, Peter, 145
Job hunting, 211-26
See also Resumes
getting first job, 222-25
networking and, 221, 226
Jones, Bill, 76
Journalism
See also Online journalism; Photojournalism; specific aspects of journalism
public relations and, 180, 183-84
Journalist's Creed (Williams), 80
Judgments, 93

K

Kansas City Star, 82
Kansas City Times, 82
Kaplan, John, 71
Kelly, Mike, 78
Kenney, James H., Jr., 71, 117, 121, 123, 223
Kerouac, Jack, 104

L

LaBelle, Dave, 120
Land, Mary Jean, 186
Law of unintended consequences, 165
"Lawyering" media, 157
Layering, in online journalism, 230-31
Leads, 6, 88-89
in broadcast stories, 139, 140
editing, 104-5
of feature story, 97
in news releases, 186

Legal issues, 155-65
confidential sources, 156, 160
defamation, 161-65
example of, 156-57
First Amendment rights, 158
"lawyering" media, 157
in news gathering, 158-60
privacy, 160, 161
tips for non-lawyers, 162
Lenses, 122, 124
Lewis, Anthony, 165
Lewis, Greg, 124
Libel law, financial threat from, 165
Library, as research tool, 26
Light, in photography, 124, 125
Limbaugh, Rush, 143
Listening
in advertising, 199
covering big story and, 77
speeches and meetings, 68, 69
Little, Darnell, 230-31, 233
Local angles
in photojournalism, 119-20
in research, 29
Local officials, as idea sources, 15-16, 17
Location
broadcast writing and, 144-45
as idea source, 15-16, 21
London Free Press, 225
Long-form television stories, 148-49
Los Angeles Times, 58, 224

M

McLuhan, Marshall, 192
Malice, in defamation, 164, 165
Manners, 79-80
Maps, as research tool, 26
Marietta *Daily Journal,* 180
Media
See also specific media
legal constraints on, 157
public relations and, 185
Media relations, 187-80
Meetings, 67-69
open meeting laws, 160
planning and zoning meetings, 20
preparing to cover, 19, 68
tape-recording, 68
Meier, Peg, 44, 48, 52
Mental health, importance of, 79

Mercer, Michael L., 59, 211, 213, 223
Messages, in advertising, 195
Meyers, Mike, 48, 49, 51, 52
Miami Herald, 59
Miller, Avram, 195
Milwaukee Journal, 168-70
Minneapolis *Star Tribune,* 44, 48, 52-53, 54, 160, 224
Minnesota Public Radio, 47
Minutes of public meetings, as idea sources, 19
Misappropriation, 161
Modified chronology, 90
Money, ethics and, 173
"Muckrakers," 170
Murray, Donald, 89
Muskegon (Mich.) *Chronicle,* 225

N

"Narrowcasting," 192
National Association of Press Photographers, 169
National Geographic, 131
Natomas (Cal.) *Journal,* 173
Networking, in job-hunting, 221
News
    identifying, 139-40, 203-5
    photojournalism and, 119-20
News gathering, legal issues in, 158-60
Newspaper, in-house television station, 58
Newspaper morgue
    plagiarism and, 172
    as research tool, 26
Newspapers
    codes of ethics of, 168, 169
    newspaper style, 137-38
    opinion polls by, 59
News release. See Press release
Newsroom, communicating with, 65-66
News services, as internet research tool, 37
Newsweek, 136
New York Times, 81
    attribution in, 9, 10
    defamation case, 161-64
    ethics and, 189
    interviews, 51
New York Times v Sullivan (1964), 161-64
New York Times v United States (1971), 158
"Niches," 193, 194

Nieman, Lucius, 168-70
"No special access" rule, 159
Notes
    See also Tape recording
    interview notes, 50, 54, 55
    keeping or destroying, 162
Noun-pronoun agreement, 109
Nut graph, 97

O

Obituaries, 62-63
Objectives, in resumes, 215-16
Objectivity, 143
Observation, writing and, 206-7
Omaha World Herald, 78
Online job-hunting, 214, 215
Online journalism, 227-33
    See also Internet; World Wide Web
    Chicago Tribune internet edition, 228, 230-31
    story writing, 58
    website development and, 231-33
    writing for, 233
Online research, 29, 37
On-the-job profiles, 15
Opelika-Auburn News, 222
Open-ended questions, 49
Open meeting laws, 160
Opinion polls
    by newspapers, 59
    using, 29
Orange County (Cal.) *Register,* 58, 224

P

Parallel construction, 111
Paraphrasing, 70, 94
Partial quotes, 92, 94
Paxton, Mark, 223-24
People
    government reporting and, 68-69
    as idea sources, 14
    interviewing. See Interviews
    personality profiles, 45
    in photojournalism, 119
    story-building and, 81
"The People Versus Larry Flynt," 158
Personal contacts
    as idea source, 16-17
    in media relations, 187
Personality profiles, 45
Photographers, 169

See also Photojournalism
    broadcast writing and, 145-46
    graphic crime-scene photos, 174
    tips for, 128
    as writers, 71-72
Photojournalism, 117-32
    captions, 130-31
    decisive moment in, 129-30
    digital photography and, 131-32
    equipment for, 122, 124
    features, 120-22
    first jobs, 222-23
    human element in, 119
    ideas, 131
    importance of photographs, 118
    news, 119-20
    picture stories or essays, 122
    sports, 120
    techniques of, 124, 126, 128-29
Photojournalism: Content and Technique (Lewis), 124
Physical health, importance of, 79
Picture essays or stories, 122
Pittsburgh Post-Gazette, 224
Plagiarism, ethics and, 171-72
Planning, in public relations, 182
Planning and zoning meetings, covering, 20
Police
    covering, 59-60
    as idea source, 14-15
    terminology, 59, 60
Political involvement, ethics and, 173
Portrait photographs, 121
Potter, Ralph, 175
"Potter Box," 175-76
Powell, Jody, 185
Powell-Tate (public relations), 180
Preparation
    generally, 76
    for interviews, 46-47
    in media relations, 187
    for meetings, 19, 68
    practicing sports photography, 120
    in public relations, 184
Press releases, 186, 188
    plagiarizing, 172
    requesting, 18
Primary sources, backgrounding and, 45

"Prime Time Live," 159, 171
Print stories, 6
Privacy
    of background information, 156
    invasion of, 173-74
    legal issues of, 160, 161
    personal illness and, 174, 175
Professional organizations
    See also specific organizations
    codes of ethics of, 168-70, 172-73
Proofreading, 105
    news releases, 187
    resumes, 214
    techniques, 109
PRSA. See Public Relations Society of America (PRSA)
Public figures, actual malice standard and, 165
Public records
    community records, 16, 28
    government documents, 28-29
    police and court records, 60, 61
    privacy issues and, 161, 174
    as research tool, 28
    writing obituaries and, 62
Public relations practice, 179-89
    codes of ethics, 189
    commonalities with journalism, 180, 183-84
    defined, 180-82, 182, 183
    media relations, 187-80
    RACE formula, 184-85
    work samples for resumes, 220
    writing basics, 185-87
Public Relations Society of America (PRSA)
    enforceable code of ethics, 169, 189
    media relations and, 180
Public trials, access rule and, 160
Pulitzer Prize, 71, 76, 82, 89, 171
Punctuation, 90, 110

Q

Questions
    See also Interviews
    broadcast writing and, 142-44
    difficult interviewees and, 51-52
    hostile sources and, 52-53

importance of, 206
kinds of, 49
preparing for interviews, 46-47
Quotes
See also Attribution
in broadcast stories, 137
in captions, 130
correct usage, 92-94
evaluating, 69-70
key quotes, 53
rules for usage, 94
support quotes, 46
types of, 92
use in feature stories, 96-97
writing for impact and, 72

R

RACE formula, 184-85
Radio
host's view of broadcasting, 143
Minnesota Public Radio, 47
tips for radio reporters, 144
Radio-Television News
Directors Association, code of ethics of, 169, 172
Rampton, Sheldon, 182
Reaction interviews, 46
"Readers," 139
Reading to write, 201-7
to accommodate audience, 205-6
advertising writing and, 198
identifying news, 203-5
observation and, 206-7
to reach reader, 202-3
in research, 88
Recycled material, ethics and, 172
Redundancy, 107
Reed, Maryanne, 148-49, 224
References, listing in resume, 217-18
Reference works
grammar books, 106
researching, 37
Relationships
establishing, 77-78
with interviewees, 47
teams in broadcasting, 145
Repetition
in feature stories, 97
of quotes, 92, 93-94
Reporting, 57-72
See also Beats
first jobs, 222, 223, 224, 225
newsroom and, 58-59

by photographers, 71-72
using quotes. See Quotes
Research, 23-30
computer assisted, 35-36, 38
for documentaries, 149
example of, 30
fundamental materials, 26-27
government documents, 28-29
importance to advertising, 197
for interviews, 46
localizing findings, 29
online research, 29, 37
in RACE formula, 184
reading to report, 88
resume writing and, 213
sloppy researching, 24-25
web sites, 37
Resolution, 3, 4-5
Responding, process of, 3, 4
Resumes
cover letter for, 218-20
employer criticisms of, 214
including references, 217-18
preparing to write, 212-14
stating objectives, 215-16
videotape reels, 221
work history and skills, 216-17
work samples, 220
writing, 213, 213-15
Reuters, 37
Revision, 97-98, 104-5
Risley, Ford, 65, 167, 224
Root Stand (online newspaper), 233
Ross, Lois, 2-3
Rotary Club, as idea source, 15
Rotzoll, Kim, 175
Rule of thirds, in photography, 126, 128, 128
Rules, being wary of, 83-84
Run-on sentences, 110
Ryan, Leland "Buck," 69

S

St. Paul *Pioneer Press,* 46, 49, 52, 222
Schie, Ron, 191, 225
Schlagheck, Carol, 23, 224
Schools
See also Education beat
as idea source, 17-19
Schroeder, Paula, 47
Schultz, Don, 192
Script preparation

in broadcast writing, 138-39, 147
guidelines for, 148-49
Search engines, 35-36, 38
Selective focus, in photography, 128
Self-reliance, 76
Senior citizens, as idea source, 16
Sentence construction, 107
Sentence fragments, 109
Sequence
examples of, 6-8
importance of, 5-6, 11
Setting, 3, 4
Shield laws, 160
Simplicity, 78-79
Slang, 94
Slug, 138, 186
Sneed, Michael, 83
Society of Professional
Journalists, 180
code of ethics (1973), 168, 169, 172-73
job hunting and, 221
SOTs (sounds on tape), 147
Sound bites, 147
Sounds on tape (SOTs), 147
Sound technicians, in broadcasting, 145
Sources
See also Idea sources
in broadcast stories, 137
confidentiality and, 156, 160
hostile, 52-53
for police and court beat, 60
primary sources, 45
in public relations, 185
Southwest Missouri State
University, 109
Speaking fees, ethics and, 173
Specialization, 145
Speeches, 67-69
Spell-checker programs, 106
Spelling
See also Grammar;
Vocabulary
checking, 106-7, 214
phonetic, 149
Sports, photojournalism and, 120
Spot news, photojournalism and, 119-20
Spot news leads, 110
*Standard and Poor's Register of
Corporations, Directors and
Executives,* 26
Standups, 146, 148
"Stardom," 143, 145
State government

researching documents, 28-29
Sunshine Acts, 160
State laws, defamation, 161, 162, 164
Stauber, John, 182
Stilted words, 93
Stock ownership, ethics and, 173
"Stop Digging Here"
formula, 186
Story, 2-3
See also Big story; Feature
stories; Story structure
classic stages of, 6
elements of, 3, 11
as event, 5
finding. See Idea sources
importance of sequence, 5-6
problems with, 8-9, 11
Storyboards
in advertising, 194
in online journalism, 230
Story structure, 87-98
See also Story; Storytelling
ending, 95
forms of organization, 90, 92
lead, 6, 88-89
revising, 97-98
using quotes, 92-94
Storytelling, 1-10
See also Story; Story
structure
in online journalism, 230
Strategy development, in
advertising, 197-98
Students, as idea sources, 18-19
Style
AP style, 187, 215
in broadcast writing, 136-38
newspaper style, 137-38
use of sentence
fragments, 109
Subject-verb agreement, 108
Sullivan, L. V., 162, 164
Summary leads, 89, 110
Sunshine Acts, 160
Support quotes, 46
Supreme Court
"no special access" rule, 159
privacy issues, 161
protection of press, 158-59
on "reporter's privilege," 160

T

Tait, David, 1, 63, 225
Talk shows, 143
Tape recording
See also Notes; Videotaping

interviews, 49
meetings, 68
sound bites, 147
Technology
See also Computer(s);
Internet; World Wide
Web
in advertising, 193, 195
Telephone numbers,
researching, 26, 37
Television
anchor's view of
broadcasting, 145
interviews for, 52
long-form stories, 148-49
magazine programs, 148
networks, 136, 145
newspaper's in-house
station, 58
time pressure in, 52
writing scripts, 147
Theme format, 92
Thesauri, as research tool, 27
Thomas, Tyrone, 232
Time contrast format, 92
Time Online, 214
Toxic Sludge is Good For You
(Stauber and Rampton), 182
Traditional outline, 92
Transitions
in feature stories, 97
quotes and, 69-70

Truthfulness
in advertising, 198
ethics and, 170
Typecasting clichés, 9
Typographical errors, in
resumes, 214

U

Unger, Robert, 75, 225
U.S. Census Bureau, 229
U.S. Constitution. See First
Amendment rights
USA Today, 174, 175
Usenet, 39
Utilitarianism, 170

V

Vance, Donald R., 192
Veil of ignorance, 170
Verbs
active verbs, 89, 112, 141
in broadcast stories, 137, 141
subject-verb agreement, 108
Videotape log, 146
Videotaping
for broadcasting, 145-46
resume reel, 221
Vocabulary
See also Grammar; Spelling

communication and, 207
of police and court beat,
59, 60
troublesome words, 91
Voiceovers (VO), 147
Volunteerism, job-hunting
and, 217
VO (voiceovers), 147

W

Wahoo (Neb.) *Newspaper,* 225
Wall Street Journal, 169,
173, 230
Walsh, Jim, 49, 50
Washington Post, 80, 171,
173, 233
Weather information,
researching, 37
Weaver, Margaret, 109
Wernsman, Robert, 62, 166,
201, 225
WETM-TV (Elmira, N.Y.),
148, 224
Wild art, 120-21
Will, George, 173
Williams, Walter, 80
Winans, R. Foster, 173
WNBC-TV (New York City),
225
WOKR (Rochester, N.Y.), 148
Wood, Dave, 44

Wordiness, 107-8
Work samples, sending with
resume, 220
World Wide Web, 34-35
See also Internet; Online
journalism
advertising on, 192
web sites, 37, 231-33
Writing
See also Broadcast writing;
Story; Story structure
for advertising, 198-99
as craft or art, 113
descriptive, 89
for impact, 72
in public relations practice,
185-87
resume as sample of, 212
resumes, 213, 214-15
to reveal news, 203
WTAE-TV (Pittsburgh, Pa.),
148

Y

Yardley, Jonathan, 171

Z

Zyman, Sergio, 196, 197

Check out these related journalism titles from CourseWise Publishing

Is Public Relations boring ???

???

Hardly. Why, then, do so many **textbooks** treat this important and exciting topic in such a **dull** fashion? Why is this dynamic course taught from over-written, **stuffy**, theory-laden textbooks that cost students far too much? Are you interested in a **fresh** approach?

This September **CourseWise** is publishing:

WALKING THE HIGHWIRE: Effective Public Relations

by Professor Merry Shelburne, PIO at Glendale Community College.

Here's what's **unique** about Merry's book:

✓ HIGHWIRE is short, snappy and sassy. The razor sharp writing goes right to the point. Reviewers summarized Merry's writing as "delightful", "energetic" and "dead-on".

✓ HIGHWIRE is a hands-on learning tool written by a practitioner who's been teaching the course for fifteen years. "Here-it-is" and "this is how you do it" is the approach, prompting another reviewer to write: "Please let me know when it's ready".

✓ HIGHWIRE is a worktext. It's a paperback that's chock-full of tear-out exercises. An ongoing case highlights the ins and outs of daily PIO work.

✓ HIGHWIRE is contemporary. Relevant examples are drawn from recent headlines, including President Clinton's visit to the author's school, the 96 Olympics and the handling of the TWA Flight 800 disaster.

✓ HIGHWIRE provides instructors and students with a hassle free way to harness the web. The on-line chapter, **cyberPR**, covers the how-to's of webPR and supplements with integrated web sites.

✓ HIGHWIRE is affordable. The suggested student price is **$24.99 !** That includes the on-line chapter. Adopting instructors receive an on-line Instructor's Manual featuring additional exercises.

✓ HIGHWIRE is appropriately fun! Finally, a tool that helps you do the serious shovel work this course deserves, but in a upbeat manner that helps students learn.

WALKING THE HIGHWIRE: Effective Public Relations

Contents

Chapter 1: What is Public Relations?
Chapter 2: Types of PR Jobs & Activities
Chapter 3: How Communication Works
Chapter 4: Understanding The Media
Chapter 5: Developing Credibility
Chapter 6: Training Your Bosses & Co-Workers
Chapter 7: Walking the HighWire
Chapter 8: Setting Policy
Chapter 9: The Contact List
Chapter 10: The News Release
Chapter 11: Media Alerts, Advisories, Calendars, and Feature Ideas
Chapter 12: The Broadcast Media
Chapter 13: The Public Service Announcement
Chapter 14: Direct Mail
Chapter 15: Advertising
Chapter 16: Developing Experts, Getting Products Mentioned
Chapter 17: The Press Conference & Press Kits
Chapter 18: cyber.PR
Chapter 19: Dealing with Dignitaries
Chapter 20: Don'ts
Chapter 21: The PR Campaign: Set Realistic Goals
Chapter 22: The PR Campaign: Define Your Audience
Chapter 23: The PR Campaign: Consider Your Budget
Chapter 24: The PR Campaign: Develop a Plan
Chapter 25: The PR Campaign: Implement the Plan; Evaluate Effectiveness
Chapter 26: Crisis Management: How to Prepare
Chapter 27: The PR Role in Natural Disasters

To obtain an **examination copy** of this or any other CourseWise publication, please call The Houghton Mifflin Sixth Floor Media: 800-565-6247.

For more on CourseWise, please visit our web site: www.coursewise.com or write the journalism publisher, Tom Doran: tomd@coursewise.com. Thanks for your interest in CourseWise!

PERSPECTIVES: OnLine Journalism
Edited by Prof. Kathleen Wickham
(University of Memphis)

From the **CourseWise Perspectives Series**, a new reader featuring cutting edge coverage selected and developed by our Academic Editor and Editorial Board including:

Prof. Jay Brodell (Metro State-Denver)
Anders Gyllenhaal (Raleigh News & Observer)   **Neil Reisner** (Miami Herald)
Prof. Chris Harper (Ithaca College)   **Prof. Steven Ross** (Columbia)
Prof. Eric Meyer (U of Illinois)   **Prof. Kathleen Wickham** (U of Memphis)
Steve Miller (New York Times)

A BETTER HYBRID: Trends Emerging from the Technology

"By juxtaposing the best of the new model—computerized access, delivery, and a packaging of information—with the best of the old model—insightful reporting in a well written story—a better hybrid model that combines the best of both is created." From "The Evolution of the Newspaper in the Future" by Chris Lapham

ON THE E-BEAT: from the Newsroom Corner to Center Stage

Explores how both the business and jobs within the business are changing as a result of new technologies. Readings examine a range of developments: from C.A.R. to changing expectations of online readers.

ONLINE CAREERS: A Specialty or a Recasting of the Mold?

"No one can forecast whether multimedia journalism will become just one more specialty, or fundamentally remake the mold. But for newspaper people restless about the future, taking a taste of new media seems wise." From "The New Journalist" by Charles Stepp

A NEW WILD WEST: Where's the Law? And Whose Ethics?

Is the online legal and ethical arena different from its print and broadcast counterparts? Readings explore rules, regulations and debates that apply to the new Wild West.

DIGGING BEHIND THE SCREEN: 2 Controversies in Online Journalism

Spotlights a controversial series from *The San Jose Mercury News*, and *The Dallas Morning News* coverage of the McViegh trial.